SUBURBAN LIVES

Suburban Lives

Margaret Marsh

Rutgers University Press
New Brunswick and London

Library of Congress Cataloging-in-Publication Data

Marsh, Margaret S., 1945–
Suburban lives / by Margaret Marsh.
p. cm.
Bibliography: p.
Includes index.
ISBN 0-8135-1483-5 (cloth)—ISBN 0-8135-1484-3 (pbk.)
1. Suburban life—United States—History. 2. Women—United States—Social conditions. I. Title.
HT352.U6M37 1990
307.74'082—dc20 89-36060
CIP

British Cataloging-in-Publication information available

Selections from Mary Augusta (Carr) Cumings Diaries are reprinted courtesy of the Schlesinger Library, Radcliffe College, Cambridge, Massachusetts. Epigraph to Chapter 5 is from "The One Thing That Can Save America," by John Ashbery, Self-Portrait in a Convex Mirror. *Reprinted courtesy of Viking Penguin, Inc., and Carcanet.*

Portions of this book previously published in journals are reprinted by permission of their editors: "Suburban Men and Masculine Domesticity, 1870–1915," American Quarterly *(June 1988), copyright 1988 by the American Studies Association; and "From Separation to Togetherness: The Construction of Domestic Space in American Suburbs, 1840–1915,"* Journal of American History *(September 1989).*

For Lu Horner

and

In Memory of Allen R. Horner,

1944–1988

It ended . . .
With his body changed to light,
A star that burns forever in that sky.

Anonymous Aztec Poet,
"The Flight of Quetzalcoatl"

Contents

Acknowledgments

This book has been seven years in the making; during those years friends and colleagues have helped me considerably, and several institutions have provided financial support. I am grateful to the National Endowment for the Humanities for a year-long Fellowship for College Teachers in 1983, and to the University of Pennsylvania, particularly former provost Thomas Ehrlich and Professor Drew Faust, for welcoming me that year as a Visiting Scholar. The Research and Professional Development Committee at Stockton State College also provided travel funds and summer research stipends over the course of several years, for which I thank the committee members, President Vera King Farris, and then Vice-President Neil Kleinman.

Most of my intellectual debts are to individuals who helped me in various ways—by reading drafts of the manuscript in whole or in part, by commenting on sections as they were presented at seminars or conference sessions, or by serving as reviewers for two earlier articles that presented parts of this research. I wish to thank John Alviti, Clifford Edward Clark, Jr., Demetrios Constantelos, Allen Davis, Deborah Gardner, David Goldfield, Helen Lefkowitz Horowitz, David Horowitz, Kenneth Jackson, Barbara Klaczynska, T. J. Jackson Lears, Colleen McDannell, Richard Polenberg, Gail Radford, and Gwendolyn Wright. William Lubenow, who read every one of these chapters in more drafts than I wanted to write or he wanted to read, deserves special thanks. The members of Columbia University's Seminar on the City, at which I first presented some of the ideas that appear in this book, helped me to shape and develop those ideas.

Stockton student Michael Ciarrocchi provided bibliographical assistance. My colleague Wendel White, in Photography, is responsible for several of the reproductions of nineteenth-century illustrations used here. For three of the years that I worked on *Suburban Lives,* I was also serving as Dean. During that time, Nancy Messina, my administrative assistant, and Dorothy Mastro, my secretary, bore additional responsibilities at times when this book got more of my attention than my administrative paperwork. Others who typed early drafts of this manuscript (before I learned about personal computers) or assisted in various ways include Virginia Burkley and Beatrice Hancox. The late Jane Smith Taylor, whose grandfather was the developer of one of the suburbs considered here in some detail, allowed me access to her personal collection of material on that community, and lent me several illustrations for use here. Her assistance was invaluable.

Dedicated and skilled librarians from several institutions eased my research, including Susan Naulty at the Huntington Library in San Marino California, the entire staff at the Schlesinger Library at Radcliffe, and closer to home, the Interlibrary Loan staff at Stockton. Kathy Tassini, Librarian of the Haddonfield Historical Society, located local sources on family and community life so necessary to a work of this kind; her colleague Douglas Rauschenberger, Director of the Haddonfield Public Library, also found important local documents.

Kenneth Arnold and Marlie Wasserman, Director and Editor-in-Chief, respectively, at Rutgers University Press, dispensed sympathetic understanding and hard-headed, practical advice in just the right proportions. I feel especially fortunate to have been able to work with them on this project from its earliest stages.

Finally, and most importantly of all, I want to thank my husband, Bob Marsh, whose support of and interest in this book sustained me during the inevitable times of frustration, and whose love enhances my life in hundreds of ways. My sister Wanda Ronner and her husband Peter Ronner encouraged and advised me. Kathleen Sammartino, my cousin, cheerfully walked around numerous suburbs with me and came to hear me give papers about them; and my brother- and sister-in-law Barry and Hope Marsh braved the winter winds of Chicago to make sure I saw every single Frank Lloyd Wright house and turn-of-the-century suburban community in the metropolitan area. To all of them, I am very grateful. This book is dedicated to my friends Lu and Al Horner. Al died of cancer on December 16, 1988. The dedication not only mourns his death, but celebrates his life.

POMONA, NEW JERSEY
June 1989

Introduction

Frederick Lewis Allen, writing in *Harper's* in 1954, observed that the suburbs of post–World War II America "were built for the young people of an intensely domestic generation, who . . . take their parental duties seriously." Like most social observers of the 1950s, Allen took for granted a close connection between suburbs and a particular ideal of family life. The new suburbs belonged to the "valiant World War II heroes and their blushing brides," and, by the mid-1950s, their two, three, or four young children. Television shows like the *Donna Reed Show, Father Knows Best, Leave It to Beaver,* and *Ozzie and Harriet* were set in neat, suburban communities and portrayed happy, white, middle-class families in which father's work was remote and his real life took place at home, mother cleaned house and baked cookies in shirtwaist dresses, high heels, and pearls, and children's mischief was never malicious and always could be smoothed over in a half hour. These were very different from the programs set in the city. In the *Honeymooners,* Ralph and Alice Cramden had no children. And until the star, Lucille Ball, became pregnant in real life, *I Love Lucy* was also a show without children. Lucy and her Cuban-born spouse lived in an apartment in the city and might not even have been welcomed in Ward and June's neighborhood.[1]

Television, of course, is not real life. It is all the more striking, therefore, that scholarly studies of suburbia during the 1950s confirmed the images on the small screen. Whether in criticism or praise, observers suggested that what Allen had called "intense" domesticity, and others referred to as child-centeredness, or, more awkwardly, "familism," was the principal characteristic of suburban families. Images of suburbia in the press, on television, and among scholars portrayed a close connection between a specific type of family life and a certain kind of environment.[2]

Historians, when they began to examine the suburbs of earlier periods, inherited that understanding of suburban life. There is little question that this perception of a linkage between suburbanization and domesticity existed in the 1950s; but when was it forged? Had middle-class Americans, for example, always moved to the suburbs because they wanted to create a certain kind of family life? Or did they choose a suburban residence for different reasons and develop this view of family life once there? Just how did suburbanization become so entangled with domesticity that by the 1950s we could think of them as single phenomenon?

I began working on this book believing that an ideal of family togetherness was connected to the suburban vision from the earliest days of suburbanization, a view I shared in varying degrees with other historians.[3] Such an assumption seemed logical. Both the suburban ideal and what historians have come to call the ideology of domesticity emerged at roughly the same time, around the second quarter of the nineteenth century; and both could be seen as responses to the same phenomena of urbanization and the development of a commercial and later an industrial economy. But my presupposition, in the end, offers a too-static picture of suburban life; further, it does not sufficiently take into account the plasticity of the domestic ideal, which held (and perhaps still holds) different meanings for men and women, and has changed and expanded throughout the nineteenth and twentieth centuries. That there has been a relationship between suburbs and the domestic ideal is undeniable, but the relationship has undergone numerous changes. The chapters that follow are the result of my attempt to sort out the meanings of the relationship between the suburban ideal and the "intensely domestic" family.

This is not, then, a history of suburbanization in the United States, but an essay on the meanings of suburban life for the families who have lived there. We have traditionally, and properly, defined suburbs in geographical, political, or economic terms; but there is also a sense in which the idea of suburbia transcends space and civic boundaries and becomes a means to conceptualize a way of life. Houston's River Oaks, deep within the city, is more "suburban" than are the city's so-called sunshine slums on the outskirts. Some cities, especially in the Midwest and the Rocky Mountain states—Denver for example—grew by accretion; one band of suburbs surrounded earlier bands, making it possible to use some suburban terms in describing the city itself. Suburbs are physical places, to be sure, but they are also places of the heart. Although I would never suggest that suburbia is solely a metaphor for a way of life, I do insist that it is partly so.

My interest in suburban America centers on the family experience itself—domestic ideals, patterns of work and leisure, relationships between husbands and wives, and childrearing—and on the way that experience has been shaped. It begins in the early nineteenth century and closes with the beginning of mass suburbanization. It focuses on the white middle class, because that group for the most part peopled the residential suburbs until at least the 1950s. And finally it attempts, through probing American middle-class family life, to understand the connections between the kinds of values people hold and the kinds of communities they create. At a time when architects and architectural historians debate whether environmental change can create social transformation, the experience of families in suburban America—because it is both a specific kind of environment and the embodiment of a set of values—will have much to tell us about both the ability to, and the ethics of trying to, change behavior through architecture.[4]

As I began to disentangle the strands of ideology and behavior that created the residential suburb in its earliest years, the first hypothesis that crumbled was that the suburban ideal and the ideology of domesticity were but two parts of the same belief system. Instead, I will argue, they developed independently, from different political needs and from different sources. The ideology of domesticity in its earliest incarnation was primarily woman-defined, and it had at its center a cultural institution, the family. The suburban ideal of the same era was largely male-defined, and had at its center a physical space, the residential suburb. Middle-class women embraced urban life in the second third of the nineteenth century. The city, not its periphery, offered them significant opportunities for social interaction, for participation in reform or religious organizations, and for relative freedom from domestic drudgery. After all, markets, bakeshops, and not least, domestic servants were much more accessible in urban areas. Women domestic reformers did not urge their readers to leave the city, but to develop proper values within it.

The suburban ideal emerged from the agrarian ethos that had dominated Jeffersonian political philosophy and posited a necessary connection between democracy and rural life; it was not an outgrowth of the ideology of domesticity. As it began to develop in the second quarter of the nineteenth century, the suburban ideal offered a spatial equivalent for the agrarian community. Ownership of a suburban house did not make a man a farmer, but it bought him closer to nature than an urban townhouse did, and it recognized the political importance of property ownership. There is a tension here; early suburban America was created by men, and by a particular kind of man—one with a vision of American life touched by nostalgia and connected to the rural origins of the United States. For women, on the other hand, the ideology of domesticity was a break with the past. If that tension had erupted into open and sustained conflict, the American landscape might look significantly different today.

It does not look different because, despite different origins and intentions, both the ideology of domesticity and the suburban ideal attempted to recast the values of the early republic to meet the demands of a commercial and industrializing society. Toward the end of the nineteenth century, as cities grew ever larger and more "alien," and as technology made the suburbs more accessible to the city as well as more civilized, the suburban ideal and the ideology of domesticity began to come together. Advocates of both increasingly believed that the great city imperiled conventional ideas about the nature of family life as well as traditional American political values.

The end result was the creation, during the last years of the nineteenth century and the first decade of the twentieth, of a new suburban vision. At its heart was the reorganization of the ideology of domesticity so that it no longer depended on a rigorous separation of masculine and feminine spheres of activity. An important element of this was the emergence of "masculine domesticity," a set of new beliefs about the role of men in the home that prompted husbands to take on increased responsibility for the emotional well-being of their children, to spend their leisure with their wives rather than male cronies, and even to take on limited domestic duties. Masculine domesticity gave men roles in the home, but it was not feminist. Indeed, it successfully blunted the power of feminist demands in significant ways.

The second characteristic of this new vision more specifically challenged the Jeffersonian notion of property ownership. By the early twentieth century, the agrarian, property-holding suburban ideal became less important, as suburbanites gave more attention to the political significance of the location of the family. During the years before World War I, "place" was of equal if not greater importance than ownership in the residential suburbs of the middle class, as a significant number of suburbanites abandoned the values of their Victorian forebears, who had insisted that actual home ownership was necessary to preserve American democracy. By the early twentieth century, place itself resonated with symbolic meaning. In fact, upper middle-class suburbanites chose to rent their homes to a surprising degree.

World War I was followed by a decade of expanded prosperity, which disproportionately benefited middle-class over working-class Americans. The effect of the war and prosperity on suburban domesticity was mixed. The war did not, in any profound sense, alter the belief of middle-class families in suburban living. Indeed, the numbers of suburbs and suburbanites increased substantially when the war was over, and residential construction once again boomed. But there were some changes. Ownership became important again, for example. And where the emphasis in suburban advocacy literature of the prewar years had been on husband-wife togetherness, that of the twenties concentrated on the importance of suburban life for children. The role of fathers changed as a result; much of masculine domesticity had eroded. What was left was the idea that fathers should take an interest in their children, but the broader implications were shunted aside. And by the twenties, the voices of proponents of urban life seemed weaker as the planners, who had once held out the hope of a redeemed urban America, took their blueprints and their T-squares beyond the city limits, lured by the prospect of planning for square miles rather than square blocks.

The depression virtually halted residential construction, and when New Dealers brought their insights to bear on the problems of housing, the end result was an intensification of the suburban ideal. The greenbelt towns, the highway construction bills, the Home Owners Loan Corporation, and the Federal Housing Administration all supported suburban growth, much of it at the expense of the city. Franklin Roosevelt may have agreed with Herbert Hoover on little else, but they held the same reverence for the single-family, owner-occupied house, cared for by a stay-at-home wife and paid for by the male breadwinner. By the time World War II ended, it seemed as if the suburb and the single-earner, nuclear family had always been two parts of a single idea.

To outline an argument in such broad strokes, of course, is to omit its complications and contradictions. As the following chapters will show, the process was not straightforward. Urban advocacy, for example, did not disappear when most of the domestic reformers bowed to the suburban ideal in the late nineteenth century, nor was it extinct in the 1920s. And in the 1930s, powerful voices argued for a renewed urban vision. Perhaps more significantly, suburbanites themselves did not proceed to create their environment in an orderly or even consistent manner. The final portrait, it is hoped, will convey much more of the complexity than this brief preliminary sketch.

One dilemma in studying a problem that is national in scope yet intimate in scale is whether to take a microcosmic or macrocosmic approach. The former allows for particularization—a major advantage—but the sweep of the latter holds the potential for greater insight. Rather than choose a single approach, therefore, I use a method of analysis that blends the two. The book is organized in a roughly chronological order. Between the prologue and the epilogue are three sections of two chapters each. The first of the two paints a broad national picture of suburban family and community, while the second particularizes. The section on America's Victorian suburbs moves from a general overview to an examination of the lives of families—whom I would call exemplary rather than representative suburbanites—in two different suburbs of Boston. From there we move to the late nineteenth and early twentieth centuries; two Philadelphia suburbs provide intimate details of the larger issues explored in this section. For the suburbs of the 1920s and 1930s, where better to look than Los Angeles, a city suburban in intent since the 1880s and more prepared than any to take advantage of the mass production of automobiles?

The choice of none of these cities was arbitrary. Each of them has been much studied as an example of urban processes of particular periods: Boston suburbanized early, Philadelphia exemplified the age of the "railroad suburb," and Los Angeles is this country's prototypical sunbelt metropolis. I have been careful to compare the suburbanites of these cities with their counterparts in other communities in order to make my images as complete as I can. Still, there are omissions. There is no discussion of what we might call "alternative suburbs," communities of radicals such as Arden (Delaware) or Stelton (New Jersey). Working-class industrial suburbs have not found a major place in this study, nor have black suburbs. Their neglect should not be taken as an indication that they are unimportant, but rather that they tell a different story. This book is about the middle-class white families who built the archetypal residential suburbs. It is about the forefathers and foremothers of the suburban vision of the 1950s. It is about the successes and failures of that vision.

Prologue: Homes of the Virtuous

[T]he love of home is one of the deepest feelings in our nature, . . . but it must be a home built and loved upon new world, and not the old world, ideas and principles; a home in which humanity and republicanism are stronger than family pride and aristocratic feeling; a home of the virtuous citizen, rather than of the mighty owner of houses and lands.

ANDREW JACKSON DOWNING,
THE ARCHITECTURE OF COUNTRY HOUSES, 1850

The United States came into existence as a rural nation; in 1790, when the new country first counted its citizens, only about 5 percent of them lived in cities. As late as 1820, that figure had risen by just 2 percent. Although it may have been true that urbanites wielded influence far out of proportion to their numbers, such a small urban population did not cause the majority of Americans to believe that the rural republic was in imminent danger. But it was. Between 1840 and 1850 the urban sector of the population increased by over 90 percent, and in the next decade by more than 75 percent. More ominous for those who believed that agrarianism and democracy were synonyms, urban centers had proliferated. In 1820, fully a third of the nation's urbanites had lived in New York and Philadelphia. Besides those, only ten other cities had populations larger than 10,000. By 1860, New York City, which then excluded Brooklyn, had more than a million residents, and seven other cities had passed the 100,000 mark. As for the lowly 10,000 figure that had marked the largest cities in 1820, more than a hundred cities had surpassed it by 1860, and city life was no longer confined to the eastern seaboard.[1]

Changes in the roles of women, in patterns of childrearing, and in relationships between men and women accompanied the urbanization of the United States and the larger processes of which it was a part, including industrialization, immigration, and the development of the modern corporate economy. To explore the meaning of urbanization for middle-class Americans is essential for understanding how this group created and shaped the suburban United States of the twentieth century. Guiding this exploration is the idea that men and women experienced urbanization differently in the early to mid-nineteenth century, and that their divergent perceptions resulted in the development of separate and distinct attitudes toward urban life and its problems as well as its opportunities. Women responded to a rapidly changing and uncertain society by creating the ideology of domesticity, which centered around the cultural institution of the family. Men had different ideas about women's roles; although certainly not immune to the domestic comforts provided by women, they were more concerned about the relationship of the home to the nation. As a result, they responded to an urbanizing society by developing the suburban ideal, seeking to retain some elements of the agrarian ethos because it seemed the best way to preserve the republican dream of a nation governed by small property holders.

In one sense, of course, both of these sets of ideas were aspects of a single phenomenon; each served as a means to assist men and women to think about the civic dimensions of their personal lives. But in other ways they were fundamentally different, prescribing contrasting kinds of behavior and arising out of dissimilar, and gender-specific, political perceptions. This is not a conventional interpretation of the relationship between the suburban ideal and the ideology of domesticity. In general, historians appear either to have assumed that they were interdependent parts of a single pattern, or that both were end results of an inevitable process of residential decentralization. In the most literal meaning of the word, of course, a suburb is simply an area lying adjacent to a densely populated urban core. But in the United States, it has traditionally had a specific connotation. We think of suburbs in the conventional sense as middle-class residential communities from which people commute to work in a nearby city. That image is a geopolitical one, but as Robert Fishman and others have argued convincingly, suburbia is perhaps more importantly an intellectual construct; its conceptualization has shaped the suburb's physical space and sometimes transcended it.

SUBURBAN BEGINNINGS

Historians have tended to account for suburbanization by pointing to technological developments that facilitated outward movement, by emphasizing the relatively inexpensive land that lay just beyond the heart of the city, and by arguing that America's agrarian heritage had made its citizens traditionally antipathetic toward urban life. None of these things are false, but not until the publication of Kenneth Jackson's landmark *Crabgrass Frontier* in 1985 was there a definitive history of the process by which the United States suburbanized.[2] Jackson's analysis concentrates on economic, demographic, and political forces, and he describes the gradual and inexorable extension of the city itself as a driving force of suburbanization. Suggestive of his broader interpretation is his discussion of the suburbanization of New York, the nation's most important city at the turn of the nineteenth century. It had already become overcrowded. Problems that would not beset other cities for decades had become a part of living here. There was a clear need for more residential space. Its population increased by 82 percent between 1790 and 1800, by another 60 percent the following decade, 28 percent the next, and another 64 percent between 1820 and 1830. New Yorkers responded to the crush by moving to Brooklyn, which was, indeed, more accessible by ferry to lower Manhattan—the central city at that time—than most of the rest of Manhattan. As fast as the city was growing, Brooklyn surpassed it, growing 48 percent between 1790 and 1800, 85 percent in the following decade, and 63 percent the next, during which the first steam ferry made its appearance. Between 1820 and 1830, Brooklyn's population more than doubled, from 7,175 to 15,394. In addition to its easy access to Manhattan, Brooklyn offered "pleasant surroundings, cheap land, [and] low taxes."[3]

Brooklyn became, as Jackson has remarked, the "first commuter suburb." Hezekiah Beers Pierrepont, who developed Brooklyn Heights, deliberately aimed his advertisements at well-to-do Manhattan businessmen, emphasizing the relative inexpensiveness as well as the healthful surroundings of Brooklyn Heights: "Gentlemen whose business or profession require daily attendance into the city cannot better, or with less expense, secure the health and comfort of their families." By 1841, some 50 percent of the household heads who had moved to the land sold by Pierrepont and his heirs worked in Manhattan, a very high commutation figure for such an early period. The development of Brooklyn into a commuter suburb was fostered by the importance of New York City and its massive growth. Although Brooklyn would grow into a thriving industrial city in its own right by the end of the nineteenth century, during this period it owed its suburban growth to Manhattan and the steam ferry. Economic, not ideological, reasons brought residents to Brooklyn, and their lives and livelihoods were tied to Manhattan.[4]

Jackson's urban-centered interpretation of the origins of suburbia contrasts with the more suburban-centered and ideological approaches taken by such historians as Robert Fishman, Henry Binford, and Clifford Clark. Each has defined the suburbs more by their architectural, environmental, and cultural characteristics than by their spatial connection to the city. Fishman argues convincingly that the origin of suburbia can be found in late eighteenth-century London, tied to evangelical religion and the emergence of "the closed, domesticated nuclear family"; in his view, true suburbs did not become transplanted decisively to the United States until near the end of the nineteenth century. Clark and Binford, in separate studies, argue that a domestic or "residential" ideal propelled suburbanization earlier, in the mid-nineteenth century. In Binford's view, suburbanites became "caught up by the power of the residential community ideal."[5]

The transformation of the Massachusetts towns of Cambridge and Somerville from fringe communities to commuter suburbs, Binford argues, had strong ideological underpinnings. Early in the nineteenth century, the two villages had included a mixture of fringe economic activities (both agricultural and preindustrial manufacturing), summer estates of Boston's wealthy families, and a few elite commuters in substantial houses. In the 1840s, as both the fringe economic activities and the residential areas grew, so did conflict between them, and the promoters of residential suburbs won out over the advocates of a mixed community. In the first thirty years or so of the nineteenth century, these villages were in most ways independent of the city, although their agricultural and manufactured products often wound up in its markets. They were in fact "hybrids," from which some residents commuted to Boston but most had primarily local interests. It was the suburbanites, insists Binford, not Bostonians, who foresaw the possibility of "the systematic development of land for commuter residence through a combination of public and private means." This process evolved gradually. In 1840, only about six percent of the household heads of Cambridge and Somerville commuted to Boston. And even during the 1850s, "commuting to work was still a practice open only to those with high income and flexible schedules, but there were now large blocs of such people in the inner suburbs."[6]

What is particularly interesting about Binford's analysis in terms of locating the origins of suburban advocacy is that the people who created the residential ideal that he describes were almost all men, as were the overwhelming majority of those cited by Fishman and Clark for the earliest years of the formation of the suburban ideal. Binford's suburban boosters, for example, included the male editor of the Cambridge *Chronicle,* male correspondents to that newspaper, and male community leaders. It was men, not women, who insisted: "It is the ever apparent desire of the denizen of the crowded city across the river, if he has a soul not dead to everything but gain, to find a place in the country convenient to business, where his family can escape the moral and physical miasma of the metropolis."[7]

The man who wrote those lines might have been paraphrasing Thomas Jefferson, who believed that cities were "pestilential to the morals, the health, and the liberties of man." He was not alone. The men of New York's Children's Aid Society around midcentury (the women of the society, as we shall see later, had a different view) tended to believe that in the countryside lay the solution to urban ills. As Christine Stansell has argued, Charles Loring Brace, who headed the society, and the men who held much of the power in it, "looked to the past, to a rural republic, to solve the problems of the modern city."[8] Indeed, one facet of the suburban ideal of this period was its look backward. Despite its reliance on new technologies, there is an element of nostalgia, even retrogression, about early suburban advocacy.

Jeffersonian political philosophy had posited a necessary connection between democracy and rural life. But by the middle of the nineteenth century, cities had grown, and commerce and manufacturing had begun to challenge the reality of a rural democracy. Suburbs, however, could come to the rescue. Throughout this period the suburban vision was grounded in a political idea: that it was important to retain some elements of the agrarian ethos in order to maintain a society of independent, small property owners and thereby preserve democracy. If a man could not be a farmer, he could at least be close to nature, on his own plot of ground, in his own house. The works of serious male writers like Nathaniel Hawthorne and Henry David Thoreau also lauded the country and damned the city.[9]

America's agrarian heritage can take us a good part of the distance toward an understanding of the cultural dimensions of suburbanization in the years before the Civil War. Urban America had its boosters, apologists, and defenders, but the dominant value structure, in spite of the exploding urban population, had strong links with the agrarian past. Perhaps nowhere are the connections clearer than in the work of Andrew Jackson Downing, whose *The Architecture of Country Houses* went through nine printings between its publication in 1850 and the end of the Civil War. Downing sternly told his readers that "the solitude and freedom of the family home in the country . . . preserves the nation, and invigorates its intellectual powers." Like Thomas Jefferson, Downing centered his hopes for the continuance of American democracy on the preservation of rural values. Simply building a country house, however, was not enough to ensure republican virtue. The house itself must express, in size, style, and ornamentation, the morality of its inhabitants. Downing's emotional exhortation illuminates the philosophical underpinnings of the earliest suburban ideal. "[T]he love of home," he said, "is one of the deepest feelings in our nature." But the American home "must be . . . built and loved upon new world, and not the old world, ideas and principles, . . . a home of the virtuous citizen."[10]

Downing, whom historians have called "the most influential single individual in translating the rural ideal into a suburban ideal," took his actual designs directly from those of English architect J. C. Loudon, although around them he created an architectural philosophy that he insisted was distinctly American. Other American builders and architects published pattern books following Downing's lead. Among them were Edward Shaw's *Rural Architecture* and Andrew Jackson Davis's *Rural Residences*. In the 1850s, Calvert Vaux brought out the first edition of *Villas and Cottages*. Pattern books showed perspective drawings, details of external ornament, and floor plans.[11]

As historian Gwendolyn Wright has pointed out, pattern book authors "considered themselves a critical component of the creation of a democratic republic." At midcentury, they were creating it in the suburbs. They were joined in the enthusiasm for "country" life by others, not builders or architects, but men who saw themselves as shapers of public opinion. Nathaniel Willis, for example, was editor of the *Home Monthly*, a magazine based in New York City. His urban economic base notwithstanding, he lived at a house he named Idlewild, along the Hudson River north of Manhattan. Willis connected democracy to living outside the city; in the 1850s he said: "While a family *in town* may be governed and held together mainly by money, there is a republic within the ring fence of a *country residence*."[12]

Pattern books, and the ideas of the men who created the house designs and composed the accompanying text, underwent little change through the 1870s, although the influence of English landscape design had become more dominant. A consciousness of their books' suburban market had, if anything, become heightened, but their claims that the houses promoted democratic values and respite from urban cares had not abated. As the authors of *Palliser's Model Homes* pleaded, "Let us have permanent homes built in accordance with the times and of modern style, homes where the manly virtues may grow strong and flourish, and which our children will remember in after years with pride."[13] In the pattern books of the 1870s, echoing as clearly as the voices of Americans Downing, Vaux, and Davis, was that of Englishman John Ruskin, who inspired the vogue for gothic architecture and who might be called the grandfather of the arts and crafts movement. Builders and architects in high Victorian America admired Ruskin and quoted him relentlessly. Ruskin scholars have pointed out, in fact, that his influence was much more powerful in the United States than in England. Ruskin was a critic, not an architect or landscape designer; he exhorted his readers and listeners to build sincerity and integrity into their houses, and like Downing he espoused the virtuous countryside over the wicked city. Following the lead of such men as Downing and Ruskin, suburban advocacy in the decade or so after the Civil War continued to focus on themes first articulated in the 1840s.[14]

In the years after the Civil War, some suburban advocates continued to take the idea of a connection between the suburb and rural America quite literally, suggesting the keeping of small farm animals and the cultivation of fruits and vegetables for home consumption (and sometimes, although less often, for sale).[15] Not everyone, however, believed that it was necessary to have a tiny farm in order to create a proper suburban environment. Influential landscape designer Frank Scott was a case in point. Scott did not want suburbanites to turn their grounds into miniature farms. Rather, he wanted to teach them to create communities that were also large parks, where passersby as well as residents could enjoy the beauty of each lawn and garden. Suburbanites, Scott insisted, had a public as well as a private duty to create a beautiful lawn and garden. Emphatically rejecting the idea that the farm was a desirable model for a suburb, he urged "the town-sick businessman who longs for a rural home . . . to take country life as a famishing man should take food—in very small quantities." He disdained the kinds of fences that shut out a lawn from view, and he discouraged making a suburb look like a farm by suggesting that people buy their vegetables and use their space to grow trees and flowers.[16]

Scott's popular landscape manual also underscored the masculine provenance of the suburban ideal. Scott assumed that husbands wanted to live in suburbs, and that their wives would be reluctant. In order to overcome such hesitation, men would have to make concessions in order to persuade their wives to move. Unless they wanted to face wifely disapproval, therefore, men would need to choose carefully an environment in which their wives would not be isolated from social and community life. Scott argued,

> [T]he wife and family are the homebodies of a residence. . . . The business man of a city who chooses a home out of it should feel that he is not depriving them of the pleasure incident to good neighborly society. During his daily absence, while his mind is kept in constant activity by hourly contact with his acquaintances, the family at home also needs some of the enlivening influences of easy intercourse with their equals, and should not be expected to find entire contentment in their household duties, with no other society day after day than that of their own little circle, and the voiceless beauty of grass, flowers, and trees.[17]

WOMEN AND DOMESTICITY

Frank Scott did not err in his assessment. The men described above advocated a suburban ideal as a way to keep the city at some remove—for themselves as a respite from urban cares as well as a device to preserve republican virtue, for their families as insulation from the temptations of the city. At the center of the male-defined surburban ideal was a physical space, and separation from the city was crucial. But many women, especially those who espoused what historian Kathryn Kish Sklar has called "the ideology of domesticity," sought in the mid-nineteenth century to make accommodation to the urban environment rather than to leave it. They could take such a position because, for them, the physical space was less important. At the heart of the ideology of domesticity was a cultural institution, the family.

It is important that we not automatically equate the ideology of domesticity with the somewhat vaguer notion of a domestic ideal, because in reality there were two domestic ideals. Both were based on the idea of separate spheres of activity for men and women, but one was shaped by men and focused on limiting women's activity to the care of home and family. The other was shaped by women, and it held that the family, over which women presided, was the central institution in American life. If the first, at least in intention, *confined* women within the home, the second turned the home into a political platform from which women would, using influence rather than power, transform the society.[18]

How the ideology of domesticity worked in practice is a subject for a later chapter; theoretically, however, by the middle of the nineteenth century, it had created a new feminine ideal for Americans: The model woman was a wife and devoted mother whose principal responsibility was to create a domestic environment that offered an alternative to the conflict and competition of the marketplace economy. In her home, a spiritual and emotional oasis, she succored her husband and nurtured her children. In the 1830s these ideas began to dominate the advice literature, displacing an older model of family life that had held sway since the early years of the new republic and reflecting major changes in the public perception of family life. The audience for such publications burgeoned in the 1830s, as social and geographical mobility threw Americans into situations for which their upbringing had left them unprepared. For women, this decade marked the beginnings of a shift from a womanly ideal inspired by the American Revolution, toward a sentimental redefinition of womanhood. If advice literature directed at women is any indication, the displacement of the older ideal occurred rather abruptly. Two of the most popular advice-writers of the 1830s, in fact, were offering what would soon become obsolete guidance. The wisdom of Lydia Maria Child, the young republic's most influential household writer, and Eliza Farrar, its foremost authority on etiquette, was about to become passé. Neither of these women exalted the home or romanticized women's role within it.

Both Child and Farrar addressed the "mothers of the republic," to use a concept made familiar by historian Linda Kerber. In revolutionary and postrevolutionary America, some historians have argued, women became political actors. Although they did not take on male-inspired public roles, they did, in Mary Beth Norton's words, become "active—if not equal—participants in discourse on public affairs and in endeavors that carried political significance." At the same time, the emphasis that a revolutionary generation placed on the idea of civic virtue made Americans more conscious of the function of women in perpetuating that virtue. As Abigail Adams said in 1799, "If a woman does not hold the reigns [sic] of Government, I see no reason for her not judging how they are conducted."[19]

The postrevolutionary family had a public as well as private aspect. Middle- and upper-class white women seized their chance for education, and they reminded their husbands and fathers that in significant ways the continuation of the republic rested on their efforts. One might argue, of course, that all of this simply heralded the beginnings of the ideology of domesticity; but what made it different, it seems to me, was the way in which these women viewed their political roles. The mothers of the republic insisted that their family roles had an immediate and direct impact on the polity, and it was the polity that was most important. For the mid-nineteenth-century advocate of the ideology of domesticity, family and home were the most significant. There are crucial differences in emphasis here, which should become more explicit if we compare the advice of Child and Farrar, at the end of the postrevolutionary period, with that of the proponents of the ideology of domesticity.

In the early 1830s Lydia Maria Child had offered hardheaded practical advice on running a household without waste or extravagance. For her, although civic virtue was not entirely ascetic, its hallmarks remained simplicity and discipline. Unlike her successors, Child did not urge women to define themselves solely as wives and mothers because to do so was noble, or to use a term that would become popular in the 1850s, "sacred." Rather, she told them that because they were women they had no choice but to accept domestic responsibilities, so they might as well make the best of them. Child later modified some of these ideas, and ceased to behave according to the norms she had so carefully set out at the beginning of her writing career; nevertheless, in *The American Frugal Housewife* she insisted that women had only two choices. They could accept their position in life, or rail ineffectually against it. She endorsed domestic education for girls because if "early accustomed to the duties of life, they will sit lightly as well as gracefully upon them."[20]

Unsentimental and unemotional about children, Child insisted, "The sooner children are taught to turn their faculties to some account, the better for them and for their parents." She condemned "useless play," and told mothers that "[a] child of six years old can be made useful. . . . [Children] can knit garters, suspenders, and stockings; they can make patchwork and braid straw; they can make mats for the table, and mats for the floor; they can weed the garden, and pick cranberries from the meadow, to be carried to market." For Child the idea of duty, of one's responsibility to be useful, was primary for everyone, children and adults. A woman should do her best in the station in which she found herself. As she reminded her readers, "True wisdom lies in finding out all the advantages of a situation in which we *are* placed, instead of imagining the enjoyments of one in which we are *not* placed."[21]

Child's injunctions to women were strict, even rigid. Eliza Farrar presented her advice differently, with a much lighter touch; she was nevertheless equally straightforward and unsentimental. She too, viewed household duties as a necessary evil, and quoted approvingly the eighteenth-century French writer Marie-Jeanne Roland's famous statement about woman's work: "Domestic cares I never neglected; but I cannot comprehend how a woman of method and activity can have her attention be engrossed by them." Like Child, Farrar insisted that a woman must know how to run a house, since "[i]f a woman does not know how the various work of a house should be done, she might as well know nothing, for that is her express vocation." Nevertheless, domestic cares, "important as they are, must not be allowed to consume too much time, and the ready wit and ingenuity of a woman cannot be turned to better account, than in devising methods of expediting household affairs, and producing the best effect with the least expense of time and labor."[22]

Neither Child nor Farrar believed that domestic duties possessed intrinsic moral significance. Doing them well, and quickly, freed women up for their larger purpose in life. For Child, that larger purpose was to protect the revolutionary ideal of civic virtue, which she believed was endangered by lack of vigilance and by the vogue for European styles. For Farrar, it was the development and inculcation of correct, yet democratic, manners. In their advice to women on the ways to conduct family life, Child emphasized duty, while Farrar stressed affection. Nevertheless their descriptions as well as their strictures resembled one another's far more than they would resemble those of the later advice givers, who encouraged women to fill their lives with domestic cares and enshrined motherhood as the preeminent function of women.

Farrar and Child represented a point of view that became outdated even as they wrote. Accepting the notion of "woman's sphere," yet resolutely refusing to romanticize it, they misread the signs of the times. The glorification of women's maternal and domestic roles had begun to take on a life of its own. This is understandable. In the final analysis, although Child and Farrar urged women to garb themselves as Columbia, they also told them to wear their robes at home. After the early revolutionary fervor had abated, the severe restrictions on what women could actually do in the society remained. The women who advocated a new ideal for their sex understood those restrictions and decided to use them to their advantage. As Nancy Cott has argued, "The doctrine of woman's sphere opened to women (reserved for them) the avenues of domestic influence, religious morality, and child nurture. It articulated a social power based on their special female qualities."[23]

The literary domestic Catharine Sedgwick epitomized, in her

work if not in her life, the new female ideal. Whereas the idea of domesticity as a cult or creed had been noticeably absent from the writings of Farrar and Child's early work, it informed all of Sedgwick's, including *Home,* her extraordinarily popular novel that went through twenty editions in the eleven years after its first appearance in 1835. An urban morality play, *Home* exalted domestic life. And for my purposes—one of which is to distinguish the ideology of domesticity from the kind of residential ideal advocated by mid-nineteenth century suburbanites—the novel is important for its contention that urbanization had made necessary the creation of a new physical environment for domesticity. Although the family returns to the father's boyhood village at the very end of the novel, its sturdy moral values were nurtured and preserved in an urban setting. In a way unlike either Farrar or Child, Sedgwick stressed the integration of the physical and moral aspects of family influence.[24]

Sedgwick's belief in an inherent interconnection between the physical house, and the emotional construct of home which it surrounded, was absolute; she accentuated the relationship between the physical and moral environment with a subplot involving a family that did not create a character-building architectural and material involvement. Their failure resulted in the financial ruin of the family and the suicide of the eldest son. As David Handlin has said of this novel's message, "the home mirrored the moral and religious state of those who lived in it."[25] Sedgwick took the prevailing ideas of woman's duty, sentimentalized them, and added the belief that the family should create a physical space in which to bring those ideas into practice. She and others who articulated similar ideas would enjoy genuine success. As Ronald Hogeland has noted, by the middle of the nineteenth century "the home" had replaced "nature" as a source of spiritual renewal.[26]

Sedgwick suggested in *Home* that urbanization required a new conception of family life. Neither she nor other advocates of the ideology of domesticity in the pre–Civil War years were antiurban. It was not urban life itself, but the way that men and women conducted themselves in the city, which caused most of the problems. The city itself held few terrors if a man worked for his family, if his wife tended to her domestic duties, and the children took their pleasures in the home. True, the city contained snares for the weak and unwary, but moral fortitude could prevent a fall. The Barclays of *Home* possessed such fortitude, and as Blaine McKinley has suggested of the households of mid-nineteenth-century domestic fiction in general, they did so with the help of their country-bred servants. The domestic novels from which McKinley took his examples were set unabashedly in the city, but the servants came from the country and helped to preserve rural values. McKinley argues persuasively that domestic writers suggested "symbolically . . . that the pastoral virtues . . . retained their vitality in an increasingly urban setting."[27]

What was important was what a woman did in the home and how she felt about it, not where that home was located. Only five years after Eliza Farrar had warned her readers not to become "engrossed" by their domestic duties, Catharine Beecher, who soon emerged as the most influential domestic advice-giver of the nineteenth century, contradicted her: "Surely it is a pernicious and mistaken idea, that the duties which tax a woman's mind are petty, trivial, or unworthy of the highest grade of intellect and moral worth. Instead of allowing this feeling, every woman should imbibe from early youth, the impression, that she is training for the charge of the most important, most difficult, and the most sacred and interesting duties that can possibly employ the highest intellect."[28]

Beecher intended nothing less than to create a social theory that would unify the contradictions of a society both democratic and in many ways inegalitarian. Republican motherhood had not prevented divisiveness; Beecher, however, intended to minimize the differences of class, race, and ethnicity by maximizing those of gender. The central tenet of Beecher's ideology of domesticity was that the home, where women presided, was the central institution of American life, and the domestic role of women was the linchpin of social unity. As her biographer Kathryn Kish Sklar has noted, Beecher's philosophy required "the isolation of women in the home and away from full participation in the society." As compensation for having voluntarily abdicated the right to a position in the world of men, women would dominate the home; social stability would be the happy result.[29]

It was not only advice-giving women who adopted the new domestic ideal. Anna Cora Mowatt's play *Fashion*, a Broadway hit in 1845, took the same line as *Home*, but much less heavy-handedly. *Fashion* satirized the follies of weak-minded urbanites. So that the wealthy Mr. Trueblood would rescue the Tiffany family from financial disaster, silly Mrs. Tiffany and her daughter had to move out of the city and stay in the country until they could learn to behave sensibly within it. Mr. Tiffany, however, stayed on, because he had learned his lesson and could be safely trusted in an urban environment. Silliness was not a gendered quality in *Fashion*, which had its share of foolish men as well.[30]

According to these writers, the mid-nineteenth-century city need not inhibit domesticity. On the contrary, its economic opportunities could help to provide the material accoutrements to successful domesticity—a parlor organ, handsome furniture, and relative freedom from drudgery for middle-class wives, who could then devote their time to the cultural as well as emotional needs of the family. By the 1850s such advice-givers had come to believe that domestic life was not only the sphere in which women had been placed, and that they therefore might as well make the best of it, but that domestic duties were sacred and significant, and to engage in them was ennobling and elevating. To be sure, vague suggestions that a woman should not become enmeshed in domestic trivia still appeared as late as the early fifties, but they were overshadowed by the louder admonitions to women to carve out of their domesticity a domain in which they could rule and from which they could exert their power.[31]

Mary Ryan remarked astutely about the ideology of domesticity: "Any cultural construct that achieved such popularity bore some resemblance to social reality. . . . At midcentury, middle-class urban males and females were more starkly separated than in times past. Women's roles had indeed become more domestic than social, more privatized, less communal. At the same time, women did exert considerable social power from their private stations."[32] Indeed, women wanted to transfer the values of the home into public life. The ideology of domesticity was a doctrine of public influence from the private sphere. For that reason, many of its adherents believed that in a restructured and more privatized urban milieu domestic values would thrive among all social classes. Women therefore increasingly broadened the concept of domesticity, and one important field of action was the city.

The women of New York's Children's Aid Society and those of the social purity movement provide two important examples. Rather than retreating from the city to some bucolic environment, these women insisted that the city could become "homelike." Christine Stansell discovered, for example, that the women of the Children's Aid Society in antebellum New York disagreed with Charles Loring Brace and his male associates, who argued that the solution to urban ills lay in rural America. The women, contends Stansell, "viewed domesticity and true womanhood as a means to regenerate a class-divided city." These are words that Catharine Beecher would have approved. According to these middle-class reforming women, "properly established gender norms could realign the social geography of the city, strengthening the boundaries between public and private." David Pivar's analysis of the women of the social purity movement in the 1870s makes a similar argument. "Purity reformers," he noted, "located the promise of American life on the urban frontier."[33]

If such women wanted to make the world more homelike, material feminists wanted to make the home more worldlike. That is, they desired to put the growing economies of scale, introduced by industrialization, to use in restructuring the American household. Delores

Hayden, who gave them their name and brilliantly analyzed their work in *The Grand Domestic Revolution,* noted the theoretical success but practical failure of Melusina Fay Peirce, who organized an unsuccessful experiment in woman-controlled, cooperative housekeeping in suburban Cambridge, Massachusetts.[34] Those cooperative schemes that were successful were unabashedly urban rather than suburban in the 1880s (a fact that would not be lost on the feminists of the next generation). In New York the architect Philip Hubert organized Hubert Home Clubs so that groups of families could buy apartment houses. The Hawthorne, the Hubert, the Rembrandt, the Milano, the Chelsea, the Mount Morris, 80 Madison Avenue, and 125 Madison Avenue were all successful products of Hubert's work. Hubert combined "duplex units and hotel facilities," for well-to-do families. Hayden concludes: "Hubert's work inspired many feminists, utopian socialists, and futurist novelists to continue to eulogize the social, physical and economic potential of the cooperatively owned apartment hotel in the 1880s and 1890s."[35]

For the most part, however, these units, when built, did not explicitly embody notions of feminism or radicalism. They offered housing for the urban upper middle class, using industrial technology to remove laundry, food preparation, and heating from the work of the individual household. They did release women from what the late nineteenth-century women's magazines referred to as "the servant problem," and freed them from having to do their own chores when domestics were in short supply. Such urban women, in short, had every reason to prefer the city to its periphery.

As late as the 1880s some advocates of the ideology of domesticity still believed that their mission was to domesticate the urban environment, and they saw no threat to family life in cooperative housekeeping. Indeed, for middle-class wives and mothers who could afford to take advantage of urban services, the city in the third quarter of the nineteenth century, and even beyond, provided unparalleled access to social life, shopping, and educational opportunities for children. The suburbs simply could not compete on these grounds. As for the domestic reformers, well into the 1870s, they believed that they could restructure the city; they did not hold the view that urban life was inherently corrupt and inimical to middle-class family life. There were evils in the city, to be sure, but the city ideal remained valid. Social purity reformers, for example, believed they could "extend the spirit of the home" throughout the urban community. Believers in the ideology of domesticity remained convinced that the middle-class family was not in specific danger from the urban environment. As long as the proper architectural and spatial dimensions of what Gwendolyn Wright has termed the moral home were maintained, the family remained safe.[36]

URBAN DOMESTICITY AND THE SUBURBAN IDEAL

Until the end of the 1870s, middle-class Americans seemed to agree more with the women who espoused the ideology of domesticity than with the men who urged the nation to suburbanize. The ranks of suburban advocates had not swelled into enormous numbers in the decade after the Civil War, though among them were influential editors and writers, not to mention landscape designers, builders, and architects. Although it may seem logical to think of families moving to the suburbs as soon as the technology existed to take them there, in most cities the technology preceded, often by decades, the desire of large numbers of the middle classes to move there. Both railroads and streetcar companies bought up suburban land in the 1850s, 1860s, and 1870s, and proceeded to try to lure residents to the newly opened land. But it was not until the 1880s that the cultural and social impetus was there to accomplish the shift. As Victor Goheen noted of Toronto (but it was true of most North American cities) "a substantial expression of enthusiasm for suburban living was only to materialize when the city spawned a growing middle class and when this group could afford the luxury in cost and time of reaching the outer limits of the city."[37]

Why not a shift in the 1870s? Technology was not the issue; values were. In spite of the cadre of enthusiasts for suburban or "country" life (within commuting distance of the city), there were other Americans besides the women of the domestic reform movement who continued to believe that the city was redeemable. Urban reformers were convinced that apartment houses surrounded by parks and gardens, and imbued with the idea of community, could best maintain republican virtues without sacrificing economic progress or the advantages of city life. Such designs were an attempt to integrate nature with modern life, reflective of an urban ideal—the "great, compact metropolis," to use the words of David Handlin. The city would reconcile nature and progress through the creation of great parks, of which New York's Central Park and Philadelphia's Fairmount Park were two examples. Again, quoting Handlin, "No matter how they were justified, these visions usually included vast public parks around or in which apartment houses were located." Apartment houses attracted considerable interest in the 1870s. Many of them were designed with the expectation that the people who lived in them would constitute a community. Some apartment house advocates even hoped that apartment-house living could help to ameliorate the growing divisiveness that they perceived had become a constant in the cities.[38]

I do not mean to deny that technology provided the means for the American middle class to become suburban in the long run, or that some urbanites (and not only women) rejected the suburbs because the city was more, well, civilized. If some reformers and other defenders of urban America expected to save urban life through censorship, and others by marrying nature and the city with the creation of the apartment house, others chose the city because they found the suburbs to be remote, uncomfortable, and lacking in the amenities that upper middle-class urbanites, at least, could take for granted. One city dweller, discouraged by his family's residence in "a flat where the upper floor lodger distilled slops through our ceiling, where the under floor came home drunk every evening, and the back floor played the piano and wind instruments until morning" decided to move to "the joyous country." The family did not stay. "We went full of expectation, dreaming of fresh butter. It took but four short, animated weeks, to demonstrate to our satisfaction that the joyous country, as seen in the suburbs, is a delusion and a snare. It is no country—it is no city." The snares of the suburbs included inadequate public services, inconvenient and uncomfortable mass transit, a sense of isolation, and the feeling that the residents lived in identical little boxes. The author told of coming home late one night, and mistaking someone else's house for his own, a joke that made the rounds again in the 1950s.[39]

Toward the end of the century, the ideology of domesticity and the suburban ideal, which had developed independently and from different political bases, fused together to create what sociologists have sometimes rather inelegantly called suburban familism. That fusion would become the dominant theme of middle-class suburbanism in the early part of the twentieth century, and the next few chapters explore how that happened. But in the immediate post–Civil War years, there was at least one important hint of the change to come—Catharine Beecher herself, the principal architect of the ideology of domesticity, began to believe that the family thrived best in a suburban environment.

The American Woman's Home, on which she collaborated with her more famous sister, the novelist Harriet Beecher Stowe, was published in 1869, an expanded and enlarged version of the earlier *Treatise on Domestic Economy.* Beecher had not abandoned her belief in separate spheres or in the importance of women's domestic role for protecting and preserving the family. But in *The American Woman's Home,* the Beecher sisters viewed that home in an expanded setting. They still agreed with Catharine Sedgwick that the physical home reflected and even created an appropriate social and moral environment, but they went further; not only the individual home, but also the surrounding neighborhood, must express domestic peace and tranquillity. It was beneficial, they contended, for "men toiling in the cities to rear families in the country."[40] By the country they meant the suburbs, reached by commuter railroad.

Like *A Treatise on Domestic Economy, The American Woman's Home* insisted on clearly enunciated and distinct gender roles as essential to make the home the central force in American life, but the later book paid much more attention to the location of that home. *The American Woman's Home* could not be described as antiurban, but the Beecher sisters had developed reservations about the city. From the 1830s, when Sedgwick first published *Home,* creators of the ideology of domesticity emphasized the material aspects of a sacred domestic environment. Most continued to argue, as had Sedgwick, that although the old-fashioned village house was more likely to produce families of uprightness and integrity, careful parents could produce the same results in a city home reflecting architectural morality. For them, the physical house was inextricably linked to the rectitude of the people who lived there. If the appropriate physical environment could no longer be found in the city, then the city house would no longer be able to instill the proper virtues.

The Beecher sisters had begun to consider whether the location of the home might be nearly as important as the home itself. What had happened in the years between 1840 and 1870 to change the symbolic meaning of "home" so that it seemed now almost to require a suburban environment in order to promote the domestic values and virtues? In the first place, domesticity in its earlier forms had not solved the problems it was created to address. Catharine Beecher had, in the 1840s, expected the ideology of domesticity to unify a nation torn by sectional and economic strife. Domesticity would cut across class, ethnic, racial, and sectional lines, and gender differentiation would become a dividing force that paradoxically would bring about unification. It did not work, as the Civil War graphically demonstrated. Beecher remained convinced, however, that her insistence on the primacy of the home, and on the preeminence of the woman who managed that home, was the appropriate way to adjust to a complex, rapidly changing society. Although committed to the fundamental idea of domesticity, Beecher was not rigid in her notions of how to accomplish her goals. Late in her life, she began to move toward the idea that the proper home might require a distinct physical as well as psychological space. The then embryonic suburb would guarantee that physical space. Nevertheless, she never insisted that a suburban location was essential for the model family. Although believing that suburbs facilitated domesticity, she never claimed outright that her readers should leave the city.[41]

If she had lived long enough to read Edward Bellamy's *Looking Backward,* she might have. Bellamy's novel created an urban utopia. His city was clean, its inhabitants productive and content. And the women who lived in it did no housework. They held jobs and took their meals in neighborhood restaurants. Charlotte Perkins Gilman, the great early twentieth-century feminist and grandniece of Catharine Beecher, adopted Bellamy's brand of socialism, as did thousands of other men and women. Bellamy's novel illustrated a society in which the kind of domesticity Catharine Beecher had preached about all her life, had become obsolete. It appeared in 1888, and by then some women's rights advocates were just beginning to make a connection between the rejection of separate spheres and urban life.[42] Perhaps the Beecher sisters saw it coming.

Making America suburban was a complex process, and so was the creation of what we have come to call the suburban ideal, which has invoked different images during different periods. Some suburbanization, such as the early development of Brooklyn, seemed predicated on simple economics; it was cheaper and more convenient to live in Brooklyn and ride the steam ferry to Manhattan. But perhaps the experience of Somerville and Cambridge were more predictive of the future, as the men who lived there turned their backs on the mixed economy of the fringe community and promoted a residential ideal. From the 1840s, when this ideal emerged, through the 1870s, the suburban ideal emphasized the political importance of retaining some elements of agrarianism in order to preserve America's republican heritage, the need to be close to nature, and the necessity of respite for careworn husbands. The ideal was resolutely masculine, and it suggested that the suburbs were necessary for the nation's political health. During this period, domestic reformers were more concerned with the house itself, and its ability to create a moral environment, than they were with moving the house from the city. In the post–Civil War period, the suburban ideal would become more privatized and less communal, and the domestic ideal shifted from social housekeeping to what Sheila Rothman has called "educated motherhood," but for most suburban residents of the years immediately after the war, that ideal had not yet become completely formed.

PART *One*

FAMILY AND SUBURB IN VICTORIAN AMERICA

CHAPTER ONE

Moulding the Moral Nature

Man is appointed by his maker to sail upon the ocean, *to circumnavigate the* globe, *to cover the earth with fruitful fields, and colossal* workmanship. *He is called to the* field, *the* forum, the halls of state. *But woman has a more* sacred appointment, *a* higher *and* holier work! *She must sow the seed, and watch with ceaseless anxiety its growth, plant the tender and delicate germs of principle, and train the young tendrils of the feelings and affections. She is set to guard, to instruct, to mould the* moral nature.

L.H.G. Abell,
Woman in Her Various Relations,
1851

The ideology of domesticity did not arise out of the early suburban ideal, and neither was the converse true; the former did not shape the latter. For the future of suburbia, what was important about domesticity was the way that it prescribed specific models of family life. We must remember that the ideology of domesticity was not a static construct, but one of plasticity that not only underwent change itself but also transformed the things it touched. Those changes, which are the subject of this chapter, ultimately brought the domestic ideal and the suburban ideal together to form a union that came to fruition around the turn of the twentieth century. During the middle third of the nineteenth century, however, the women who shaped the concept of domesticity gave their attention to the social construction of family life and to the intimate domestic space in which that family life occurred. They prescribed a modified patriarchal family, one softened by love and mutual obligation, as the model for middle-class Americans.

I want to begin exploring the changes in the values of these middle-class families, therefore, by examining the words of the prescribers. Historians have become wary of advice literature and popular fiction as historical evidence, because used alone, they cannot help us to understand whether their strictures were followed. An exact correlation between advice and behavior, however, is not the only way of judging the former's truth or usefulness. There are other ways to check validity. In the first place, the extraordinary popularity of such works demonstrates that people wanted to know what kinds of beliefs were culturally acceptable. Furthermore, what people believe is just as important as the way they behave. Although our behavior may contravene our beliefs, the perception of the gap between belief and behavior is what shapes conscience. And finally, men and women presumably read these books in order to know if what they did or wanted to do would help them achieve a social goal, whether it was presiding over a household or becoming a success in business. The advice literature may have taught them to be insincere, for example, but that very insincerity had a social impact.[1]

DOMESTICITY PRESCRIBED

In the mid-nineteenth century, it was an article of faith among middle-class Americans that healthy family life required a household over which a mother presided, for which a father worked, from which young boys were expected to sally forth and conquer the world, and within which young girls were to prepare themselves to follow in their mother's footsteps. Advice-writers helped their readers to figure out not only how to do this but why it was so important. We have already seen how in the 1830s a significant change occurred in the ways women advice-givers defined the meaning of women's household roles. Under the influence of the ideal of republican virtue Eliza Farrar and Lydia Maria Child had urged women to perform their domestic responsibilities diligently because it was their duty; by the early 1840s, as that ideal was transformed, such women as Catharine Sedgwick, Sarah Josepha Hale, and Catharine Beecher had told them that those responsibilities constituted the means of social salvation. The result was the ideology of domesticity, which had the immediate effect of isolating women's work in the home while at the same time making them answerable for the moral vision of American society.

In the earliest construction of the ideology of domesticity, its advocates declared that women would preside over the society from the home. One need only recall how some of the early female reform societies of the 1830s were reduced to auxiliaries of male organizations by midcentury or privatized within the home to understand how domesticity operated initially to limit women's public roles at the same time that it broadened their private power. And yet, such private power was not inconsiderable. Women used it first to claim the right of preeminence in child-rearing, and they then invoked that preeminence to influence the behavior of their husbands outside the family circle.[2]

Godey's Lady's Book was one of the most important purveyors of the ideology of domesticity. A forerunner of modern magazines for women such as *Good Housekeeping* and *The Ladies Home Journal*, *Godey's* published much of its domestic advice in the form of fiction. Edited by Sarah Josepha Hale, in the 1840s its fiction showed the ways in which a woman could ruin her family permanently if she did not adhere to domestic principles. The gruesome fate of Clara in "The Open Hand" offers a nearly perfect illustration of the pitfalls of married life, as the magazine viewed them. Clara, a young woman of unformed principles, married a man of fashion. Instead of gently influencing him to develop financial prudence and steadier habits, she let him influence her and spent her days gadding about and her evenings at the theatre. Eventually they had a child; her maternal instincts triumphed and she now spent her evenings at home (alone, because her husband continued his old habits). But she wanted to share some of her husband's life as well, so one evening she went out with him, leaving their daughter with a servant. The servant, predictably, was negligent. An accident followed, the child was permanently disfigured, and Clara instantly recognized her guilt for placing her husband's pleasure above her child's needs. Too late. To compound her misery, Clara's husband failed in business. At the end of the story she had "hopelessly" resigned "herself to her fallen station," with "little prognostic of a brighter day."[3]

This story, typical of *Godey's* offerings in the 1840s, had two morals. First, the mother-child bond was inviolate, taking precedence over individual pleasures and a husband's wishes. Second, and equally important, women must take great care in their choice of a husband or they would find themselves miserable. The author of this story had no pity for Clara, who had failed in both her domestic and social duty. "The Open Hand" is a frightening story, in spite of its heavy-handed melodrama, because it contained an element of reality that no woman could escape; if she made a mistake in choosing her husband, or if she failed to influence him in the early days of her marriage, she might well suffer for it for the rest of her life.

In the nineteenth century, when few women over the age of twenty-five were employed outside the home, particularly in the middle classes, marriage *was* most women's occupation. For a woman to fail at marriage meant that she had failed in business, and American society in the second quarter of the nineteenth century had scant sympathy for those who failed. Advocates of the ideology of domesticity, however, understood that if their vision of the domestic ideal were to flourish, women would have to protect themselves. But how? Some women endorsed the Declaration of Rights and Sentiments, and threw their lot in with the women's rights movement. But most did not; in the 1850s and 1860s the "woman movement" consisted of a pioneering and radical band. It was not until after the Civil War that women's rights began to seem less than revolutionary and to attract a broader constituency.[4]

If women were not to demand legal and civil equality, how could they protect themselves against disaster? Above all, the advice-givers warned, they needed to be very careful about whom they married. Domestic writers repeatedly urged young women never to marry without love, because without love it would become even more difficult to endure the inevitable hardships of marriage. But even with love, marriage required more fortitude and sacrifice on the part of women than of men. The literary domestic Caroline Howard Gilman, who appeared to have had a happy marriage herself, suggested that a woman could never let her husband know how she really felt; she must instead seek "self-control, almost to hypocrisy," and pretend "cheerfulness when her frame is drooping," or else "languish alone."[5]

Around the middle of the nineteenth century, a woman who was unable or unwilling to marry, if she were not the fortunate recipient of an hereditary income, could expect to have to struggle making a living. And single women did not escape easily the domestic ideal. In fact, Catharine Beecher, the most important advocate of the ideology of domesticity and a single woman herself, spent much of her life making teaching a respectable (if not especially well-paying) occupation for women, using the argument that teaching simply exercised another aspect of the maternal instinct. There were, nevertheless, some advantages to being single: Beecher pointedly reminded her audiences that the duty of obedience to men did not apply to single women, who could be household heads themselves. Single women working as teachers and heading their own households, according to Beecher, did not contravene domesticity but extended its values to the larger community. But if being single had its pleasures it also had its price. Beecher herself never had a settled home, never possessed financial security, and had to depend on her family and friends to give her a home at several points in her life. A woman not gifted with Beecher's ability to announce that she was arriving for a visit of several months at her convenience, or blessed with a large family of sufficient means to support her when she was in pecuniary difficulty, had a far harder time of it. Many women lived on the sufferance of family members or eked out a living in one or another poorly paid job.[6]

To dwell on the economic difficulties of single women and the calculative aspects of accepting a husband makes marriage seem like a business. In a way it was.[7] That is not to say that husbands and wives did not love each other; still, historians who have studied middle-class marriage in the nineteenth century have given us vastly different views of it. Some have found marriages of near equality, what we might call "companionate" marriages.[8] Carl Degler has written of affectionate husbands and wives who wrote loving letters to one another when separated and placed these letters in evidence to demonstrate the existence of such companionate unions. However, such letters, written mostly during the very long absences of the husbands, do not always tell us what the marriage was like when the couple was together. And although they do show us that husbands and wives expressed their love for each other, to say that is not the same thing as saying that they had a shared domestic vision or even that they were each other's confidants and dear friends. To show that a man loved a woman is not the same thing as showing that he shared her interests or problems.[9]

This should come as no surprise. Historians Mary Ryan and Suzanne Lebsock, in separate studies of communities as far apart as Utica (New York) and Petersburg (Virginia), discovered few, if any, marriages of equality. As Lebsock commented, "The evidence from Petersburg suggests that marriage was fundamentally asymmetrical. Men retained the upper hand in almost every aspect of marriage." She "doubts whether the majority of Petersburg's wives would have classified their own marriages as companionate." And Ryan, who found that middle-class women and men in Utica accepted the doctrine of separate spheres at midcentury (although each sex interpreted it differently), suggested as well that "the model of female influence with its injunction that wives coyly persuade and slyly manipulate husbands," also brought tensions into the relationship.[10]

The dynamic of the "model of female influence" may not have given women power, but it did provide for them a central role in ordering family life. Domestic writers repeatedly asserted the significance of women's roles in the family. L. H. G. Abell told her readers that the influence of mothers and wives was "far reaching"; she hoped that such words would "soothe and even elevate" their minds. Abell called women's duties "sacred" and "dignified." Catharine Beecher and Harriet Beecher Stowe also used the word "sacred" to characterize women's work in the home. Some English writers went beyond their American counterparts in determining women's roles within the home. Domestic novelist and advice-writer Dinah Craick, for example, insisted that since men got to control the outside world, they should keep out of women's business inside the home, where the woman should be "the autocrat." Men, she said, had "no business to meddle in the management of the house."[11]

All of these writers assured women of the worth of their "calling." L. H. G. Abell insisted that "[woman] is set to guard, to instruct, to mould the *moral nature!*" Abell almost invariably used the singular; all women are Woman. And the Beecher sisters affirmed that "any man of sense and discernment," who lived in a well-run household and paid attention to what went on in it, "would conclude that no statesman, at the head of a nation's affairs, had more frequent calls for wisdom, firmness, tact, discrimination, prudence, and versatility of talent, than such a woman."[12]

The insistence on the importance of women's domestic duties sometimes rang hollow. After explaining to women the great significance of their work, domestic writers in the next breath reminded them not to be too upset if their families failed to notice. They advised their readers to remain cheerful and calm, because the whims of husbands and the heedlessness of children would invariably destroy the best plans to keep an orderly household. The message was perhaps inevitably contradictory: on the one hand, running a household was as important as governing a nation; on the other hand, husbands and children were likely to pay little attention to whatever system a woman devised. Women had to be able themselves, these writers insisted, to see that what they did was important. One of the ways that it would become so in the years after the Civil War would be for women to bring domesticity to the larger society, just as the voluntarism of the 1820s and 1830s had reorganized family life.[13]

Although it is always difficult to know how seriously readers took the strictures of the advice-givers, recent studies of mid-nineteenth-century family and community history, in particular the illuminating work of Mary Ryan and Suzanne Lebsock, have given us a picture of the middle-class family that conforms to a surprising extent to the prescriptive literature—not so much in the sense that women were real-life counterparts of fictional heroines or that people's behavior matched the strictures in the advice books, but rather that they believed in the cultural values embodied in the literary material. And they did so even when their own lives failed to conform to the patterns. Poor Lavinia Johnson, a Utica woman whose husband failed to live up to the expectations for middle-class men during the period, nevertheless comforted herself with her own adherence to the ideology of domesticity, in which she kept faith through more than thirty years of an unhappy and surely unequal marriage. We must remember, however, that the ideology of domesticity, although it accepted and made use of the doctrine of separate spheres, had its subversive element, an element that Carroll Smith-Rosenberg, among others, has often brilliantly illuminated. Where men thought of separate spheres as a description of a reality in which women did not interfere in public affairs, women increasingly insisted that their voluntary abdication of positions in the world of men made them the moral arbiters of male standards.[14]

We know less about men's family roles during the middle of the nineteenth century. In our own version of separate spheres, historians until recently have tended to focus on the private lives of women and public life among men. Possibly men were relatively unimportant in the home during this period. As Mary Ryan observed for Utica, by midcentury "the idea of fatherhood itself seemed almost to wither away as the bond between mother and child assumed central place in the constellation of family affection."[15] This is not to suggest that the male slate is absolutely blank. During the 1830s, 1840s, and 1850s there was advice literature for men, written by men. This literature fell into different categories. One was the marriage manual genre, written mostly by reform-minded physicians. Among the marriage advisors perhaps no one was more prolific than William Alcott, who wrote more than thirty books on marriage, some addressed to young single women, others to new husbands. His books were widely read, his *Physiology of Marriage* running into at least seven editions. In *The Young Husband,* first published in 1839, Alcott castigated husbands for their tendency to spend all of their leisure time away from the home. But how much time was the right amount of time to spend with the family? The dinner hour was quite enough. This was all a husband and father needed "to instruct [his family] in all the common concerns of life."[16]

Naturally, authors who wrote specifically to advise young men on marital issues had something to say about the domestic relationship, and Alcott was a fair specimen. Even more interesting, however, are the general advice books written for young men, because these proposed to show how men should organize their lives as a whole. Although purportedly comprehensive, such volumes rarely concerned themselves with men's roles as husbands or fathers. Instead, they emphasized economic and social mobility, urging young men to develop the qualities of sobriety, honesty, and a capacity for hard work because these qualities were essential to economic success, not because they would help a man become a better husband or father. Neither did male writers offer suggestions on choosing a suitable wife, or on appropriate behavior toward one's children. Although the moral young man avoided prostitutes, gambling dens, and the questionable pleasures of urban life, the advice manuals offered him no specialized assistance in settling his personal life.[17]

A British writer, William Rathbone Grey, did express anxieties about the future of marriage, suggesting that prostitution made many men "lo[a]th to resign the easy independence, the exceptional luxuries, the habitual indulgences of a bachelor's career, for the fetters of a wife, the burden and responsibility of children, and the decent monotony of the domestic hearth." Grey's portrait of youthful decadence was not unusual for the period, but the explicit expression of the fear that it would deter young men from marrying was. Unlike Grey, American writers of advice for young men generally contented themselves with painting lurid pictures of corruption, without correspondingly urging their readers to embrace "the decent monotony" of domesticity. Most male advice writers in the 1840s and 1850s did not exhibit misgivings about their readers' future domestic lives; books by women did, but they addressed a different, mostly female, audience.[18]

One of the few men who did take up the question of domestic duties of husbands at midcentury, temperance writer T. S. Arthur, did so for the readers of *Godey's Lady's Book.* Arthur's series on "model husbands" explored the impact of husbands' temperaments on domestic life. His "bad model" husband had a foul temper, paid no attention to his children, and was selfish and inconsiderate, leaving his wife alone night after night while he went out with his male cronies. A "better specimen," although he began married life impatient with his bride's inability to manage the household to his satisfaction, learned to subdue his selfishness and thereby bring about an improvement in *her* domestic abilities. If for Arthur a "better specimen" of a husband was one who could learn to subdue his anger, a "good model" had none to subdue. The ideal husband took delight in his family, spending his evenings at home reading with his wife and children. Arthur insisted that men had domestic obligations that included helping around the house in emergencies, as well as showing attention to their wives and children, and taking their pleasures in the home with the family rather than in clubs and taverns with their male friends. Arthur, however, was atypical; significantly, he published these articles in a magazine read mostly by women. Still, his contention that men set the tone and pace of family life, and had the power thereby to make their wives and children happy or miserable, was an unwelcome reminder to those readers of the unequal nature of power even among those women fortunate enough to have "a good model" husband.[19]

T. S. Arthur endorsed a companionate marriage within a patriarchal context. Catharine Beecher also endorsed marital companionship and patriarchy, but with a difference. She defined male superiority in such terms as to make it an almost disagreeable burden, and perhaps this represents the real difference between the ways that men and women who thought about these questions looked at those attributes defined as masculine or feminine in the mid-nineteenth century. "Every boy," Beecher warned, "is to be trained for his future . . . position [as husband and father] by labor and sacrifices for his mother and sisters. It is the brother who is to do the hardest and most disagreeable work . . . and perform the most laborious drudgeries. . . . [He] is to give his mother and sisters precedence in all the convenience and comforts of home life."[20] To contemplate such preparation for his future should have been enough to make any boy think twice about male superiority.

The "convenience and comforts" of home were things to which both the advocates of the suburban ideal and domestic reformers gave considerable thought. But although the former were concerned more about the location of the model home, the latter wanted to make sure that its interior design proclaimed the appropriate messages. As Colleen McDannell has argued, for American middle-class Protestants, particularly for women (as they had come by this period to dominate daily religious practices), the home assumed the character of sacred space. While the men who wrote about architecture and landscape design in pattern books and in popular literature in general articulated a vision of suburban home as refuge, the women domestic reformers thought of the home as a workplace. Both were correct, for men and women had very different roles and functions in the house. Women performed their sacred (to use a word favored by numerous domestic writers) duties in the sacred space of the home. But a home that was both refuge and workplace was a complicated one. It was necessary to create an interior environment that promoted both.[21]

SEPARATE SPHERES BY DESIGN

How did American Victorians create a home that reflected its sacredness (to use McDannell's terminology) or morality (to use Gwendolyn Wright's)? One way to come to grips with the issue is to examine the houses themselves.[22] Popular pattern books of the 1860s and 1870s suggest that a typical, freestanding middle-class residential design was of a tall and rather narrow house, with a basement and two stories capped by a full attic. Its interior arrangement both protected family privacy and encouraged separation *within* the family (see table 1.1). Most designs included an entrance hall, which in larger houses would have been of substantial proportion, with seating arrangements and often a fireplace. The hall and parlor presented the public face of the family. Sixty-one percent of a sample of seventy pattern-book houses had both a parlor and sitting room on the first floor. Another 20 percent had three or more first-floor living areas, adding on a conservatory, library, or study. Only 19 percent of the designs offered just one living area on the first floor.

The design and function of the rooms suggested not only a separation between the family and outsiders, but also a good deal of internal familial segregation. Although the majority of middle-class houses did not have billiard or smoking rooms, the study was commonly viewed as a male refuge, where a man could "keep his gun, his top-boots, his fishing rod and his horrid pipes."[23] Twenty-one percent of the sample houses had basement kitchens; in theory if not always in practice, kitchens were still supposed to be the domain of servants. The second floor sheltered more intimate functions, although occasionally house plans included semipublic areas on the

Table 1.1. Use of Interior Space in Victorian Suburban Houses

	NO.	%
1 story	0	0
1½ and 2 story	70	100
Entrance halls	70	100
Kitchens		
Basement	15	21
First floor	55	79
Dining rooms		
Basement	6	8
First floor	62	89
No separate d.r.	2	3
No. of first-floor living areas		
1	13	19
2	43	61
3 or more	14	20
Living areas on second floor	3	4
Bedrooms		
1–2	0	0
3	8	12
4	19	27
5–6	22	31
7 or more	21	30
1½ or 2 story houses w. first fl. bedrooms	8	11
Bathrooms		
0	15	22
w.c. only	5	7
1	49	70
1 plus w.c.	1	1
2 or more	0	0

Sources: Calvert Vaux, *Villas and Cottages* (1864; reprint, New York, 1970); E. C. Hussey, *Home Building: A Reliable Book of Facts* (1875; reprint, Watkins Glen, N.Y., 1976); Palliser, Palliser, & Co., *Palliser's Model Homes* (1878; reprint, Fenton, California, 1972).

Notes: N = 70; percentages are rounded.

second floor, such as sewing rooms or studies. Children shared a common playroom. They apparently shared bedrooms as well, although boys and girls seem to have been separated. Servants slept either in a back bedroom on the second floor or in the attic. Seventy-one percent of the sample houses had a bathroom, while another 7 percent had an indoor water closet. Bathrooms were rationed sparingly; no house had more than one.

Their design for separation was the most striking thing about the house plans of this era—a separation that becomes even more interesting when one considers that at least one early London suburb had houses designed on a quite different model. According to Robert Fishman, in suburban Clapham at the turn of the nineteenth century, the houses took on a very different form from the one that became common in the United States a few decades later. In Clapham, "families knew very little of that segregation by sex and age which was to mark the Victorian Age later in the nineteenth century." Among these early English suburbanites—Evangelicals in whose families fathers led the daily prayers and took the lead in spiritual guidance—men were a genuine presence in the household. In contrast, by the middle of the century among American middle-class Protestants, women had taken charge not only of home religion but also of society's "moral nature," and the interiors of houses had become quite different.[24]

There was one striking exception to the conventional interiors described above: Catharine Beecher's model Christian home, which both resembled a church and could serve as one. Beecher's house is significant not so much because its open floor plan was in contrast to the typical middle-class house of the age, but because of the people for whom it was designed. She created her plans initially for households run "for and by women"—teachers who would give lessons in the parlor, and who might have the opportunity, in areas without a minister, to preach in it on Sunday. Without men, there was no need for elaborately segregated spaces.[25]

These house plans are extremely suggestive, but one should beware of interpreting them too literally. Although the other evidence for the middle decades of the nineteenth century confirms the practice of gender and age separation in the home, by the late 1870s and early 1880s there may have been a change in the way families functioned in that separated space. Indeed, these segregated spaces may have masked a growing closeness between husband and wife. Certainly that was true for Charles Cumings and his family, whom we will meet in the next chapter. By the end of the century young husbands and wives would confirm their discontent with Victorian interiors by demanding new houses with open floor plans, or by remodeling the older Victorian interiors to conform to their new inclinations about family life. What we seem to have in the 1870s and 1880s is a period in which husband-wife relations were changing, but new spatial configurations had not yet been worked out. That was partly because the outlines of changes were as yet unclear, and partly, one might speculate, because there was still a need for some separate physical space in which men and women could get used to new ideas about emotional intimacy.[26]

HUSBANDS, CHILDREN, AND CHANGING IDEAS ABOUT MIDDLE-CLASS FAMILY LIFE

By the 1870s, domestic writers had begun to alter the ways in which they presented male roles and men's marital obligations to their readers. Harriet Beecher Stowe, for example, was among the earliest to make public her suspicion that women were neither men's inferiors nor their equals, but their betters. The male characters in her novels often seemed perpetual children, rather than patriarchs or even fully adult. Her attitude toward men was fraught with ambivalence, but her readers could not fail to notice her frequent creation of powerful female characters and male ne'er do wells. In *My Wife and I*, published in 1870, she had a respectable male character insist that the opinions of his wife and sister "on the meaning of a text of scripture" were far more meaningful than the view "of all the doctors of Divinity." And she solemnly declared that "sooner or later the true wife becomes a mother to her husband; she guides him, cares for him, teaches him, and catechizes him in the nicest way possible." No man who would encourage his wife to mother him and interpret his religion for him could be an object of awe in his family.[27]

Stowe, like her elder sister, was not a professed women's rights supporter, although as Mary Kelley has pointed out, she "had something to say for all sides." In her fiction the men who were happiest and most successful were those who tried to be most like women. Other writers, more explicit proponents of the women's rights movement, were more forthright. Abby Morton Diaz, a suffragist pamphleteer as well as the author of popular juvenile stories that numbered the young Theodore Roosevelt among their loyal readers, tried to persuade men that egalitarian marriages were in their best interest. Long before the term "togetherness" was coined to describe an ideal marriage, Diaz insisted that "a sympathetic couple are to such a degree one that a pleasure which comes to either singly can only be half enjoyed, and even this half-joy is lessened by the consciousness of what the other is losing." Such matrimonial bliss was possible only when the wife was "at least the equal of her husband" in intelligence, taste, and education. Diaz's argument was as political as it was personal;

she believed that truly happy marriages would have to await the granting of equal rights to women. While male writers continued to spur young men on toward the material success that would be the ultimate reward for their willingness to eschew all the enticing vices, women now questioned the masculine preoccupation with the outside world.[28]

Consider, for example, Stowe's popular domestic novel *My Wife and I,* with its sharply drawn generational contrast between the father and husband of the heroine. The father, Mr. Van Arsdell, a well-to-do businessman who supported his family in a Fifth Avenue townhouse, "considered the household and all its works and ways as an insoluble mystery which he was well-pleased to leave to his wife." His role in the family was quite simply "yearly to enlarge his means of satisfying the desires and aspirations of his family," the domestic appurtenances of which "he knew little and cared less." But if Mr. Van Arsdell was a shadow in his house, fleeing to his library and leaving everything else to his wife, his son-in-law, Harry Henderson, was a very different kind of man. Harry and his wife Eva eschewed Fifth Avenue and urban fashion for a detached, single-family house; its yard had "trees, and English sparrows, and bird houses," not to mention flowers and grape vines, those necessary adjuncts to the Victorian suburban house. Revelling in his domestic life, Harry spent his evenings with his wife planning new decorations and home improvements. (The latter were carried out by the servants, not the Hendersons.) He said of his house, "I think of it . . . when I'm at work in my office, and am always wanting to come home and see it again," and proclaimed, "there is no earthly reason which requires a man, in order to be manly, to be unhandy and clumsy in regard to the minutiae of domestic life."[29]

Among Harry Henderson's real-life counterparts was Charles Bradley Cumings, whose family life we will explore shortly. The fictional Henderson and the actual Cumings were harbingers of a new kind of middle-class man, rare in the 1870s but substantially more common by the turn of the century. The typical man of the post–Civil War era, however, was more likely to resemble Mr. Van Arsdell than his son-in-law. Maintaining a condition of affluence or stable respectability for a family without a hereditary income involved considerable risk. The salaried middle-class man with a secure corporate or bureaucratic position was still a rarity. William Robinson, another husband and father whose life we will consider in detail in the next chapter, struggled constantly, and he could not always provide even moderate prosperity for his growing family.[30]

William Robinson accepted the breadwinner role and its responsibilities; but the economic realities of the age meant that his work required his whole attention. Other men simply opted out altogether. David Lee Child, husband of Lydia Maria Child, was perhaps an extreme example of an ineffectual provider, since he failed at every occupation he tried. Nevertheless, the reaction of his wife, who by midcentury had become a prominent public figure, indicates the great importance of masculine economic success in the mid-nineteenth century, even for a capable and independent woman. Lydia Maria Child complained bitterly to David Child's sister after David died: "For the last forty-five years I have paid from my own funds, all the expenses . . . ; food, clothing, washing, fuel, taxes, etc. . . . [David] had no promptitude, no system in his affairs; hence everything went into confusion. After many years of struggling with ever recurring pecuniary difficulties, I reluctantly became convinced that there was *no help* for these difficulties." Lydia Maria Child, with a husband so absolutely unfit for the demands of the marketplace economy, took over, and retained with some considerable resentment, the role of breadwinner.[31]

Child's resentment exemplifies the contradictions of this age for middle-class men and women. She was a talented, reasonably successful writer, and first-rate editor, but having to support her husband, because of his fecklessness, angered her. Child was not alone. When Hattie Robinson married Sydney Shattuck in 1878, she left her job so that he could be the sole breadwinner. After a period of living with the bride's mother, the young couple bought a suburban house, and Shattuck, in business for himself, prospered. But his business failed, and although he spent years trying to recapture his early success, it always eluded him; at the time of his death the couple lived in a shabbily genteel boardinghouse, his wife having become a bitter, querulous, and nearly friendless woman. After his death, she was forced to throw herself on the charity of a niece.[32]

These few examples, although they do not indicate that middle-class men were abandoning the breadwinner role in any numbers, suggest the precarious nature of middle-class status. Statistical portraits have made a similar point. As Michael Katz has said of the male citizenry of Buffalo, a comparatively prosperous city that nevertheless witnessed a downward mobility rate of twenty-seven percent in the 1850s and forty-three percent in the 1860s, "Neither staying wealthy nor falling, many men struggled from year to year, their economic state marginal and fluctuating."[33] Both men and women might be unable to live up to their assigned (or hoped-for) roles. When they failed to do so, they were likely to become dispirited and resentful.

Despite the fact that domestic men of the kind admired by Stowe as yet were few, there are clear indications that women's expectations of men's domestic obligations were beginning to rise as early as the mid-1870s. Abby Diaz remarked that women were always asking her why, if women required education for motherhood, men should not have similar training for fatherhood. Men, she responded, did indeed need such training, but *she* was too busy to provide it. She concluded tartly: "If men feel this need, there is nothing to prevent them from assembling . . . to inquire how they shall best qualify themselves to fulfill the duties of fatherhood. [I am] . . . under the impression that men's clubs do not meet especially with a view to such discussion." Harriet Beecher Stowe took a gentler tone, but she was equally convinced that men ought to learn more about their emotional responsibilities as husbands. "[W]e have heard much said of the importance of training women to be wives," she noted, adding that she would like to have "something to be said on the importance of training men to be husbands."[34]

By the 1890s sympathetic anecdotes had begun to appear describing families in which the men shared domestic duties. Popular author Margaret Sangster expressed delighted approval of a family of her acquaintance in which "everyone shared the housework, even the boys," while in another household the son, "a manly young fellow," did the ironing. Her moderate tones notwithstanding, Sangster, a widely read writer on household affairs respected by men and women alike, did not scruple to remind men of their domestic duties. Men, she said, should help out around the house and stop expecting their wives to wait on them. One of Sangster's friends complained that she was tired of picking up after her husband, who every day "manages to give my drawing room, sitting room, and library an appearance of having been swept by a cyclone. One traces him all over the house by the things he has heedlessly dropped." Sangster urged her to tell her husband to pick up after himself, since a good husband would surely make an effort to reform, at least "to some extent."[35] Such advice, and the relationship that it implied, was far removed from a world in which a father's convenience was of principal importance.

By the 1890s, wives had developed higher hopes regarding their husbands' contributions to family life. Where midcentury domestic writers had begged husbands not to "sear and palsy" their wives' hearts by a "tyrannical and overbearing manner," their counterparts in the eighties and nineties crisply reminded men that husbands too "should rise above the petty . . . irritations of the day and speak with agreeable consideration for others." Furthermore, they insisted, the work of a housewife was "just as important" as the husband's breadwinning job, and therefore his wife was entitled to his income: "She earns it just as truly, and has just as much a right to it as he."[36]

This attention to men's roles in the home eventually resulted, by the early twentieth century, in greater domestic parity. But it also damaged what historians refer to as "women's culture," that congeries of relationships that provided women with social networks, support, and influence. Women's culture, based as it was on the idea of significant gender separation, had provided a powerful source for feminism and for social reform. When husbands became involved in domesticity and began to share more of their wives' interests, they became much less alien creatures.[37]

In the 1850s, when advice-givers like Catharine Beecher and L. H. G. Abell had told their readers that a domestic woman would not forget her duty to have female friends and companions, they made it clear that women's own emotional well-being required them to socialize with other women. But by the 1890s the justification for the maintenance of women's outside interests was different, and emphasized the importance of the husband-wife bond. Too great an absorption in one's domestic duties, argued this later generation of advice-givers, would damage a woman's relationship with her husband. Women who confined themselves to the household and to the unremitting care of children were in danger of becoming inadequate wives.[38]

When domestic writers admonished women not to neglect their husbands, or prefer the company of their children to their mates, they did not intend to suggest that children had become unimportant. On the contrary, parent-child relations toward the close of the nineteenth century, at the end of two centuries of changes in child-rearing patterns, engendered enormous concern, to judge from the printed matter pertaining to them.[39] Sorting out the reasons for the changes is an extraordinarily difficult problem; historians have wrestled with it during the last twenty years in much confusion and even more disagreement. Scholars agree that in the eighteenth and nineteenth centuries, upper- and middle-class Europeans and Americans became more sentimental about their children and more loving toward them. And they have further connected this changed attitude to a lowered birthrate, although they do so in different ways.

Edward Shorter and Randolph Trumbach have argued that families became smaller as parents developed more powerful emotional ties to their children. J. A. Banks, a leading British scholar who specializes in the study of birth control, reverses the argument. He contends that parents in specific occupational groups in Victorian England were "pioneers of the smaller family." The household heads in these families were, with certain exceptions, "army and navy officers, authors, editors, journalists, accountants, physicians, surveyors, registered practitioners, civil mining engineers, painters, sculptors, artists, barristers, [and] solicitors." An important part of Banks's argument is that the men in these groups, in England, once they had become established in their careers, had a security of income not matched by other socioeconomic groups.[40]

According to Banks, there were two forces pushing these men. (He argues controversially that men, not women, made the initial move toward smaller families.) First, men of this class found the expenses of a family increasingly prohibitive, which pushed them to desire fewer children. Second, they and their wives perceived that the sons would most likely not follow a father's career, so they desired to educate them for social and occupational change. At the heart of this argument is the contention that these husbands and wives no longer had children to perpetuate the family line, but had only the number of children that they could afford to educate for independence. Mark Stern, in his study of Erie County, New York, found a similar pattern among what he called "business class" families.[41]

Historians of the United States have demonstrated that family size began to decrease in the early nineteenth century, and that at the very least it was accompanied, if not caused, by a changed attitude toward children within middle-class families. Bernard Wishy's *The Child and the Republic* has shown how child-rearing manuals depicted children in the mid-nineteenth century as capable of being good, sweet, and lovable; and how, toward the end of the century, childhood was portrayed as a golden age of innocence that parents had a duty to preserve and protect. It is not only in child-rearing literature itself, but in the whole complex of advice and didactic fiction that filled the bookshelves of educated Americans, that the transformation of beliefs about bringing up children appears. The popular minister Henry Ward Beecher, who later changed his mind (perhaps under the influence of his sister Harriet Beecher Stowe) on the question of child depravity, thought in the 1840s that "knavish propensities are inherent: born with the child and transmissible from parent to son." Daughters, too, could be born wicked; Beecher described prostitutes as innately evil creatures, drawn to sin despite parental love and watchfulness.[42]

Mid-nineteenth-century advice-givers, the men who told their juniors how to reach success and material prosperity, and the women who explained to female readers how to perform their dignified and sacred domestic duties, had alike believed that parents earned gratitude and respect simply by bringing their children into the world. Catharine Beecher, L. H. G. Abell, John Angell James, and others stressed the duties of children, not their rights. James, like Henry Ward Beecher a minister, informed his youthful readers of their obligations in unequivocal terms. It would take, he said, "very much" to satisfy parents—"much, to reward a mother's pangs in childbirth, [and] much, that will be an adequate reward for a father's incessant toil to provide for his family." Parents, according to James, raised their children in the expectation that "surely I shall have a rich reward one day for this." Never once did James even hint that parents might forfeit the respect of their children; nor did he have anything to say to his readers about how they should treat their own children. Obligation flowed in only one direction, from child to parent.[43]

The Reverend James was without doubt or ambivalence. Some other writers (more often women), while they shared his general outlook, tried to uphold parental infallibility without taking all the pleasure out of childhood. Catharine Beecher attempted to assist parents through the thicket of authority and love. Beecher granted absolute parental authority: "The parent [should] take the attitude of a superior in age, knowledge, and relation, who has a perfect *right* to control every action of the child, and that too, without giving any reason for the requisition." In almost the next breath, however, she told her readers that children "should have the reasons for most requisitions kindly stated; never, however, on the demand of it from the child, as a right, but as an act of kindness from the parent."[44] Although kindly parents chose to give their children reasons, they were under no obligation to do so.

The overall tone of Catharine Beecher's child-rearing advice is one of parental right tempered with kindness. In theory parental rights were absolute, but if parents wanted to raise children who were obedient, unselfish, and devoted, they would have to forgo the full exercise of those rights. Nevertheless, in her eyes the wishes of adults always came first. Beecher, who was often a guest in large families, made it quite clear that guests ought to take precedence over children, who should be trained "to be silent [at meals], except when addressed by others; or else their chattering will interrupt the conversation and comfort of their elders. They should always be required, too, to wait in silence, till all the older persons are helped." For all of Beecher's admonitions to parents to love their children, in the final analysis her attitudes were substantially in agreement with those of James. For both of them, family life was conducted for the convenience of adults. Catharine Beecher exploited the rhetoric of parental self-sacrifice, but in fact she viewed children as an always disagreeable, and sometimes barely tolerable burden. Perhaps not surprisingly, she urged an early removal to school for all children: "With a suitable teacher, it is no matter how early children are sent to school." In short, the advice-givers' view of the middle-class household illustrated a life centered around the convenience of adults, but with the long-term benefit of the child in view. Every member of the family had responsibilities, but the rights belonged to the grown-ups.[45]

Harriet Beecher Stowe, who was a pivotal transitional figure in much of this literature, had different ideas, to which she gave full voice in the 1870s. Stowe described childhood a generation after her brother Henry Ward Beecher could still speak of youngsters' depravity, as "lovely and loving . . . , with its truthfulness, its frank sincerity, its pure simple love." Children were "sweet and holy."[46] This quote is from 1870, but Stowe had been creating saintly children since *Uncle Tom's Cabin*. Little Eva was just the first of a number of children who were too heavenly to live. The difference was that in the 1850s she had created *individual* children who led perfect lives, while in 1870 she had begun to use that literary device as a symbol for the inherent innocence of all children.

By the 1890s, the new idea was full-blown. Some writers carried the idea of childhood as a golden age to the point where children could be looked to as teachers and guides. Best-selling novelist and former kindergarten teacher Kate Wiggin surely went to extremes when she begged, "Dear little one, . . . thou has a treasure that the years have stolen from me—share it with me!"[47] Such an earnest, perhaps desperate, seeking in a child for the wisdom that adults ought to possess seems excessive; but not everyone placed such heavy burdens on children. Wiggin's sister and fellow teacher took a more reasonable position, arguing that children on the whole "have a tolerably clear sense of right and wrong, [and] need . . . only gentle guidance," but that there were exceptions, "poor, blurred, human scrawls, blotted all over with the mistakes of other people."[48] Regardless of such doses of common sense, Kate Wiggin's plea for salvation at the hands of a child—any child—was far more extreme than Stowe's portrayal of child-saints like little Eva.

Before the turn of the century, advice-givers began to tell middle-class parents that children had rights and that adults owed them not only understanding but also respect. Kate Wiggin counseled adults to be as polite to children as they were to other adults, and to grant their small sons and daughters privacy and consideration. "The child," argued Wiggin, "has a right to a place of his own, to things of his own." Margaret Sangster agreed. She told adults that they should never "needlessly interrupt a child in its occupations," and that "we should thank them for what they do as precisely as we apologize and acknowledge and are courteous to our older friends." Parents, according to these writers, must of course teach their children "obedience and truthfulness," but they also must give them "sympathy and freedom" while they were learning how to grow up according to adult guidelines. If parents followed all this advice faithfully, it was implied, their children would become happy and responsible adults. If they acted otherwise, then they had only themselves to blame if their offspring grew up willful, disobedient, or selfish. Parental failure, not innate depravity, created bad children.[49]

The adult-centered, middle-class household of the mid-nineteenth century had begun to give way before the turn of the twentieth century to one in which children took a more central place. There were fewer of them, but they had more rights and privileges, and the weight of responsibility for their shortcomings rested squarely on the shoulders of their parents. In the next chapter, I explore the ways in which the world of the advice-givers, domestic novelists, and suburban visionaries (including builders, architects, and pattern-book publishers) interacted with the world of real suburban Americans, as I examine the lives of two suburban families whose histories spanned the Victorian age in America.

CHAPTER TWO

The Minutiae of Domestic Life

There is no earthly reason which requires a man, in order to be manly, to be unhandy and clumsy in regard to the minutiae of domestic life.

HARRIET BEECHER STOWE,
My Wife and I,
1870

As we saw in the last chapter, Harriet Beecher Stowe put the words quoted above in to the mouth of Harry Henderson, Eva Van Arsdell's husband in *My Wife and I.* In the same novel she insisted on the need for "training men to be husbands." We know that Stowe was not alone in her demand that men share more fully in the daily domestic round of duties as well as pleasures; but we also know that those who echoed her wishes, at least during the second third of the nineteenth century, were other women, not men. And yet, by the turn of the new century, men would respond favorably to women's desires for greater mutuality, and indeed would articulate their own domestic hopes. Thus far, I have endeavored to trace the lineaments of American middle-class domestic life through the mid-nineteenth century as it appeared in fiction, advice literature, and in the kinds of houses in which families played out their daily dramas. In the years between the 1830s, which marked the emergence of the ideology of domesticity among women, and the 1890s, in which the outlines of a new domestic ideal began to be visible within the middle-class, the relations between men and women had changed in ways both subtle and profound. These changes were necessary preconditions for the creation of the new domestic ideal.

The ideas of the last two chapters might be summarized as follows: Middle-class men, seeking to hold on to a set of republican political and social values that urbanization threatened to erode, created a suburban ideal that stressed separation from urban life, protection of wives and children from city evils (both real and fancied), and property ownership as a safeguard for political independence. Middle-class women, seeking to make the family the preeminent institution in American life, created a domestic ideal that exalted the spiritual influence of the home, eventually turning the home into a power base from which women would, it was hoped, transform the moral character of the nation, working from the family outward. But as both of these ideas developed, the nation changed—becoming more urban, industrial, and heterogeneous in terms of class and ethnicity. Middle-class families also changed; there were fewer children, mothers increasingly took on outside interests, and fathers relied less on their own entrepreneurial skills and more on working with others to earn a livelihood.

Until now, I have drawn these changes with broad and sweeping strokes, locating evidence for them in fiction, advice-literature, community studies, and economic data. But my aim is not only to understand in general terms what happened to the suburban ideal and the ideology of domesticity—both transformed by and transforming America's urban landscape—that caused them to merge, but also how their fusion took effect in the intimate drama of daily life.

What follows are two stories of families whose reasons for choosing the suburbs, whose lives once they moved to them, and whose political and personal choices exemplify the process by which suburbia transformed itself from a substitute for a vanishing rural ideal to the physical setting for the creation of a new kind of middle-class ideal of marriage and family life. The two families lived in suburban Boston, a city that suburbanized early, and whose suburban residents were the nation's first, in historian Henry Binford's words, to become "caught up by the power of the residential ideal."[1] The case study is both an analytical and a rhetorical device; I use it here to emphasize points made earlier as well as to illuminate details not so sharply etched when the subject is viewed more largely. Neither of these families was representative of all Victorian suburbanites, but both of them exemplified the pattern of suburbanization in the nineteenth century. The Robinson family illustrated the dominant motifs of the era while Charles and Augusta Cumings were harbingers of the new suburban domesticity that did not fully emerge until the early twentieth century.

THE ROBINSON FAMILY AND THE MODEL OF FEMALE INFLUENCE

William and Harriet Robinson's suburban drama took place in Malden, a fringe community of Boston just beginning to suburbanize in the 1850s. Harriet Hanson (1825–1911) grew up in the mill town of Lowell, where her widowed mother kept a boardinghouse for mill workers. She began working in the mills at age ten. As a young woman, she had literary ambitions; a friend of Lucy Larcom, she wrote for the *Lowell Offering* and struggled to educate herself, succeeding in graduating from high school despite considerable obstacles.[2] Her aspirations to write notwithstanding, Harriet Hanson was a conventional young woman, who expected to marry and have a family, not to seek her fortune independently. She fell in love with William Robinson, a Lowell journalist, and married him in 1848. His prospects looked good; as acting editor of the *Lowell Courier,* he appeared to have every chance of professional advancement. But, like many middle-class men of his generation, his occupational life was a constant struggle. Shortly before the wedding he left this job to take on the editorship of a campaign newspaper for the Free Soil party. A committed antislavery man, he pinned his journalistic future on the Free Soil, and later, the Republican party.

He also pinned his wife's hopes of prosperity and security on his choices. The newspaper business in the mid-nineteenth century was unstable; papers started and folded with almost predictable regularity. As an antislavery journalist, William chose to make a precarious livelihood even more so. It never occurred to him to ask his wife whether the economic well-being of his family should take precedence over his political and journalistic ideals, or his choice of where the family ought to live. When he had been out of a regular job for months, long enough to worry his wife considerably, he was offered a reporter's job in New York, for the more than adequate compensation of $25 a week. Despite his wife's expressed wishes to the contrary, Robinson refused to leave Massachusetts. As a result, he remained without steady employment for nearly five years, from 1857 to 1862.

William Robinson suffered from the unpredictability of mid-nineteenth-century professional life as well as from his own political and personal choices. Earlier, when the couple was first married, they had settled in Boston, taking rooms in a Boston boardinghouse. At that time, Harriet Robinson hoped for a long and comfortable stay in the city, but her husband's career dictated otherwise. Within a few months William was out of a job, dismissed by his Free Soil allies; he thereupon decided to move back to Lowell, to start his own paper. They never again lived in Boston, although Harriet had enjoyed her urban life very much. Her husband earned a good income, and she appreciated the relative freedom from domestic chores. Nevertheless, once again they were in Lowell, their income halved and their family growing. In 1850 their first child, Harriette, was born, and in 1851, William Robinson's fortunes underwent a temporary change for the better when he won election to the Massachusetts House of Representatives.[3]

During the legislative session, Robinson commuted daily to Boston. Train service between Lowell and Boston was direct and rapid, designed for the convenience of businessmen with interests in the mills and in the city. Politically and personally ambitious, Robinson struggled to make a name for himself, tackling two jobs. Each morning he got up at 6:30 to catch his train to Boston, where he arrived after about an hour's ride; he did not return to Lowell until eight at night, whereupon he put in two or three hours' work on his trice-weekly paper, the *Lowell American*. Harriet helped him with the paper, but she had first one baby then a second, with no household help but her mother, who lived with the family. Both Robinsons were exhausted and overworked, and he still had difficulty supporting the family.[4]

The failure of the *American*, and the infirmity of William's mother, who lived in Concord, resulted in the Robinsons' move to the town identified with Emerson, Thoreau, and Hawthorne. While the family lived in Concord, William again commuted to Boston, this time to work variously as assistant editor, writer, and (briefly) editor at the *Boston Telegraph*. The Robinsons were unhappy in Concord, and after William's mother died in 1856 they saw little reason to remain. In a town of luminaries, the Robinsons, status-conscious but prickly and quick to take offense, did not shine. When William was not offered membership in the Social Circle, a club to which the socially and politically influential belonged, and which his grandfather had helped to found, the Robinsons determined to move.[5]

They moved to Malden, a five-mile commute to Boston, in 1858. Malden, which had been an incorporated town since 1649, was at this time just beginning to emerge as a residential suburb. In the 1840s, Malden town boosters had started to see its suburban possibilities—the Boston and Maine railroad provided access to the city—and the town attempted to attract suburban commuters as well as continue to develop its earlier industrial base. Like the residents of other towns surrounding Boston during these years, Malden's leading citizens made a conscious choice to create a suburb. They boasted of its "woody heights and rocky glens, and smoothly rounded hills . . . affording numerous prospects combining the charms of city, sea, and country," all close to the city itself. According to the town's promotional literature, Malden offered "spots for the rustic cottage, or the ornate country seat." Throughout the middle years of the nineteenth century, Malden retained this mixed character. The skilled and unskilled workers who toiled in the town's rubber shoe factories were still able to find housing, but increasingly Malden attracted clerks and agents of various kinds, as well as a group of professionals and business owners.[6]

Malden's commuters could choose to ride to Boston on the horsecars, which ran every half hour during the day and early evening, and every hour after 7:30 in the evening. Or they could take the train, which was equally convenient and just a little more expensive—twelve cents to the horsecars' ten-cent fare. But William Robinson had no need of daily commuter services for a while. Before the family moved to Malden he had lost yet another regular job. For five years the family survived on what he could earn as a freelance journalist, which was not very much. It was not until Robinson stopped trying to make a living as a full-time journalist (although he continued to be a part-time columnist) that he brought his family some economic stability. In 1862, with children ranging in age from three to twelve, William took the position of clerk of the Massachusetts House of Representatives, a job he held until 1873, two years before his death.[7]

William Robinson's struggle to earn a living working for himself was typical of nineteenth-century, middle-class men, whether they were professionals or proprietors. As Michael Katz said of the male citizenry of another city, middle-class men often "struggled from year to year," rarely getting ahead, and often falling behind. Hard work and ambition were nearly as likely to bring downward as upward mobility. Robinson accepted the breadwinner ethos, unlike some of the men we met in the last chapter, but he was unable to meet its demands on a consistent basis. Harriet Robinson accepted her husband's choices, perhaps having read Caroline Gilman's warning to women that if they complained too much, they would "languish alone." Instead, she tried to be philosophical about it, and in her diary spoke of the importance of sacrificing for an ideal. (William had the ideal, and got the credit for it. She did the sacrificing.)[8]

Once the Robinson family settled in Malden, William and Harriet lived there for the rest of their lives. Malden was principally William Robinson's choice, although Harriet had been just as eager as he to leave Concord. He preferred small towns, disliked cities in general, and thought of himself as a devotee of country life. Before his marriage Robinson had lived for a while in Washington, and according to biographer Claudia Bushman, "immersed as he was in politics, the country boy still yearned for his rural home." In Malden, the Robinson family attempted at least a partial re-creation of the rural ideal, each year managing to have a large fruit and vegetable garden. Although a hired gardener did all the planting and weeding, Harriet preserved the food herself—a hot, tiring, and time-consuming job. She also kept hens, and earned a small income from the eggs. The garden and the chicken coops had both economic and symbolic value for the family. The Robinsons believed that they had "created the ideal garden/farm"; for Harriet, it was a renewal of "the rural life her family had not known for generations." In spite of their shared belief in a rural ideal, Harriet Robinson's notion of that ideal was becoming more and more suburban. Unlike a typical farmer, but very much in tune with the advice of the Beecher sisters in *The American Woman's Home,* she set nearly as much store by her flowers as her vegetables; and indoors she grew petunias, verbenas, nasturtiums, and mignonettes. In their attempt to recapture country life, but softened and civilized by flower gardens and with the culture of the city nearby, the Robinsons were very much the suburbanites.[9]

Living in Malden, where they could have hens and a vegetable garden and where they purchased their home out of savings and a personal loan from a friend, also helped to shield them in part from some of the economic difficulties brought on by the breadwinner's vicissitudes. Except for the earliest years of their married life, the Robinsons did not endure real hardship, even when William was out of a regular job. Until 1862, when her husband began to earn a regular salary of $1,600 a year (which became $3,000 by the early 1870s), Harriet Robinson economized carefully to make the most of a small income for her growing family. (The Robinsons had four children.) But she did not forego such things as domestic help. When her mother was living with them, which was for most of the year, she hired women to come in and help with housework by the day. But whenever her mother was away on long visits to Harriet's brother, the Robinsons found day help inadequate and engaged a live-in domestic. They did so whether or not William enjoyed regular employment. In the early sixties, the Robinsons began to dispense with live-in domestic help altogether and rely entirely on day workers. In making this decision, according to the family biographer, Harriet Robinson had been influenced by the advice of Harriet Beecher Stowe's *House and Home Papers.* From then on, women came in during the day to do the laundry and to help clean the house all year around. During spring cleaning time they came every day; at other times the family had help in for a couple of days a week.[10]

In addition to regular domestic help, the Robinson family also took regular vacations, again regardless of William's job situation. The vacations were lengthy ones, usually a month with the children at the seashore in Manomet, Massachusetts. Although the family had not, for most of the Robinsons' married life, endured the kind of privation that working-class families routinely faced, it was nevertheless true that Harriet Robinson's life changed greatly for the better when her husband achieved some security in his clerkship. Such security allowed her to take, with confidence, a more active role in the local community. In Lowell and Concord she had had few friends and had belonged to no social clubs. In Malden she began to develop a richer social life, joining a church and going often to Boston for shopping expeditions. She and her family gave parties, and had neighbors over on summer evenings to play croquet. Her daughters, Hattie and Lizzie, gave parties too, and their mother made the refreshments.

If part of Harriet Robinson's ability to enjoy living in Malden in the 1860s had to do with her family's less precarious economic situation, another part had to do with the fact that the family lived in a community with people much like themselves. In Lowell, one suspects, Harriet felt herself to be socially above most of the mill workers, yet less accomplished than some of her friends such as Lucy Larcom.

In Concord it was obvious that both Robinsons yearned to move in the same intellectual circles as Emerson and Hawthorne but were not welcome. In Malden, their neighborhood was filled with people like themselves, respectably middle-class but hardly pretentious. Several of the women living in the district were teachers; there were some professional men, some clerks, and some salesmen. The neighborhood was small and friendly. Only thirteen families lived on Lincoln Street, where the Robinsons' generously proportioned but unimposing house stood in the midst of similar houses.[11]

For the family's first ten years in Malden, Harriet Robinson's children, house and garden, shopping trips to Boston, church, and neighborhood socializing kept her fully occupied. She appears to have been content, both in her community and her family. If she was dissatisfied with her husband's lack of worldly success, she did not record it. If she wished that he had spent more time with her and less with his political cronies, she complained very little. Perhaps she felt she had little to complain about. William Robinson, after all, loved his family; had he been asked, he might have said that his idealism was theirs as well. Nevertheless, the fact remains that *his* personal and political goals determined the kind of life that the family led. True, he lost some jobs because a paper went under, or his own failed. But he lost others because he fell out with editors or publishers. His final falling out, with the powerful Massachusetts politician Benjamin Butler, cost him his clerkship, which had provided the family with tangible middle-class respectability for eleven years.[12]

His writing and political activism took most of William's time, form the earliest years of his marriage. When the newlyweds had lived in Lowell he was often gone for thirteen hours a day and spent another two working at home. But even after prosperity came, William evidently spent so much time with his political cronies and allies that some of them were unaware of his family's existence. Wendell Phillips, with whom he had worked for years in the antislavery movement, was surprised to find out that he was married when Robinson introduced Harriet, to whom he had by then been married for twenty-one years. "Your wife! I did not know you had a wife! I thought you were a crusty old bachelor!" the startled Phillips exclaimed. Harriet was rankled. William loved his family, but he clearly did not dote on them. And in common with most men of his era, he seemed to pay very little attention to the house. It was not without good reason that women's domestic advice books included sections on plumbing, heating, and carpentry. Like many other housewives, Harriet Robinson was the one to decide when to install indoor plumbing, add the cellar, build an addition.[13]

In Malden, her children nearly grown, her husband in a stable job, her place in the community established, and her house completed to her satisfaction, Harriet Robinson felt able to turn her attention to the wider world. In the late 1860s, she became one of the pioneers of the women's club movement and an early advocate for women's suffrage. In common with women like Harriet Beecher Stowe and Frances Willard, Harriet had come to believe that it was necessary for women to use more than moral suasion to bring domestic values to the larger society. In 1868 she joined Lucy Stone's American Woman's Suffrage Association, organizing meetings in Malden and in other Massachusetts communities. The following year she was invited to join the New England Women's Club. Despite this notice by some of the leading lights of the women's movement in Boston, Harriet preferred to center her suffrage and club activities in Malden. She was one of the founders of Malden's women's club, The Old and New Club, and she and her daughter Harriette became prominent clubwomen and suffrage workers in their own community.[14]

As long as William was alive, Harriet Robinson devoted most of her attention to her family, and her suffrage and club work was subordinate to her role as wife and mother. But after his death in 1875 she became considerably more active in club work, while continuing to work for suffrage. She centered her activism in Malden, but she often served as the local representative on national boards and at conventions. She began to lecture on her experiences as an early mill girl, and published two books on Lowell. She also wrote *Massachusetts in the Woman Suffrage Movement,* which, with some additions and deletions, was incorporated into volume three of *The History of Woman Suffrage.* She composed some poetry and drama, too, but she never became a successful or well-known writer. She paid to publish most of her books, and she earned no money from them.[15] In her widowhood Harriet Hanson Robinson became a respected figure as clubwoman and suffragist. Like the more famous Julia Ward Howe, Robinson became active once she was freed from the responsibilities of marriage and child-rearing, when she was no longer a suburban housewife.

Harriet and William Robinson became suburbanites as a result of his distaste for urban life and desire to replicate, as much as possible, a rural existence. And Harriet, although she had very much enjoyed her brief experience as an urbanite, also liked living in Malden. Living only five miles from Boston, her house just two blocks from the train station, she went downtown for all her major purchases, for concerts, and the theatre. She belonged to an urban club, as well, but most of her social and political life was centered in Malden, where she engaged in significant public activity in an environment of comforting familiarity. Harriet and William Robinson, in their reasons for choosing to live in a suburb, in their attempts to create a pastoral environment, in their economic struggles, and in the pattern of their relations with each other, characterized mid-nineteenth-century, middle-class suburban family life. For M. Augusta and Charles Bradley Cumings, suburban life would have a different meaning.

THE CUMINGS FAMILY AND THE MODEL OF MARITAL TOGETHERNESS

Mary Augusta Carr (1837–1904), having been born and brought up in Portsmouth, New Hampshire, left her family in the early 1860s to marry Bostonian Charles Bradley Cumings.[16] The newlyweds then settled in Boston's South End, not too far away from Charles's parents, who lived on Rutland Square. They stayed in the South End, renting various houses and changing addresses every couple of years, until 1877. When the Cumingses arrived in the South End, it was at the height of its popularity as an upper middle-class, urban residential district. Although Boston's wealthiest and oldest families did not make their homes here, bankers, merchants, lawyers and other professionals rented or purchased the newly built townhouses that lined the streets and more imposing squares. The influential ministers James Freeman Clarke and Theodore Parker built their churches here.[17] Charles Cumings, son of a successful merchant and himself secretary of an insurance company, lived in the South End with people much like himself.

Augusta and Charles Cumings were typical of South End residents during its heyday in the 1860s and early 1870s. Charles's father Bradley Cumings was a commission merchant, a partner in the firm of Eaton, Cumings, and Company. The elder Cumings was both intelligent and fortunate; having taken the risks of self-employment, he enjoyed its rewards. In a world in which failure, or at least downward mobility, was as likely as success, Bradley Cumings was one of the successful ones. His son, however, did not follow his father's example. He left no record of his reasons, but Charles Cumings chose to become what we would call in the twentieth century a company man. By the early 1900s, Charles's occupational decision would become a commonplace. But in the middle of the 1800s, it was less so. Beginning his career by working for others, he never ceased to do so. As a very young man, his first job was as a clerk for the accounting firm of Manning and Stanwood, after graduating from the private Brimmer school. (Aspiring young businessmen of Charles's generation—he was born in 1838—did not attend college.) In 1863 his great-uncle, Charles Wells, hired him to be secretary of the Massachusetts Mutual

Fire Insurance Company. When Charles Wells died in 1866, the directors named the nephew president; Charles would remain in that job until the directors dissolved the company in 1899.

Bradley Cumings died in 1876. The year before, during his illness, Charles, Augusta, and their daughters had moved into the house on Rutland Square. After his death, they stayed with his mother for a year, after which she moved into an apartment and they moved to the suburbs. The Cumings family left the South End in 1877 at the height of the upper middle-class exodus. The South End had unfortunately enjoyed an all too brief moment of fashion. The panic of 1873 had affected some residents, those who had mortgages on their houses. Banks who repossessed those houses unloaded them quickly. The South End might have been able to withstand the impact of the panic, but in the next few years the Back Bay was developed, and it soon eclipsed the South End as the residential choice of the newly well-to-do. By the 1890s, the South End had become the city's lodging house district, where respectable but struggling single young clerks and other white collar employees rented rooms while they worked in the city's insurance companies, banks, and mercantile firms.[18]

Not everyone who left the South End ended up in the Back Bay. Many moved to the newly emergent upper middle-class suburban enclaves. Unlike Malden, these were not suburbanizing towns, but older villages and rural areas in which prosperous families built imposing houses and landscaped their grounds to make their neighborhoods look like parks, as Frank Scott's *Suburban Home Grounds* had so persuasively urged. The Cumings family was among their number. While spending the year following the death of the elder Cumings on Rutland Square, Charles and Augusta were having a house built for themselves on Greenough Avenue in newly suburbanizing Jamaica Plain, where they would stay for the rest of their lives.

As a Boston guide book proclaimed about their new community a decade after the Cumingses' arrival, "No suburb of Boston is more easy of access, more charmingly situated, for many reasons more delightful of residence, than is Jamaica Plain"; it added, "Professional men abound; this seems to be a favorite suburb for their residence." Charles Dole, a Unitarian minister and the Cumingses' pastor, who had moved here from Maine in 1876, claimed that Jamaica Plain was well-to-do, liberal, and had a wholesome environment. In short, it was "the best that suburban Boston could give."[19] The Cumings family agreed, staying put for more than thirty years, after more than a decade of biennial address changes.

Whereas Malden had begun life as an independent village and retained its independent identity as it moved into the orbit of suburban Boston during the mid-nineteenth century, Jamaica Plain started out as a residential suburb. It had had few of its own institutions, and depended on the new suburbanites to create them. This is not to suggest that Jamaica Plain had been completely undeveloped land before being discovered by prosperous Bostonians. It had been a part of West Roxbury, which in 1851 seceded from Roxbury proper because it wished to retain its rural character. That was not possible, and West Roxbury, not having the kind of committed local leadership that would fight against annexation, and experiencing the first wave of suburbanites who were insisting on public services, became a part of Boston in 1873. Although indisputably urban today, well into the twentieth century Jamaica Plain remained suburban. In fact, as early as the 1880s Jamaica Plain already looked very much like the ideal, early twentieth-century residential suburb.[20]

For most of its new residents, Jamaica Plain's separation—both physical and psychological—from the urban work environment, and from the urban workers, was an advantage. The Cumingses and their neighbors were indeed in an enclave of people very much like themselves. Some noticed the growing socioeconomic isolation with misgivings. Charles Dole, for one, suggested worriedly that Jamaica Plain in the late nineteenth century was becoming "in a sense . . . too prosperous. . . . In Jamaica Plain, the well-to-do folk were beginning to follow a rather perilous modern fashion of clustering away from their unprosperous fellows."[21]

Charles Dole, along with his friends Augusta and Charles Cumings, lived among the "well-to-do folks." The residents of Greenough Avenue, a street of new houses, were much like them. Charles and Augusta, in their early forties when they moved here, found the neighbors to be much of the same age and, not surprisingly, similarly prosperous. The wives all "kept house," in census parlance, although none of them did so without the help of servants. Many of the men owned their own businesses, although there were two other salaried household heads. Charles and Augusta had three children, which made theirs one of the larger families in the neighborhood, but nearly all of the houses had one or two children near the ages of the Cumings girls. The neighborhood was comfortably middle to upper-middle class, and the Cumingses fit in.[22]

When Augusta was a young wife living in the South End, her life revolved around her babies—she had her daughters between 1866 and 1873—and her husband appears to have shared her delight in their first steps, first words, and childish mischief. Augusta Cumings kept a daybook, given to her as a gift every New Year's Day by Charles. Both of them wrote in it, and together these books provide us with an intimate picture of the daily life of the Cumings family. During the years in which they lived in the South End, the daybook included numerous entries about the events in the children's lives: their weight, the number of teeth, the date they were weaned, their first steps and some of their missteps. A typical entry recorded the time that Mamie, aged one and a half, eluded the family and the servants for a "clandestine" trip up two flights of stairs.[23]

When Charles made an entry in the daybook, his precise, deliberate script offered a constant contrast to Augusta's hurried scrawl. He appeared to enjoy entering the milestones of their little girls' lives. It was he who wrote, "Lulu walks alone for [the] first time." Lulu was M. Louise, the couple's second daughter, born in 1867. Gertrude, their youngest, arrived in 1873. The landmark days of the children's lives, including their first days at church, school, and Sunday School, found a place in the daybook. There were also meticulous records of the children's illnesses—mumps, measles, whooping cough, chicken pox, influenza, and scarlet fever. Charles and Augusta worried about childhood illnesses to the extent that they called a physician whenever the children seemed unwell. If one of the girls was truly sick, they had the doctor come every day. During these periods, although Augusta stayed with them most of the time, Charles often took over to give his wife a break.[24]

But if Augusta Cumings was devoted to her children during her years in the South End, she had other interests as well. Members of her family came from Portsmouth and other places to stay with them periodically. She recorded in her daybook the frequent appearance of the dressmaker, and showed an interest in the latest fashions. And, fond parents that they were, Charles and Augusta nevertheless took several trips without the girls. In her travel notes Augusta Cumings comes alive as a curious, lively, and friendly woman who liked to travel and enjoyed new experiences. In 1871, for example, they traveled to the Shaker community at New Lebanon, New York, toured the community and talked with its members, whom Augusta found very interesting. On other trips they went to Philadelphia, New York, and the White Mountains. Sometimes they traveled with another couple, sometimes alone. And they also took the children on vacation. When Mamie was fourteen, she went to New York with her parents, but the younger girls stayed behind. Before the family moved to Jamaica Plain, the Cumingses spent part of the summer at Topsfield, with Charles commuting into Boston to work. But after they moved, they spent their summers in Jamaica Plain.[25]

The children's doings, the family visits, wearing new fashions, travel—all these remained constants in Augusta's daybook after the move to the suburbs. But suburban life made several changes in the things that interested the family. Moving to Jamaica Plain meant more to them than a simple change of address. Perhaps most noticeable, the new house took on an almost animate existence. Neither Augusta nor Charles had taken much interest in their rented dwellings, but the house they had built for themselves became extremely important.

Throughout 1877, as construction proceeded, Charles recorded the events, always capitalizing the "H" in house. Once they were settled, he took note of their suburban "firsts." Although it was his wife who noted that they had purchased a lawn mower, the very next day's entry contained, in his meticulous script, "Papa cut the grass [for the] first time." His entries included notes on landscaping, although his wife was the one who kept track of when they expected the gardener.[26]

Charles Cumings took great pride in his new suburban house, and unlike William Robinson he was involved in doing things around it. The bulk of the added domestic responsibilities, however, were his wife's. When the family had lived in the city, Augusta Cumings never recorded domestic matters (except for the things having to do with the children). Nor did she take much interest in formal social calls. All of this changed in Jamaica Plain. Now she recorded in the daybook when she hired a new servant and when the current domestic help left. (Whether this meant that she found servants harder to keep in the suburbs, or just that it mattered more to her, is impossible to tell.) She marked down the schedule of her spring cleaning, which she would have to supervise despite the fact that she had two servants to do the work. She collected recipes for the first time as well. And she kept a record of the formal calls she received, checking them off as she returned them. All of these kinds of entries were new.

Augusta Cumings did not appear to resent the new obligations that moving to the suburbs imposed on her. She took pleasure in the domestic interests that she and her husband shared. She enjoyed the surroundings, taking the kind of interest in nature close to hand that she used to reserve for her vacation trips. Once in the suburbs, she frequently mentioned day outings in which the whole family took part, such as a Christmas walk with the family in the nearby woods. Still, Charles's proud little entries about the house and lawn stand in contrast with her hurried notations about new work to be done. For him, the house was a pleasant and restful retreat, his work around it a recreation; for her it was a responsibility, which she had not had to this extent during their years in rented city dwellings.

Most of their time in their new suburban community seemed to be taken up with their children, each other, and their house, although both Charles and Augusta were involved in outside activities, sometimes together, sometimes separately. Augusta and daughter Louise joined the Tuesday Club, a women's club in Jamaica Plain, when it was established in 1896. And Charles, from the time he moved to their new house, had been active in both his church and the community. Along with his pastor Charles Dole he worked for years as an officer of the Jamaica Plain Friendly Society, which dispensed careful and supervised benefactions to the worthy poor. When she was old enough, his daughter Louise joined him in the Society as a "friendly visitor."

Interestingly, the Friendly Society was the only civic group in Jamaica Plain, and perhaps one of the few in metropolitan Boston, to contain almost equal numbers of men and women. And the women, although they made up the whole team of full-fledged visitors (the men were associate visitors), also served as officers and members of the executive committee. Charles Cumings also numbered among his interests and activities the Appalachian Club (he and his wife enjoying trips together to the mountains), the American Unitarian Association, a Boston social club and historical society, and the Eliot Club of Jamaica Plain, a men's club that met for dinner and a speech once a month.[27]

M. Augusta Cumings died in 1904, Charles three years later. At the time of his death, a friend wrote in the *Jamaica Plain News*, "He was a useful and valuable citizen but not a public man."[28] The same might have been said of his wife. She showed a genuine interest in her neighbors, joined the women's club to which most of them belonged, and cheerfully entertained members of her larger family on long visits. Nevertheless, the reader of her daybook cannot help but get the impression that Augusta and Charles were mostly interested in each other and their children. Their daybook entries are a study in contrasts: Her thoughts ran ahead of her pencil (and she always wrote in pencil), and sometimes her entries are nearly illegible. His writing was always precise, and he was as likely to write in ink as in pencil. Yet they covered much of the same ground. He was as interested as she was when their babies walked, or talked, and as concerned when they got sick. His travels alone away from the family were both rare and unwelcome. Gertrude was sick in December of 1876 when "Papa went to Portsmouth which made little Gertrude feel rather bad when bed-time came." He came home a day or so later "much to Gertrude's joy as well as the rest of the household."[29]

For Augusta Cumings, although moving to the suburbs increased her household cares, it also increased her husband's participation in them. If she jotted down when to expect the gardener or how much she was paying the new maid or which rooms needed to be cleaned next, he took note of the new beech trees he had bought and the shrubberies he had arranged to have planted. The greater burden was hers, to be sure, but he was not an absent husband. Charles Cumings had no desire to follow the example of Charles Dole, who almost yearly left his wife "cheerfully [sic] at home . . . look[ing] after the children," while he took lengthy vacations to Europe or the American West. Dole even managed to be away visiting friends at a summer resort when his youngest child was born. Dole was a professed advocate of women's rights, but unlike Charles Cumings he did not share at all in his wife's domestic burdens.[30] It would be hard to imagine Charles Cumings setting off for a six-week jaunt to Europe without his wife or to see him leaving his children for that long a time.

Like Harriet Beecher Stowe's fictional Harry Henderson, Charles Cumings was not "unhandy . . . in regard to the minutiae of domestic life." Putting his family duties and pleasures first, Charles Cumings was in many ways a man before his time. In the nineteenth century, as Suzanne Lebsock has suggested, what such historians as Laurence Stone and Carl Degler have called marriages of affection may have ended up producing more conflict than harmony, as women attempted to take advantage of a husband's love to exercise some power in the relationship, while men retained all of the actual power. Although in the 1870s Abby Diaz wished to see "sympathetic couple[s] that were . . . one," and domestic writers like Harriet Beecher Stowe invented at least one husband capable of providing the sympathetic understanding for which Diaz and others wished, for the most part actual husbands appear to have been more like William Robinson than Charles Bradley Cumings—loving their families but keeping their distance from the minutiae of domestic life.[31]

By the early twentieth century, however, there would be a change. Middle-class husbands and wives, especially in the suburbs, would try to resolve these marital complications by having husbands take on a share of the nurturing and emotional tasks of female domesticity, a subject the next chapters will treat in considerable detail. Charles Cumings was a harbinger of what I call "masculine domesticity." Not until the power relations within middle-class marriages underwent subtle shifts, not until the rise of the corporation provided relatively secure jobs with predictable patterns of mobility, and not until suburbs were viewed as the appropriate physical space for the creation of the companionate family, would the conditions exist for masculine domesticity to be a discernable model for the husband and father. But Charles Cumings was an early example of the kind of man for whom such a model would be attractive. He was an organization man during the heyday of American entrepreneurialism; he was a private man during the great age of the men's club; and he involved himself in the details of his children's lives in a time when middle-class men on the whole believed along with Charles Dole that children were a woman's responsibility. By the first decade of the twentieth century, Charles Cumings would have a lot of company; in the 1870s and 1880s he was a precursor of things to come.

It would be an oversimplification to call either the Robinsons or the Cumingses representative or typical of suburban families in general during the second half of the nineteenth century, but they do exemplify the ways in which the meaning of suburban life was being transformed for middle-class Americans. Through these brief biographical studies I have attempted to explore the ways in which relatively ordinary men and women experienced the changes evident in prescriptive literature and in the prescient observations of social commentators. Neither the Robinsons nor the Cumingses were entirely typical, yet some parts of their lives were replicated by countless other Americans. The kinds of transitions and accommodations to which they had begun to adjust, and to redefine for themselves, affected all of middle-class America during these years. By the first decade of the twentieth century, out of the sum of these changes, a new ideal of middle-class family life, centered firmly in the suburbs, would emerge. Those developments are the subjects of the next two chapters.

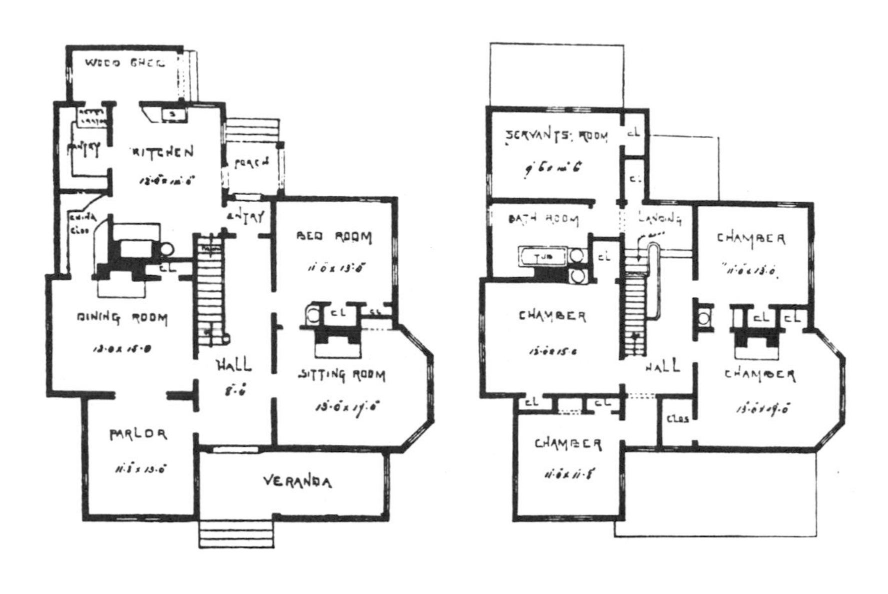

Houses from the Pallisers' designs were built by the thousands in the United States. According to them, this house should have cost about $3,000 in the 1870s. From Palliser, Palliser, and Co., Architects, *Palliser's Model Homes*, 1878.

These houses, designed by the noted Philadelphia architect Samuel Sloan, are from the 1850s. The grounds of each house were to be planted in a "pleasing lawn and garden, with shade, fruit and ornamental trees, and various sorts of shrubbery and flowers." The interior plans included both a parlor and a library on the first floor, six bedrooms on the second and third floors, and one bathroom. Sloan's "ready villas," although never built, embody the romantic architectural ideas popularized by Andrew Jackson Downing during the mid-nineteenth century. From the *Plan of the Haddonfield Ready Villa Association,* 1854. Courtesy of the Historical Society of Haddonfield.

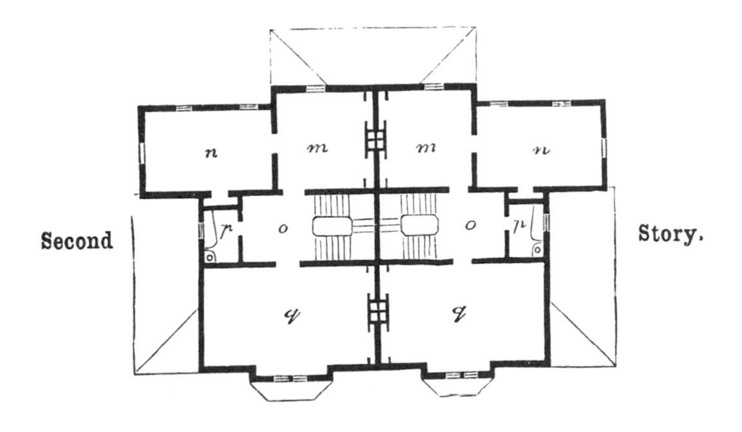

Second Story.

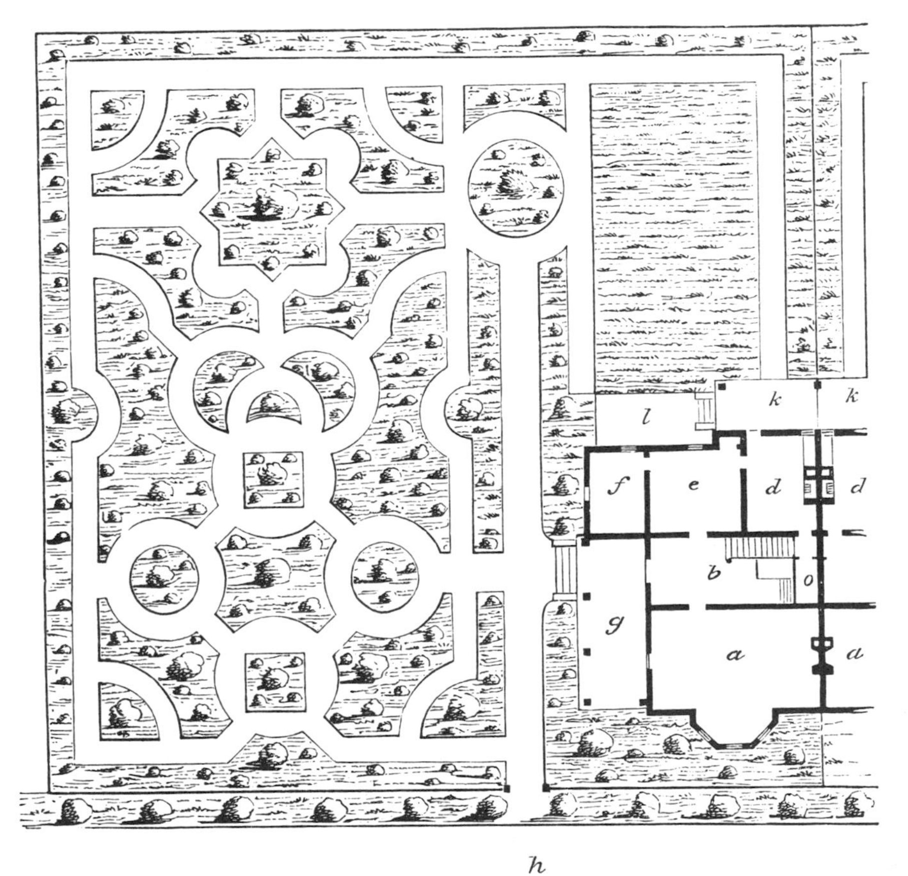

h

i

Ground Plan of Designs No. 5 and 6.

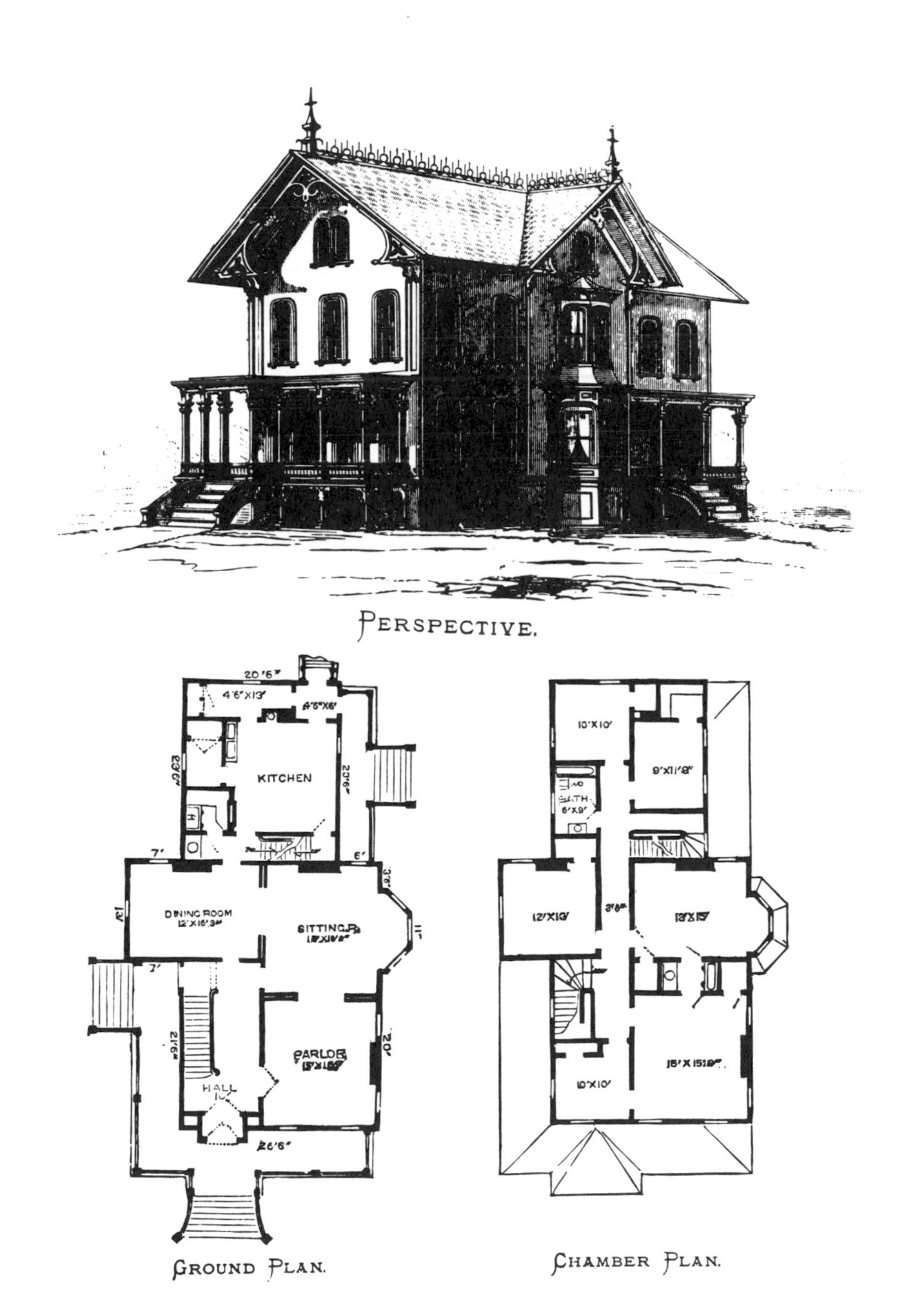

More expensive than the *Palliser's* design, this house from E. C. Hussy's *Home Building: A Reliable Book of Facts . . .*, published in 1875, was estimated to cost, "at New York," $7,000. More expensive materials and ornamentation, as well as the cost for plumbing both the kitchen and the bathroom, accounted for the higher price tag. In room size and interior design, the houses were not particularly different.

Idlewild was Nathaniel Willis's country house on the Hudson River. Willis, editor of the *Home Monthly,* was an ardent advocate of "country" life, but not an isolated rural environment. Idlewild was linked by rail with New York City, where the offices of *Home Monthly* were located. From Martha Lamb, *Home of America,* 1875.

Frank Scott, the prominent landscape architect, urged suburban families to give their neighborhoods a parklike environment by "throwing front grounds open together," thereby creating broad, open vistas. From Frank Scott, *The Art of Beautifying Suburban Home Grounds*, 1870.

In the early twentieth century, a reaction set in against houses that looked like this. Joy Wheeler Dow was one of a number of American architects who began to seek in the nation's colonial past for an architecture that evoked what he called the "Anglo-Saxon" home feeling. This is an illustration of a "bad" house, according to Dow's lights. From Joy Wheeler Dow, *American Renaissance*, 1904.

PART
Two

PROGRESSIVE SUBURBANITES

CHAPTER THREE

Homemakers Male and Female

The home is man's affair as much as woman's. . . . When God created homemakers, male and female created He them.

MARTHA AND ROBERT BRUÈRE
INCREASING HOME EFFICIENCY, 1912

As the nineteenth century ended and the twentieth began, there were some aspects of the relationship between husbands and wives that changed very little, if at all. Men were still the breadwinners, women their economic dependents. Fewer than 5 percent of married women held jobs outside the home, and most of these were working-class wives, not members of the middle class. But as we saw in the last chapter, beneath the surface one finds a complicated pattern of changing relationships. I explored its beginnings in the domestic writings of the late nineteenth century, and in the daily lives of the Robinson and Cumings families. Those changes culminated in the creation, in the early twentieth century, of a new model of middle-class marriage and family life, centered in the suburbs and in many ways redefining them.

Although one might read the story of the suburbanization of the United States as an almost inevitable outcome of technological innovation and the availability of relatively inexpensive land, historians such as Robert Fishman have pointed out the pitfalls of doing so—England suburbanized, after all, without cheap land, while the French chose to redesign the cities for the bourgeoisie and allot the suburbs to the working class. And in the United States? In the nineteenth century this country's suburban advocates had combined agrarian nostalgia, an idealized vision of the linkage of pastoral life to republican virtue, and an image of a sturdy, property-owning yeomanry in a package that recast the values of the early American republic to meet the needs of a commercial, industrial, and urbanizing society. The women who advocated the ideology of domesticity, using different means and without abandoning the city, had tried also to respond to change without abandoning the past.[1]

By the early twentieth century, however, many of these women, having failed to make the city conform to the values of domesticity, came to agree with suburban proponents that the city itself was dangerous, and these two formerly separate and distinct ideas combined into one. In the years before World War I a new suburban domestic ideal took hold. This new suburban vision changed middle-class family life—it reorganized domesticity so that it no longer depended on the strict adherence to separate masculine and feminine roles—and it also redefined the residential suburbs, so that the ruralized suburban vision of the mid-nineteenth century gave way to one emphasizing the importance of place as well as, perhaps more so than, property ownership.

This new ideal developed within a social and spatial context familiar to historians: By 1900, middle-class women, despite the fact that most did not have careers in the traditionally masculine sense of the word, had made genuine incursions into the male sphere as it had conventionally been defined. At the same time, middle-class men's lives had been transformed, as they increasingly worked for salaries rather than for themselves. Cities had changed too, as many of them teemed with vast numbers of immigrants from southern and eastern Europe. Finally, the residential suburbs themselves had become—in terms of services, access to the central city, and social life—much more urban.[2]

THE DANGEROUS CITY PERCEIVED

If we try to look at the great city of the early twentieth century from the vantage point of a native-born, white, middle-class American, whether male or female, we can see how a new domesticity might be viewed as a solution to a large number of seemingly different kinds of problems. When these men and women took stock of urban society at the dawn of the twentieth century, they saw filthy factory districts, crowded immigrant ghettos, reports of anarchist terrorism and socialist electoral encroachment, black migration from the rural to the urban South, and the beginnings of movement to the North. In addition, there were visible and prominent urban feminists demanding opportunities identical to those of men, while ordinary middle-class wives and mothers were spending their mornings at the department stores and afternoons at the women's clubs. The success of machine politics seemed to confirm that republican values had eroded, and the optimistic assessments of nineteenth-century domestic reformers that domestic ideals could redeem the city no longer seemed realistic. Their efforts to reshape what Christine Stansell has called the social geography of urban America had failed; by the turn of the century a "ubiquitous and aggressive working class culture" had taken strong hold of the city.[3]

For Americans who took this point of view, the great city appeared as a danger, both to the family and the polity. That perceived danger, based on an overt anxiety about the erosion of the pastoral landscape and undergirded with subtextual fears of urban feminists, radicals, and immigrants, was at the heart of the new suburban advocacy. The optimism of the past, that the great city could be reshaped to conform to domestic and small town ideals, had come to seem misplaced. In the early 1880s the pastoral and the urban had not seemed utterly incompatible. The urban park movement was at its height, and architects of apartment buildings—in their own parklike settings—insisted that they built communities, not isolated flats. But by the turn of the twentieth century, urban advocates tended to be radicals, or reformers wishing to create a nation of urban sophisticates who would live in city apartments, take nature sparingly in urban parks and gardens, and relegate their domestic duties to "trained professionals." Such a prospect was unacceptable to most Americans.[4]

Immigrants shared the title of urban villain with political radicals. Suburban advocates blamed the immigrants of southern and eastern Europe for the dirt and density of the city; they assumed that the newcomers chose to live in squalor instead of joining a building and loan association to save for a house. (The irony of that attitude, as we shall see later, is that immigrants were more likely to be home owners than native-born, white, middle-class Americans.) Sneered one prominent childrearing expert, "The revolting creatures of the slums in a vague way want to be decent, but they don't want to *enough*."[5] Echoing this theme, magazine editorials in the early twentieth century reviled immigrant families who took the streetcar to the outskirts of the city for recreation. There, according to the editorials, they literally trashed the pastoral landscape: They "bring their babies, their baby carriages and their baby milk bottles; they bring newspapers to look at and they bring food tied up in untidy bundles. And there they pass a pleasant afternoon, filling the air with talk in strange harsh languages, and when they retire they leave behind them exactly everything which they do not wish to carry away. . . . Is this fair?" The question was rhetorical. "The American citizen," concluded this editor, "is entitled to greater consideration than the foreigner." Such views—combined with the emergence of residential covenants that prohibited Jews, blacks, and in the West, Asians, from living in certain suburbs—highlighted American ethnocentrism, as did suggestions by such prominent architects as Joy Wheeler Dow that people of "Anglo-Saxon descent" possessed the greatest reverence for "the dwelling place."[6]

Nevertheless, some ambivalence lay behind this condemnation of the living habits of urban, working-class immigrants (and to a somewhat lesser extent, of blacks as well). At the same time that such attitudes encouraged native white Americans to leave the poor to their ghettos, they also spurred philanthropists to urge the poor to adopt middle-class standards, so that they too could aspire to a suburban house. On the one hand, living in slums was said to breed radical violence: The American public saw radicals, especially anarchists, as tenement dwelling immigrants—"the offscourings of Europe"—who prowled the streets terrorizing law-abiding men and women.[7] On the other hand, the "cure" for revolutionary behavior was respectability and a single-family dwelling. Many middle-class Americans, as historians have routinely pointed out, believed in the transforming power of the single-family home for those with radical tendencies. Elaine May goes perhaps a little too far when she argues that "suburbs encouraged rather than resisted ethnic mixture," but she captures the ambivalence of suburban advocates, who were repelled by foreigners, blacks, and, depending on the location, Asians, and yet wanted them to have aspirations similar to theirs.[8]

In the early twentieth century such a wish was not always related to compassion for the poor, and was not, at least among many suburban advocates, associated with an argument that the society as a whole ought to take responsibility for their plight. For example, the editor of *American Homes and Gardens* wrote what at first glance appeared to be a sympathetic account of a poverty-stricken neighborhood in Washington, D.C. The editor, however, blamed the victims of those terrible conditions for their own circumstances. If these families, he insisted, had saved a portion of their pittances they would not have been in such destitution: "A year or two ago," he concluded piously, "the magazine world was treated to an extended series of articles showing how homes were built or purchased on incomes not much greater than those cited here and on savings made from such incomes. . . . The contrast . . . is nothing short of amazing."[9] Poverty was a sad situation, in short, but it was up to the poor to help themselves.

Ethnocentrism was one important facet of middle-class, anti-urban rhetoric of the early twentieth century. Fear of radicalism was related to it. Newspaper editorials were quick to draw connections between the slum and dangerous ideas. Revolutionary anarchists, in particular, in spite of the smallness of their actual numbers, were favorite journalistic targets. Since many of them were immigrants concentrated in urban slums, their very existence reinforced the connection in the public mind between radicalism and the foreign born. Newspapers all over the country reported radical offenses—real and imaginary—against convention and against the state. Although anti-radical hysteria did not characterize suburban home magazines, except for the occasional editorial endorsing suburban homes as a cure for working-class political discontent, other newspapers and magazines aimed at the middle class returned to this theme again and again. Interestingly, although there were anarchists on the farm as well as in the city, newspapers characterized them (to use a more modern term, but one that captures the meaning of this period, too) as urban guerillas, whose war cry was, in the words of economist Richard Ely, "away with religion, away with the family, away with the state."[10] The Haymarket Bombing of 1886, in Chicago, and the Lexington Avenue incident in New York in 1914, in which three young anarchists blew up themselves and a comrade while producing a bomb to use against John D. Rockefeller, symbolized for the newspapers the terrorist nature of radicals, anarchists in particular, who made the cities dangerous.[11]

For the American public, the anarchist was a foreign-born bomb thrower who lived in a slum and lurked in dark alleys, waiting to assault a respectable citizen. Although this was an irrational notion, Americans viewed anarchists with a mixture of horror and outraged fascination. Perhaps the reason lies in the fact that anarchists took to their limits fairly widespread American apprehensions. While many Americans worried about governmental efficacy, anarchists rejected government; while ordinary people worried about the future of the family in the face of feminist demands or rising divorce rates, anarchists disdained marriage and conventional family life altogether; and while Americans worried about the concentration of money and power in the hands of a few, and feared for their personal autonomy, revolutionary anarchists called for the removal, by assassination if necessary, of the powerful few.[12] Writers in what we might call the "advocacy press" of suburbia (the home and family magazines) rarely articulated a fear of radicalism, but the prominent newspapers of the day did, and in those pages columnists and editors made it clear that urban America was in a state of collapse, and that radicals should take a lot of the blame for that collapse.

Fear of foreigners linked up with antiradical hostilities to form one element of America's worries about the future of its great cities. But radicalism was also connected, perhaps more obliquely, to anxieties about the direction of what had been called in the nineteenth century the "woman movement." This was potential subversion closer to home, as white, middle-class, mostly Protestant women were forcing changes in family and community life. The new suburban ideal owed much to a desire to do something about the changes in the behavior of middle-class women. After all, even if it *were* possible to explain the demographic facts of residential decentralization and urban deconcentration by technological development and immigration, to do so does not account for the way in which middle-class suburbs took on the social and cultural geography that gave rise to "intensely domestic" families. To begin to make sense of these kinds of changes it is necessary to explore the intersection of the female-based ideology of domesticity with the male-defined suburban ideal.[13]

In the 1890s the women's rights movement had begun to engender mass support, attracting women with a wide range of political viewpoints and social attitudes. And by the end of the first decade of the twentieth century, it had become clear that some adherents intended to take the women's rights cause some steps further. It was then, as Nancy Cott has perceptively pointed out, that some women began to describe themselves as "Feminists." Cott's discovery—that "although continuity in the suffrage campaign obscured the important transition, the new language of Feminism marked the end of the woman movement and embarkation on a modern agenda"—helps us to understand why it became important in this decade, rather than earlier, for those with more traditional views about gender roles to try to root women ever more securely in the family. At the center of the new "Feminism" (almost always capitalized in the heady days of its first appearance) was "freedom for all forms of women's active expression, elimination of all structural and psychological handicaps to women's economic independence, an end to the double standard of sexual morality, release from constraining sexual stereotypes, and opportunity to shine in every civic and professional capacity."[14]

Feminism raised a specter that advocates of domesticity feared; here were women demanding that the individualistic consciousness so central to the nineteenth-century ideal of liberalism apply to them as well as to men. It should come as no surprise that feminism flourished in an urban environment. Two of the most important organized expressions of the new ideology—Heterodoxy and the Feminist Alliance—were creations of New Yorkers. And it was urban feminists who insisted that in order to create an environment in which women's individualism could flourish, the household itself required radical restructuring. Charlotte Perkins Gilman's now familiar design for an apartment house in which all cooking, cleaning, and daily childcare were the tasks of people trained for those jobs was particularly threatening because it was designed for a family in which each person, including the wife and mother, maintained a separate identity. Gilman believed that the traditional family was anachronistic in an urbanized, industrial society. Like the other feminists of her day, she demanded that women seek for themselves the sense of individual achievement and separate identity that had been heretofore reserved for men.[15] Americans today are still uncomfortable with this idea, as is evident from the cultural and institutional barriers to gender equality that continue to exist. But perhaps if middle-class men and women had made different choices during the Progressive Era, these problems might not have come down to us in the same form.

It may seem surprising that Gilman—radical as her ideas seem even to some present-day observers—enjoyed considerable popularity in the years before World War I. But she was a sought-after lecturer among club women, and her writings received considerable attention, finding a place on the discussion lists of dozens of programs in suburban women's clubs. For her and her supporters to demand an architecture of independence was to challenge, in the most fundamental sense and in spite of all of Gilman's denials that she had no wish to destroy the family, the conventional idea of what family meant. Nevertheless, feminism, as represented by Charlotte Perkins Gilman and others like her, while it challenged, did not replace the "woman movement." "Women's Rights women" continued to believe in an updated and revitalized ideology of domesticity: They encouraged women to involve themselves in the outside world, and they took care to express that interest in the name of the preservation of the family. The concept of "family protection," for example, justified the women's rights activities of the Woman's Christian Temperance Union under Frances Willard's leadership as well as many of the suffrage and reform activities of women's clubs, and it continued to do so throughout the first two decades of the twentieth century. Women's rights women, less radical but considerably more numerous than the new feminists, continued to hold the view that men and women had distinct psychologies, and that the reproductive function was the chief cause of differences in the behavior of men and women.[16]

Even if most women's rights women did not accept Gilman's argument that an obsolete social system kept women isolated in domestic drudgery, and that the physical manifestation of that isolation was the single-family house, many did relish the comparative freedom of urban life. With or without feminist architecture, urban life, whether in apartment buildings or row houses, afforded middle-class wives and mothers a respite from some domestic demands as well as opportunities for social and political activity. Suburban advocates as early as the 1870s had recognized this when they suggested that husbands generally favored the suburbs more than did their wives, and that men found it necessary to persuade their wives to give up city life. Cities gave women scope, as they became active not only in women's clubs but also in temperance and social purity movements and the drive for suffrage. In larger cities, the department stores served as quasi-clubs for women, with lounges and dining rooms where they could meet their friends for lunch, or rest or read. Some department stores even had a place to leave the children.[17]

It became obvious to all but the dullest observers that middle-class wives and mothers were having fewer children and spending more of their time in women's clubs, reform organizations, or the suffrage movement. As such women moved ever farther beyond the confines of the family, apprehension about women's changing roles turned in some quarters to fear. Although the club movement had been growing since its creation in the late 1860s, department stores had deliberately sought the woman shopper since at least the 1870s, and apartment houses had been built in increasing numbers since the same era, it was after the turn of the century that social commentators began to connect the growth of such institutions with the "decline" of family life.[18] Magazine editorials began to remind women that "civic betterment" ought to begin at home, with beautifying the house and yard. *American Homes and Gardens,* too aware of the popularity of women's clubs among its own readers to risk an outright attack, instead damned the club movement with faint praise, first commending clubwomen for "concern[ing] themselves with the life and the things around them," and then informing them that "[n]ot all of this new energy has been wisely directed . . . : there has been much done that need not have been done."[19]

The sharpest attacks were not against the women's clubs, but against apartment life, particularly in its newly popular form, the apartment hotel.[20] These buildings were not based on the designs of Charlotte Perkins Gilman, who wanted to remove even childcare from the mother's supervision, but they still were seen as a threat. The *Architectural Record,* which often welcomed innovation, did not welcome this one. In a much quoted and cited attack on urban apartment hotels, it damned these symbols of the city for removing the duties of housekeeping from women and thereby destroying American family life. Taking note in 1903 of the phenomenal growth of plans for apartment hotels in New York City alone—from 11 in 1900 (already "much larger than any preceding year") to 46 in 1901 to 44 in the first ten months of 1902—The *Record* expressed its shock and dismay that families, and not only businessmen or suburban dwellers who spent a month or two in the city and then returned to a more wholesome environment, were choosing this manner of living on a permanent basis. "The apartment hotel," the *Record* insisted, "[is] the consummate flower of domestic irresponsibility." And there was no question about which member of the family bore the blame for that irresponsibility: "A woman who lives in an apartment hotel has nothing to do. . . . She cannot create that atmosphere of manners and things around her own personality, which is the chief source of her effectiveness and power." Club life and outside interests, the *Record* averred, were very poor substitutes for the pleasures of creating a home.[21]

THE ATTRACTION OF THE SUBURBS I: MASCULINE DOMESTICITY

If urban life offered so many attractions for women, how could they be persuaded to choose the suburb instead? In part, of course, the suburbs themselves had become more "urban," as we shall see in the next chapter. But even more, the growing interest of upper middle-class men in domestic life made women their willing partners in deciding on a suburban way of life. Most women—many women's rights women, too, particularly those more interested in social reform movements than in absolute gender parity—still thought of themselves as mothers, if not literally, at least symbolically. Perhaps "nurturers" is a better word; some women nurtured their families, others the poor, and others the state. Such women began to favor suburban life, and to espouse the new domestic ideal, to a great extent because of the emergence of what I call "masculine domesticity."[22]

We have met a few fictional and actual precursors of the domestic men of the early twentieth century in the last chapters, but in general, historians are not used to thinking of men in domestic terms. To characterize middle-class American men as domestic requires us to modify some widely held assumptions about the nature of middle-class manhood at the turn of the twentieth century. The images that typically come to mind whenever we think about American men of this period include a bored clerk or middle-manager in some impersonal office of a faceless corporation, pushing papers or counting the company's money, longing nostalgically for a time when a man could find adventure and get rich at the same time—by becoming a robber baron, or conquering new frontiers. Or we conjure up a vision of Theodore Roosevelt, the delicate child who grew up to relish big-game hunting and war, and whose open disdain for softness and "effeminacy" made him the symbol of rugged masculinity in his own time.

We owe the identification of this association of the corporate drone with the flamboyant Rough Rider to an influential essay by historian John Higham, who argued that one of the most significant American cultural constructs at the turn of the century was a growing cult of masculinity, attended by the insecurities of middle-class men about their own virility and "manliness." Beginning in the 1890s, Higham argued, the country witnessed a national "urge to be young, masculine, and adventurous," when Americans rebelled against "the frustrations, the routine, and the sheer dullness of an urban-industrial culture."[23] He cited the growing popularity of boxing and football, a disaffection from genteel fiction, and not least, the rise in the level of national bellicosity, as important indicators of a new public mood.

An understanding of the cult of masculinity has provided historians with rich insights about the nature of what it means to be male in American society.[24] But it is not a general-purpose explanatory device, unless we wish to define an entire generation of middle-class men—young and middle-aged, married and single, urban, suburban, and rural—in terms of anxieties about manliness. Those anxieties, and the men who faced them, undoubtedly existed, but in the suburbs of the early twentieth century, we see a different kind of man—an apparently contented suburban father, who enjoyed the security of a regular salary, a predictable rise through the company hierarchy, and greater leisure. (Harried commuters today tend to forget that in the early part of this century, commuting times on the railroad to the suburbs of most cities, with the exception of some of New York's, averaged thirty minutes or less.)[25]

None of this should be taken as a suggestion that the cult of masculinity did not exist; but it does not tell the whole story of middle-class manhood. (Or of working-class manhood, either. Although working-class families are not the subject of this book, as historian Kathy Piess has reminded us, for *all* social classes, "the complex passage from Victorian culture to modernism involved . . . what might be termed the shift from homosocial to heterosocial culture.") Like the idea of masculinity itself, masculine domesticity[26] is difficult to define; in some ways, it is easier to say what it was *not* than what it was. It was not equivalent to feminism. It was not an equal sharing of all household duties. It emphatically did not extend to the belief that men and women ought to have identical opportunities in the larger society.[27] It was, however, a behavioral model in which fathers agreed to take on increased responsibility for some of the day-to-day tasks of bringing up children and spend their time away from work in playing with their sons and daughters, teaching them, taking them on trips. A domestic man also made his wife, rather than his male associates, his regular companion on evenings out. And while he might not dust the mantel or make the bed except in special circumstances, he took a significantly greater interest in the details of running the household and caring for the children than his father had been expected to take.[28]

Masculine domesticity could not exist without a marriage of companionship. And although the idea of companionate marriage had been developing during the nineteenth century, historians disagree profoundly about its actual presence. In reality, both the ideology of domesticity and the patriarchal ideal had promoted more gender separation than togetherness. Masculine domesticity also called for an economic system that provided sufficient job security for middle-class men so that husbands could devote more attention to their families. And as we shall see later in this chapter and the next, it required a special physical location in which the new attitudes toward family could find their appropriate spatial expressions. We saw the beginnings of masculine domesticity in the last chapters, in the prescriptive literature of Harriet Beecher Stowe, Abby Morton Diaz, and Margaret Sangster; and in the quiet domestic life of Charles Cumings. But it was not until the early twentieth century that these three forces—cultural, economic, and spatial—came together with enough power to integrate men more fully into the middle-class home.

By the early twentieth century, middle-class men had begun to think about marriage in ways different from their fathers and grandfathers. The changing nature of occupational patterns among them had resulted in reduced job risks, regular hours, and more secure careers. Men had time and emotional energy to spend on their families. Women had long been trying to bring about a change in men's attitudes toward home and family life. Abby Diaz, readers will recall, as early as the mid-1870s tried to persuade men that egalitarian marriages were in their best interests. She was ahead of her time; but by the 1890s other women had come to agree with her, and by the early twentieth century, male advice writers took up the same theme. For the first time, men advising other men began to give considerable attention to the duties and the pleasures of men in the household. The male editors of *American Homes and Gardens* did not hesitate to remind men of their domestic responsibilities. Others stressed family togetherness. As an anonymous father, writing in *The Independent* in 1906, argued, not only the family but the larger society benefitted when "father and son . . . take their social enjoyments *en famille.*" James Canfield expressed similar views in *Cosmopolitan,* when he enumerated "the three controlling desires of every normal man." Men's domestic needs were uppermost in Canfield's mind. A man's "home must be more than a mere shelter. . . . He must be able to make his house a home by adding a hearth—and there is no hearth for a man but the heart of a woman."[29]

Although male advice-givers rarely expected or desired men to take on the administrative or physical duties of running a household, they did urge fathers to trade the burdens of patriarchal authority and work-induced separation from family life for emotional closeness to their wives and the pleasures of spending time with their children as companions. Naturally, there were dissenters; however, even criticism could inadvertantly highlight the new domesticity of suburban men. Richard Harding Davis, writing for *Harper's,* found his married suburban friends boring because they had no interests beyond each other, their house, and their suburban pleasures. Davis found their contentment incomprehensible.[30] What seemed to men like Davis a stifling existence appeared to others to offer a life of quiet contentment.

Companionate marriages did not have to be completely egalitarian in order to require new roles for both men and women.[31] Martha Bruère, an influential Progressive Era home economist, and her economist husband Robert, investigated the households of early twentieth-century, middle-class America, using case studies of urban, suburban, and farm families. Reformers who discouraged parsimony and encouraged consumption in the pursuit of "cultivation and comfort," the Bruères believed that "[t]he home is man's affair as much as woman's. . . . [W]hen God made homemakers, male and female created He them!"[32]

There is a considerable cultural chasm between middle-class society of the mid-nineteenth century, in which women took responsibility for the home and for the emotional tasks of parenthood while men took on the role of firm patriarch or detached observer, and that of the early twentieth, in which men could be referred to as "homemakers." That shift could not have occurred without a shift in the occupational patterns of middle-class men. Charles Bradley Cumings, that early practitioner of many elements of masculine domesticity, was an organization man, not an entrepreneur or independent professional. The connection between Cumings's occupation and his domesticity is significant. As the century came to a close, and the American middle-class shifted away from its mid-nineteenth century base of entrepreneurs, independent professionals, and clergy, other men could be like Charles Cumings. By then, particularly in the suburbs, the typical early twentieth-century, middle-class father was salaried and had some security in his position, more or less regular hours, and relatively predictable patterns of occupational mobility.[33]

As middle-class men gained respite from the economic pressures that had plagued the previous generation, they had the time to give their families greater attention. The importance of male domestic roles was taken seriously. As Martha and Robert Bruère insisted, "A knowledge of housekeeping is not a matter of sex, but science," which "all ought to know, men and women alike." High schools, they argued, should require boys to take home economics courses, because men should also become "homemakers."[34] Others shared the Bruères' views. The male editor of the suburban-oriented magazine *American Homes and Gardens* announced in 1905, "There is no reason at all why men should not sweep and dust, make beds, clean windows, fix the fire, clean the grate, arrange the furniture" and cook. The editor refers to domestic servants, not husbands. Still, he intended to make a point about male involvement in the home, and not merely about servants; he continued the same theme in his editorial for the following month: "The responsibility for the home is not [the woman's] alone," he insisted, "but is equally the husband's."[35]

It is not clear that the average middle-class man, young or old, was induced to sweep and dust on the word of a magazine editor, or sign up for home economics courses on the advice of the Bruères. Nevertheless, men were becoming more involved in the internal workings of the household, perhaps to the disgust of Richard Harding Davis, but to the delight of their wives. Joan Seidl, who examined the diaries and letters of Minnesotans at the turn of the twentieth century, including St. Paul suburbanites, discovered that husbands of the early twentieth century took a far greater interest in the home than did those of the 1880s. Her focus is on house decoration; she discovered that in the earlier period men cared little about it, but by the first decade of the century they were active participants. The recently married Helen Sommers, for example, wrote her sister in 1909 about decorating the house that she and her husband had chosen: "Harry & I are working every thing out together." Household decoration, according to Seidl, was a symbol of the growing involvement of men in the home. "Most remarkable," she argues, "given the standard interpretations of the period, is the degree to which husbands took an active role in domestic arrangements. . . . Fixed hours of work allowed leisure for Walter Post to dry the dishes and for James Andrews to paste up the wallpaper."[36]

Greater involvement in the internal workings of the home was one aspect of this change in male roles, but it was not the whole of it. Women wanted more from men than for them to share in the process of making decisions about household furnishings. They also wanted them to be nurturing fathers. In the 1890s some of them had already pinned their hopes on the next generation. Kate Wiggin, who before she wrote *Rebecca of Sunnybrook Farm* had been a kindergarten teacher, attempted to develop "the father spirit" in little boys. At school, her charges played a bird game, in which "we had always had a mother bird in the nest with the birdlings." Wiggin then introduced a "father bird" and similarly reorganized other games. Finally, she incorporated the boys into "doll's day," previously a girls' game only. Wiggin asked one of the boys to play "father" and rock a doll to sleep. To her delight, all the other little boys then wanted to play.[37]

Wiggin published her kindergarten techniques and they enjoyed wide circulation. One might deduce from this that the imagined sight of thousands of little boys rocking dolls to sleep sent men scurrying to their sons' rooms, if only to confiscate the dolls. Indeed, one of the most powerful motivations for greater fatherly involvement with their children was a desire to balance the preponderant female presence in the lives of young children, especially boys. But it is important to remember that the word is balance, not overshadow. Masculine domesticity, as it had evolved by the early twentieth century, was incorporated into the concept of manliness, as men became convinced that in order to have their sons grow up to be "manly" they should involve themselves more substantially in their children's upbringing. In so doing, they turned nurturing, at least during this period, into a "manly" activity.[38]

Advocates of masculine domesticity encouraged fathers to form direct and intimate bonds with their children of both sexes, by playing games with them, taking them on camping trips, and simply spending time with them. Of course, before the entrenchment of the ideology of domesticity in the second third of the nineteenth century, fathers had maintained a large role in family government, but in the earlier period the emphasis was on obedience, discipline, and the importance of the father's role as head of the household. In the early twentieth century the stress was on friendship; fathers were encouraged to be "chums" with their children, especially, but by no means exclusively, with their sons. Male writers on parenthood differed from their female counterparts in that they placed greater importance on independence, approving of boys having, from about the age of seven on, a sort of freewheeling companionship with other boys—a "gang" or "bunch," to use the terms of the period. They argued that fathers could encourage such freedom because the new closeness of father and son would prevent the boy from falling into evil ways. His father would play baseball with him, take him and his friends camping and swimming, and in general play the role of a caring older companion rather than a stern patriarch.[39]

Within this new definition of fatherhood, one could argue that the concepts of masculine domesticity and "manliness" were more complementary than they might seem at first glance. There are a couple of ways to look at this question. If we focus on the organized movements to turn boys into "manly" men—the scouts and other groups like them—we see adult men channeling and directing the energies of their charges into safe outlets. And if we turn our attention to middle-class adult men themselves, it appears that while they might have had a more aggressive fantasy life, their actual behavior within the family had become more nurturing and companionable. Take the rage for football, which men avidly watched. Who played it? The young. As Foster Rhea Dulles pointed out in his classic history of American recreation, "few adults found themselves able or willing to play football" in the early twentieth century. "The game was primarily for boys." This is not to deny that some men were frustrated by the new male domesticity. Historians such as John Higham, Peter Filene, and T. J. Jackson Lears have done an excellent job of chronicling that frustration. But how widespread was it? Lears tellingly viewed the aggressive masculinity of the martial ideal, for example, as an aberration, an antimodernist reaction to the changes of late nineteenth- and early twentieth-century society.[40] One might legitimately see the popularity of football and boxing, and the reading of adventure novels, as elements of a vigorous fantasy life, rather than as a rebellion against domesticity, masking it to some extent but not negating it.

At least one of the proponents both of manliness and masculine domesticity faced the issue of possible contradictions between them squarely and concluded that in fact the two were not antagonistic. Senator Albert Beveridge, in his advice book for young men, told the story of a "resourceful Oriental" who had suggested that "the influence of women on the Occidental man is effeminizing our civilization." Beveridge countered with his own view: "Even if what this Oriental assailant of our customs terms the overcharge of femininity in Occidental society does mellow us," he said, "it does not follow that it weakens us."[41]

Perhaps no single individual epitomized the connections between the cult of masculinity and masculine domesticity more powerfully than Bernarr Macfadden. A major figure in the mass culture of the early to mid-twentieth century, Macfadden amassed a publishing empire based on his ownership of *The New York Daily News* and the magazines *True Story* and *True Romance.* In the early part of his career, in the years before World War I, he published *Physical Culture* and books on health and what we now call "fitness." Macfadden addressed his gospel of "physical culture" to women as much as to men. And by the same token, just as women ought to develop physical strength, so too men ought to develop their nurturant capacities, since both had emotional and nurturing functions within the family.[42]

According to Macfadden, a man should share as much as possible in the rearing of his children, and he should begin by being present during their births. Men who did not want to share their wives' experience of childbirth, or who did not choose to spend time with children, he believed, were men who could not be trusted. "Whenever you find a man who is without an innate love for children," he told his readers, "you may rest assured that there is something wrong with his character." An early biographer of Macfadden claimed that his subject regularly devoted his evenings to his family, always leaving work "between five and seven. . . . He is a home-loving soul. . . . Sane, happy American family life is one of his ideals . . . and his [seven] children are a constant source of pleasure to him." Whether Macfadden's friend and authorized biographer accurately described his subject's habits is less significant than that it mattered deeply to Macfadden that readers believe in the overarching importance of his family life. In the mid-nineteenth century, a self-made man like Macfadden would have stressed his arduous climb up the ladder of economic success, and the tenacity required to keep him at the top, rather than his willingness to set his business cares aside at a specific time each day in order to be with his family.[43]

Both Senator Beveridge and Bernarr Macfadden assumed that there was a necessary connection between a man's embrace of domesticity and a desire to live in the suburbs. Each viewed suburbia as the "natural" habitat of domestic man. Macfadden believed that the purchase of a "modest little home" gave a young married man a sense of stability, as well as the necessary physical distance from urban temptations. Having come to New York City from the Midwest to make his fortune, Macfadden himself moved to the suburbs at the first opportunity, and held resolutely antiurban sentiments. And Beveridge devoted an entire chapter of his advice book for young men to "The New Home." In it he insisted, "'Apartments' cannot by any magic be converted into a home. . . . [B]etter a separate dwelling with [a] dry goods box for table and camp-stools for chairs than tapestried walls, mosaic floors, and all luxuriousness." Furthermore, once the young man had got himself a wife, a nice suburban house, and some children (because "a purposely childless marriage is no marriage at all"), he "will spend all of [his] extra time at home," listening to his wife play the piano, reading, and not least, playing with the children.[44]

Masculine domesticity was a successful response to the challenges posed by an educated and civic-minded womanhood within America's middle class. Husbands appeared to be promising—at last—to become companions in marriage and partners in childrearing. Whether consciously or not, and my guess is that men had a pretty good idea of what they were offering, the advocates of masculine domesticity offered a way for moderate women's rights women to accommodate within the family their desire for civil and political equality. Whether these women would have been drawn into the camp of the feminists is problematic, but that they were not satisfied with things as they had been is clear. Now, their husbands had come to acknowledge the importance of the domestic sphere, not only rhetorically, but also by assuming specific responsibilities within it. But there was a catch. In order to have companionate marriages, women would have to agree to share only partially in the world of men.

It was not the first time, nor would it be the last, that women faced this dilemma. Here was a new domestic ideal, which offered women the opportunity to cultivate outside interests (but not the right to play the same roles in society as men). And while it retained the position of breadwinner for husbands, it also required them to assume some of the nurturing responsibilities that had traditionally belonged to women. That it emerged now—when feminists argued for women's individualism, when nativist fears about the declining birthrate of white Protestant women had reached near frenzy, and when anxieties over the divorce rate had become a national issue—should come as no surprise. Nor is it surprising that many women accepted the idea, given the continued strength of the idea of women as nurturant and care-giving.[45]

Because the city was viewed as the center of anonymity and individualism, the suburbs took on new meaning as the locus of this new domesticity. In suburbia husbands and wives could be companions, not rivals, and the specter of individualist demands would retreat in the face of family togetherness. There was scholarly support for these arguments as well. Sociologists who specialized in the study of the family during the first decade of the twentieth century contended that urban life and family stability had become incompatible. In 1908 the American Sociological Society devoted its annual meeting to questions about the family. Although the scholars in attendance were not entirely agreed about the nature of the changes that were affecting the family, a number of the participants warned explicitly that city life and family togetherness had become contradictory.[46]

THE ATTRACTION OF THE SUBURBS II: BUILDING NEW "HOMES OF THE VIRTUOUS"

If suburbanization was seen, in one sense, as a way to preserve the American middle-class family, it was also an attempt to recast American democracy, by recreating, relocating, and modernizing the small town or village. In the suburban "home town," it was hoped, women would channel their civic energies into mothers' clubs, and would join together on the basis of their children's needs, not their own individual interests. And suburban fathers, with more secure careers in corporate or other organizations, as well as the built-in restrictiveness of commuters' schedules, would spend free time with their families. Their children, with mother at home, and father accessible, and a cheerful, detached house as a base, would be less tempted to find unwholesome pleasures outside the home. The new suburban domestic ideal intertwined ideas about the importance of the single-family house, companionate marriages, "expert" mothers, and masculine domesticity with longings for a pastoral landscape and visions of restoring a vanished countryside, as well as with nativist fears and anxieties about the corruption of family life in urban America.[47]

The new domestic ideal found physical expression in a new suburban architecture. If middle-class domestic architecture produced in the second and third quarters of the nineteenth century encouraged separation, suburban houses in the early twentieth century almost compelled family togetherness. There was a wide variety of exteriors in the early twentieth century.[48] Many of the home magazines favored styles colonial in inspiration, but there were also the newly popular Craftsman houses and bungalows. Frank Lloyd Wright designed some of his most memorable houses during this period as well.[49]

These houses, despite a wide diversity in the way they looked on the outside, had a great deal in common, as architectural historian Gwendolyn Wright has pointed out. The interior layouts of the houses in Gustav Stickley's *Craftsman* magazine, despite the overlay of quotations from Peter Kropotkin and William Morris, resembled those in the very conventional *American Homes and Gardens*. Frank Lloyd Wright's domestic architecture in this period made the same appeal to family unity and togetherness as the more pedestrian designs of less talented architects and builders, and in many ways his work epitomized the interconnected values of suburbanism and family togetherness.[50] For Wright, Stickley, and the numerous architectural writers of the conventional home magazines, the important new idea about domestic space was that the house should express togetherness and family activities, not provide special spaces for individual activities. (Some houses did have small "dens," however, presumably for the times when father brought work home from the office, or when the parents wished time alone.)[51]

Although the exteriors of the houses differed, the interiors were surprisingly similar, and this marked a major shift from the domestic architecture of the mid-nineteenth century. Victorian houses had been designed for separation, but dramatic changes had occurred. The most striking thing about early twentieth-century suburban houses was their design for togetherness. Delores Hayden erred when she argued that although the gothic designs favored in the Victorian era went out of fashion in the early twentieth century, "the interior organization of spaces replicated the Victorian homes."[52] An examination of a sampling of house designs for middle- to upper middle-class suburbanites, culled from two of the most popular home magazines of the period, shows why (see table 3.1). In 63 percent of these houses the separate parlor, study or library, and sitting room had given way to one large living room.

Although it is true that suburban houses had become smaller to accommodate families of more modest incomes who were moving to the suburbs, expensive houses also began to have more open floor plans. Early twentieth-century writers in home magazines stressed the symbolic importance of the living room as the visible symbol of family togetherness. Durando Nichols told his readers to insist that their architects or builders "eliminate the hall and parlor . . . and build in their place a living room." According to Nichols, "[The] living room . . . is now regarded as the most important room of the house. . . . [It] is the executive chamber of the household, where the family centers." Gustav Stickley so wholeheartedly agreed with these sentiments that he lifted without attribution several paragraphs from this article and presented them as his own in his 1909 book, *Craftsman Homes*.[53]

Frank Lloyd Wright would later claim sole responsibility for the greater openness of interior floor plans:

> Dwellings [at the beginning of the twentieth century] were "cut up," advisedly [sic] and completely. . . . The "interiors" consisted of boxes beside or inside other boxes, called *rooms*. . . . I could see little sense in this inhibition. . . . So I declared the whole lower floor as one room, cutting off the kitchen as a laboratory. . . . Scores of doors disappeared and no end of partition. . . . The house became more free as "space" and more livable too. Interior spaciousness began to dawn.[54]

Always grandiose, Wright ignored the fact that his early designs shared many attributes with those of other architects in that period.

Table 3.1. Use of Interior Space in Suburban Houses, Early Twentieth Century

	NO.	%
1 story	6	7
1½ and 2 story	75	93
Entrance halls	48	59
Kitchens		
Basement	0	0
First floor	81	100
Dining rooms		
Basement	0	0
First floor	71	88
No separate d.r.	10	12
No. of first-floor living areas		
1	51	63
2	30	37
3 or more	0	0
Living areas on second floor	6	7
Bedrooms		
1–2	10	12
3	27	33
4	31	39
5–6	13	16
7 or more	0	0
1½ or 2 story houses w. first fl. bedrooms	1	1
Bathrooms		
1	68	84
1 plus w.c.	1	1
2	12	15
more than 2	0	0

Sources: American Homes and Gardens, 1906–1912; *Craftsman,* 1901–1906. These magazines pictured an excellent variety of different kinds of popular middle to upper middle-class house designs.

Notes: N = 81; percentages are rounded.

His image of himself as a misunderstood prophet notwithstanding, Wright was a popular architect whose houses appeared in several magazines, including the *Ladies Home Journal.* His designs were more innovative than any that appeared in the *Craftsman,* and generally far more expensive, but he was not alone in his abhorrence of the closed-in, cut-up, privatized living areas of the Victorian house.

Designers of Craftsman homes, bungalows, and the boxy structures (in the middle-class home magazines) that we have since come to call foursquares, shared with Wright a distaste for the segregated social spaces that had characterized the floor plans of the 1870s. Eugene Gardner's *The House that Jill Built,* written early in the 1890s, heralded the new philosophy. Jill, the heroine of Gardner's architectural romance, on being informed by an elderly relative that a husband needed a private space "where he can revel to his heart's content in the hideous disorder of a 'man's room'," retorted to her husband, "I shall never allow you to set up a den . . . all by yourself." The younger generation intended to discard, within the house at least, the physical manifestations of separate spheres.[55]

A small, efficient kitchen and multiple bathrooms were added to the open floor plan to complete the interior changes in the houses of the Progressive Era. Some continuities remained. Although in many houses the entrance hall had shrunk to a mere vestibule leading into a hallway, nearly 60 percent of the new houses still had them. Finally, smaller family size and the decline of the live-in servant notwithstanding, 55 percent contained four or more bedrooms. In the end, however, the changes far outweighed the continuities. In the Victorian era family members were segregated from each other as much as the family as a whole was protected from intruders. In the early twentieth century the social areas of the first floor became accessible to casual visitors as well as to family and intimate friends. But the second floor had become less accessible. Hardly any two-story house plans called for first-floor bedrooms, and few had second-floor social areas—sitting, smoking, or sewing rooms.

By the early twentieth century family members spent less time in segregated social spaces, but upstairs, the private areas had become more private.[56] The rage for decorating children's rooms with special child-oriented furniture, wallpaper, and accessories suggests more than the obvious conclusion that middle-class parents had decided that children had a right to possessions designed specifically for them. It also points, perhaps obliquely, to the idea that children no longer automatically shared women's space, as they had in the earlier period. Instead, private space was shared by men and women.[57]

A new domestic architecture was not the only manifestation of the spatial dimensions of a new suburban domestic ideal. Another was the growing importance of place rather than property ownership within the suburbs. Historians have recently begun to discover evidence suggesting that working-class Americans in the late nineteenth and early twentieth centuries bought houses in larger numbers than did middle-class families. Although Stephan Thernstrom's 1964 pathbreaking study of Newburyport, Massachusetts, demonstrated that at least some immigrants became home owners, it was not until the late 1970s and early 1980s that historians began to suggest, in the words of Olivier Zunz, that "homeownership at the turn of the century was neither particularly middle-class nor American." Zunz's detailed study of Detroit is an excellent case in point: "The first striking feature" of the statistics on turn-of-the-century home ownership, he contends, "is that working class immigrants owned their homes proportionately more often than middle-class, native white Americans." On the suburban fringes of the city, one new upper middle-class neighborhood had a rental rate of over 60 percent.[58]

Other historians have made similar discoveries. Most of these studies have been specifically about the immigrant working class and raise tantalizing questions about the relationship of home ownership to upward mobility.[59] But what about the opposite of this problem, that of the dimensions of middle-class patterns of renting? As the next chapter shows in detail, in the two turn-of-the-century Philadelphia suburbs studied, ownership figures confirm the new picture that historians are discovering. Home ownership did not appear to be of primary interest to a substantial number of middle-class suburbanites. This was a major departure from the tenets of the Victorian advocates of suburbanization, who had stressed the importance of actual home ownership as a necessary concomitant to the preservation of democratic institutions. By the early twentieth century, however, it was the place itself that resonated with symbolic meaning. Property ownership was not as crucial as it had once been.[60]

Both "space," in the sense that the new suburban houses had interiors designed for family unity, and "place," in the sense that the advocates of the new domestic ideal, male and female alike, insisted on the importance of suburban living, were important in defining the environment for the ideal middle-class family of the early twentieth century. In considering the question of space, it will not do to minimize the significance of the changes in interior design that promoted togetherness, or to dismiss the cultural significance of these changes by arguing that such technological developments as central heating, for example, or the higher cost of building houses with bathrooms, were principally responsible for open floor plans. In the 1890s, when large houses without central heating were still common, "pocket" or sliding doors were used to a greater extent than heretofore as a device to allow most of the first-floor rooms of a house to open on each other, at the same time letting them be closed to conserve heat. And among those houses that did have central heating in the early 1890s, floor plans were much less open than in houses of the same size and price range as those built a decade later.[61]

If a new kind of space became important in the suburbs of the middle class by the turn of the twentieth century, so too did the idea of place. In the redefined space of the suburban house, families ideally would spend their evenings together—reading aloud, playing word games, talking. And in the suburban place, they would enjoy both outdoor life and a sense of community. The next chapter, which examines family and community life in two middle-class suburbs, confirms that these families did indeed want to spend their leisure together. Nationally, family-oriented recreation was extraordinarily popular. Croquet and roller skating attracted more interest than baseball; and some baseball enthusiasts had even apparently tried to make it a family sport, with girls and boys, as well as their parents, playing it on the lawn. Bicycling did not become a craze until it became a sport for the entire family as well. In short, the most popular forms of recreation were those families could enjoy together. Suburbs institutionalized the relationships that marked the companionate family by creating various kinds of clubs, such as "wheel clubs," athletic fields used by both sexes, and tennis and golf clubs. (If early twentieth century photographs and real estate advertisements are reliable, men played golf with their wives, not business associates.)[62]

Suburban couples, of course, did not do everything jointly; togetherness was not absolute. What is at issue is the degree of change that occurred over the course of the last quarter of the nineteenth century or so. And if we compare these husbands and wives of the early twentieth century to the generation that preceded them, the change is considerable. The new domestic ideal, centered firmly in the suburbs, represented family and community togetherness in the face of an urban society that promised individual achievement, anonymity, and excitement. Although urban advocates continued to show strength throughout the early years of the century and well into the 1920s,[63] the association of suburbs with the ideal of close-knit family life also gathered more force.

The "virtuous republic" that was the goal of America's revolutionary generation had been predicated on a strong, property-holding, and independent yeomanry. As the earliest suburban advocates transformed it, a man need not be a farmer, but he could at least be close to nature, on his own plot of ground, and in his own house. In Andrew Jackson Downing's words, the suburban man, along with his family, would live in a "home of the virtuous citizen," one "built and loved upon new world . . . ideas and principles." But toward the end of the nineteenth century, as the suburban ideal underwent yet another change, the advocates of the new suburban domesticity succeeded in appropriating for the middle-class residential suburb at least the rhetorical distinction of preserving the American family. It is the task of the next chapter to show how the new suburban ideal translated from idea to reality, by exploring the lives of the residents of two suburban communities.

CHAPTER FOUR

Breathing the Air of Domesticity

Here [we] breathe the air of domesticity, thrift, and progress.
Haddonfield as a State Normal School Site,
1917

American families who contemplated moving to the suburbs took with them the images presented in the last chapter. If they believed the magazines, took to heart the advice of men like Senator Albert Beveridge, and heeded the wisdom of childrearing experts, they could hope that suburban life would bring domestic contentment and family togetherness in an environment that was both physically proximate to the city and psychically distant from it. To urban sophisticates suburbia may have been boring, and to the new feminists stifling, but for men and women whose mothers had single-handedly held the emotional reins of the family, and whose fathers' economic struggles often left them no time to spend with their children, the situation was quite different. The new suburban domesticity could be seen as an opportunity to reconstruct family life. The new suburbs, lushly landscaped, safe, homogeneous and purged of the poor, the radical, and the ethnically suspect, offered seemingly foolproof environments for raising model children. The houses themselves, with their open floor plans, intimated that here there would be no disturbing secrets. In the new suburbs, middle-class Americans created an ideal of family and community life that was, on the one hand, nostalgic and, on the other, geared toward an industrial society. These families wanted to enjoy the fruits of industrial growth, but without sacrificing the vision of a traditional village community.

Such, at least, was the image. But what of the reality? What kinds of lives did suburban families create at the turn of the twentieth century? To answer such questions, one must turn to actual suburban communities. And just as an examination of Victorian suburbs seemed to demand a look at some suburbanites from that most Victorian of American cities—Boston—the contemplation of turn-of-the-century suburbs brings Philadelphia immediately to mind. Other cities might do nearly as well, but Philadelphia has its special attractions for understanding this period in which the new suburban domesticity emerged. It was a major industrial city in the late nineteenth century, and although its historians have traditionally concentrated on the city itself, recently a spate of interest in its suburbs has emerged. Noting that "Philadelphia was reshaped by the steam locomotive and the electric trolley," Robert Fishman has argued that this city's metropolitan growth exemplified suburbia during its "classic" period. The city's size, its reputation as a "city of homes," its industrial might at the close of the nineteenth century, and the topographical unity of much of what we would later call the metropolitan area were all important in creating suburbs that were illustrative of a national trend.[1]

Both the trolley and the railroad were important to Philadelphia's suburbanization. While clerks and skilled workers took the trolley, and later the subways and elevated lines, to and from their jobs, the prosperous preferred the more comfortable, and more expensive, train. John Stilgoe has described "the typical commuter," who "strode through the great urban terminals convinced that his way of life represented the apogee of civilization." In the first years of the new century, commuting by rail had become a way of life for bankers, brokers, lawyers, and managers.[2] Philadelphia's geography was particularly hospitable to the building of railroad suburbs. Not only was Philadelphia the largest city (in area) until Los Angeles usurped its place in the twentieth century, but it also had few physical obstacles to inhibit development. If the inner city had become crowded by the late nineteenth century, and indeed it had, the outer city offered scope for small- and large-scale developers alike. The land surrounding the city—mostly farms, country estates, and small villages—was not separated from it by inaccessible swamps or nuisance industries. By the great age of the railroad suburbs, industry was no longer scattered haphazardly throughout the area, but established in specific localities. And even the Delaware River, which separated Philadelphia from New Jersey, became less of a barrier to commuters after the improvements in ferry service and the completion of a railroad bridge in the 1890s.

True suburbanization, in the sense of the deliberate creation of residential communities that (for men at least) were spatially separated from the workplace, came later to Philadelphia than to Boston or New York, the Northeast's other two principal cities. Like those cities, Philadelphia had begun to decentralize in the early nineteenth century, but those living in most of its "suburbs" were working class, both skilled and unskilled. The pattern began to change around midcentury; still, as late as 1860, the people who lived in the district of Penn, located to the northwest of the central city and in the path of the most important axis of residential growth at the time, were overwhelmingly artisans and unskilled laborers.[3] And as late as 1880, West Philadelphia, which within a quarter of a century was to become the city's first mass dormitory community, had a mixture of mills, brickyards, small villages, shantytowns, and nuisance industries, as well as a few new residential communities and a scattering of farms and country estates.[4]

Philadelphia's suburbanization began in earnest in the late 1890s, and has continued ever since. This is not to suggest the immediate demise of elite urban neighborhoods. Well-to-do Philadelphians continued to live on the traditionally fashionable streets just south of Market Street; and Rittenhouse Square was the downtown's most fashionable address well into the twentieth century. But much of the population was suburbanizing. The subway-elevated line into West Philadelphia offered a quasi-suburban alternative to the city's clerks and skilled laborers, while families of the upper-middle class had a wider range of communities from which to choose. Germantown had been since midcentury a residential enclave for the affluent, and Chestnut Hill, which like Germantown stood within the political boundaries of the city, had begun to gain a reputation as Philadelphia's most elite suburb, developed by railroad magnate Henry Houston.[5] Others of the city's wealthy moved farther out to the sites of former country estates. The affluent among the middle classes dispersed within the city not only to Germantown, but to Overbrook and Mt. Airy, and outside the city to Wayne, Ridley Park, Sharon Hill, Ardmore. In New Jersey, commuters made their homes in Collingswood, Haddonfield, and Merchantville.

Most of these communities owed their development to men with substantial connections to the railroads, either as executives or investors. The two suburbs examined here illustrate the ways in which the new suburban ideal came to practical fruition, with the help of railroad magnates, land speculators, and developers. Both communities were middle class, and both were railroad suburbs. One, Overbrook Farms, was on the inner edge of the famed Main Line of the Pennsylvania Railroad and was a planned community. The other, Haddonfield, was in New Jersey and had developed from a village to a town of some regional importance before its suburbanization at the end of the nineteenth century.

OVERBROOK FARMS: PLANNED SUBURB AND "HOME TOWN" FOR THE AFFLUENT

Planned suburbs were not a new idea in the 1890s. Llewellyn Park, New Jersey, built in the 1850s, was perhaps the first. Others followed, including Frederick Law Olmsted's famed Riverside, outside Chicago. But in the late nineteenth century there were only a few successful planned suburbs. And Overbrook Farms, conceived in the early 1890s and built over a period of nearly two decades, was one example of the ways in which a developer succeeded in creating a community of some scale and magnitude, rather than simply subdividing the land and arranging for some basic services.

Walter Bassett Smith and Herman Wendell developed Overbrook Farms. Long-time Philadelphia builders, they had been building suburban houses for a decade or more before they began Overbrook Farms. Smith, a plainspoken and laconic man, could summon up near-exuberance when he thought of the opportunities for development around Philadelphia. "New York," said Smith, "is cut off from its 'suburbs' by rivers and swamps, vast spaces that render quick access impossible; and when you get to its outlying country, it is, except a few places, flat or worse; but we have, within a half-hour's ride on more than one of our railroads, a rich and beautiful country—to one, who has not seen it, an inconceivable paradise." The success of Smith's enterprises was indeed great to elevate his feelings to such a pitch. (He was usually much more blunt, once telling potential buyers regarding Ardmore, in which he was building a new development, "Some parts are handsome, and some are not.")[6]

He had reason to enthuse. From small scale operators who constructed a few houses at a time in West Philadelphia, Wendell and Smith went on to create Pelham in Germantown, then more expensive projects in Haverford and Wayne. Overbrook Farms was one of their most important and most successful projects. In 1893, Drexel & Company, the powerful firm of investment bankers with close financial ties to the Pennsylvania Railroad, had bought approximately 170 acres on the edge of, but just within, the city. The George family had farmed the land for more than a hundred and fifty years. Now the last member of it had died in the house in which he and his father had been born; his will directed that the land be sold in order to fund the creation of a coeducational boarding school offering "a good, plain quaker education." The farm was sold, and a lavish suburb replaced the crops. At its center was the Overbrook Station of the Pennsylvania Railroad, the first suburban stop along the Main Line, and a twenty minute commute into the downtown.[7]

In the course of their careers, Wendell and Smith had built houses for families ranging from the modestly prosperous through the lower reaches of the upper class. They had never had the opportunity, however, to plan an entire community; Overbrook Farms was to be a model suburb, with churches, a community center, a shopping plaza, and open space. The builders engaged a group of prominent Philadelphia architects to design houses in different styles and price ranges. Although the developers also agreed simply to sell lots and have the buyer engage an architect, their intention was that purchasers would choose one of the houses already designed; on their part, Wendell and Smith agreed to pass along the resultant economies of scale. Their architects included Horace Trumbauer, whose commissions from the city for public buildings later included the art museum and the free library. Trumbauer, like the other architects favored by Wendell and Smith, was patronized, not by the city's old elite, but by newcomers to affluence and influence.[8]

The first Overbrook Farms houses, those completed between 1893 and 1896, were exuberant creations in various late Victorian styles, their interiors replicating the familiar patterns of separation by function and segregation by age and gender. These first houses sold for between $7,000 and $18,000, many of them in the $13,000 to $16,000 range. The majority of the houses were detached dwellings, a fact that in the suburbs of most cities could go unmentioned, because it would be taken for granted that a suburban house was a detached house. Philadelphians, however, even relatively well-to-do suburbanites, were unusual in their acceptance of "single-family attached" housing.[9]

It is difficult to account for this phenomenon; residents of other cities with a row house tradition apparently viewed attached houses as things to be borne with only when a completely detached house was unaffordable. Around Philadelphia, however, "twins," as they are called, were popular suburban dwellings. In the early twentieth century, the *Architectural Record* published an article about a group of "quadruple houses" built by George Woodward in Chestnut Hill. Woodward, the son-in-law of Chestnut Hill developer Henry Houston, said of his houses, "A slight social stigma may attach itself to the commuter of other cities if he is obliged to dwell in one of a pair of houses, but custom has decreed otherwise [in Philadelphia which] long ago set its stamp of approval upon the two family house for a suburban dwelling." Woodward insisted that quadruple houses would soon be as popular as twins. He was wrong about that, but suburban builders did continue to mix twins and detached houses in many suburban developments, including expensive ones like Overbrook Farms, where several of the first houses to go up were elegant twins.[10]

The developers planned Overbrook Farms as a community with houses in a fairly wide price range, to attract families from the upper reaches of the middle class to the very well-to-do. Interestingly, during the first two years most of those built were at the upper end of that range. Indeed by 1895 Wendell and Smith had sold at least two that cost $30,000, ten times the average $3,000 selling price for a house and lot in Philadelphia. But toward the end of the decade, beginning in the last months of 1896, they reverted to their earlier plans, and began to build houses selling for $6,500. It is possible that Wendell and Smith thought that they had exhausted the market for very expensive houses. In addition, the depression of 1894, after which housing prices fell slightly, had an impact on the entire metropolitan housing market.[11]

Interestingly, both these houses and the more expensive new designs that Wendell and Smith built at the turn of the century and afterward, differed in style from the earlier models. Even the $6,500 houses were not scaled-down Queen Annes, but were simpler in exterior ornament and more open in their interior arrangements. Overbrook Farms's desirability did not diminish for Philadelphia's upper-middle class. Even the least expensive of the new designs were more than double what an average lower middle-class family could afford; and to rent a house here cost from $50 to $200.[12] To look at the changes in style of Overbrook Farms during the period in which it was built, to examine the shift in emphasis from ownership to renting, and to explore family and community life, is to view in microcosm the changes taking place in suburban America.

In its architecture, Overbrook Farms bridged the styles between the late Victorian and those that early twentieth-century writers would call modern. And the use of interior space in these houses was somewhere between the segregation of the former era and the more open floor plans of the latter. Although the earliest houses, inside, seemed very much conventionally Victorian, there were some subtle changes: Archways replaced doors between some rooms, prefiguring the open styles of the next decade. There was a heavy use as well of sliding or pocket doors, which made it a matter of choice whether to create an open or closed environment. Or, to put it another way, sliding doors made it possible for families to move between togetherness and separation. By the end of the 1890s, many of the plans had become even more open. Horace Trumbauer designed a stone house for the developers that had both a formal hall and a parlor, with a wide archway between them. In the houses built for the developers the trend was decidedly, by the last two years of the nineteenth century, toward more open floor plans. Most of the designs had the hall opening into the parlor by means of either a square or rounded arch, although some used sliding doors. Several of the houses had the living room and dining room opening into each other, with sliding doors, but more often the dining room was across the hall. Although these houses would never be confused with those designed by Frank Lloyd Wright in the next decade, and although they still had "parlors" rather than "living rooms," they were far more open than the ones built earlier in the decade. *The Scientific American Building Edition* in 1898 said of one house designed by the architectural firm of Keen and Mead for Wendell and Smith, "The first floor plan is so arranged that the rooms can be thrown open, producing an attractive, broad, open effect."[13]

Overbrook Farms was a success from the beginning, and not only because of the kinds of houses the community contained. Wendell and Smith had welcomed the chance to create a community. In their advertisements, the developers constantly reiterated the theme of community, and the residents responded. From all indications, they involved themselves enthusiastically in community and neighborly activities. On the whole, Overbrook Farms reflected the national picture drawn in the last chapter. From the advertising literature to the testimony of residents, from the civic clubs through the recreational organizations, the community exhibited the patterns of the new suburban domesticity.

The highly successful advertising strategy of Wendell and Smith incorporated the themes of the new domesticity that the last chapter outlined. They presented their community as a planned environment, the aims of which were to develop family togetherness, to remove families from the city itself while at the same time bringing the culture and civility of urban life to the suburbs, and to build community. The developers impressed upon prospective clients that they were choosing a neighborhood and a way of life, not simply a house. The advertisements evoked a mood composed of equal parts of nostalgia and status-seeking, offering a "home town," but promising that the "town" would contain only people like them. The developers produced two lavish advertising books, in 1899 and 1905. Although both of them reiterated the themes of exclusivity, community, and domestic pleasures, the six years between them did mark some changes. In their first prospectus, the developers, reiterating an idea prevalent in the 1860s and 1870s that women did not like the suburbs, worried that wives would be more reluctant to come to Overbrook Farms than their husbands. So they promised, in a revealing phrase, that women would not be "bur[ied] alive" in Overbrook Farms, since the community possessed "all the . . . refinements and luxuries of city life." But even in 1899 that fear was outdated, and in their 1905 brochure they dropped that approach for one richly illustrative of the family-oriented recreational and social activities available for both men and women.[14]

One hundred and sixty-eight families had come to live in Overbrook Farms by the turn of the century. All of them were at least in the upper-middle class, and a few were wealthy, although not numbered among the city's traditional elite. A majority of the male household heads were company officers and executives, or financiers. Of the remainder, nearly 25 percent were professionals—physicians, lawyers, architects, engineers—and another 10 percent were managers or other white collar employees (see table 4.1). Although some of the company officers and financiers owned the firms where they worked, at least half the men were members of the new middle classes who had a profession or worked for someone else. But Overbrook Farms in 1900 also contained a fair number of entrepreneurs and owners of family businesses, most of them living in the more expensive houses on what the residents called the "north side."

Table 4.1. Occupation of Male Heads of Households, Overbrook Farms, 1900

OCCUPATION	NO.	%
Corporate officers, executives, financiers	79	51
Managers, corporate salaried employees	15	10
Contractors, builders, real estate developers	11	7
Professionals	36	24
Retired, no occupation	13	8
Total	154	100

Source: Manuscript Census Data, 1900, Enumeration District 904.
Note: Percentages are rounded.

As the map shows, Overbrook Farms was bisected by the tracks of the Pennsylvania Railroad, the rail line that carried a majority of the men to their offices downtown. The developers had not wanted to have the community divided, but they could not obtain city approval for their plan of constructing overpasses across the tracks for all the streets. As a result, there were only two through streets in the suburb. Wendell and Smith built the north side first, and that is where most of the elaborate Queen Anne houses are found. The south side developed at the end of the 1890s, although in 1900 there were still more families across the tracks. What is perhaps most interesting in terms of the argument this book makes about the changing nature of domesticity, the north side retained more of the characteristics of the Victorian suburb than did the south side. That is to say, home ownership was higher (77 percent versus 41 percent); more entrepreneurs and business owners lived on the north side than did professionals and employees; and the houses were more "Victorian" in scale and design. It is the south side that exemplifies most clearly the new spatial and economic characteristics of the early twentieth-century suburban family.[15]

If the north side and south side had some important differences, in some ways their residents were very much alike. Everywhere in Overbrook Farms, households were headed by prosperous men between the ages of thirty and fifty. Family size was small; only 12 percent of Overbrook Farms residents had more than three children. Twenty-one percent had no children, and 55 percent had one or two. Wives did not have jobs outside the home (nor did female household heads). As we would expect, not a single married woman was employed, and unmarried female dependents, be they sisters, aunts, mothers, or cousins, were also mostly not in the paid work force. Two families sent their daughters to college, however, and another two had daughters working as teachers, perhaps at Miss Sayward's school, the private girl's school established at the behest of the developers.[16]

The extent of the economic prosperity of Overbrook Farms families may in part be measured by their enjoyment of live-in domestic service. At a time when the availability of live-in domestic help had declined all across the United States, almost 90 percent of these families had at least one live-in servant, and nearly a quarter of them had three or more. In Overbrook Farms, the typical domestic help consisted of one or two Irish or black women who worked as multipurpose servants. Only twelve households had "child nurses"; a few of the wealthier families had specialized staffs that might include cooks, waiters, chambermaids, gardeners, and coachmen. Six families had governesses.[17]

Between 1900 and 1910 Overbrook Farms grew by 40 percent. Most, but by no means all, of the new development was on the south side, which grew by 60 percent while the increase on the north side was just 25 percent. The upper middle-class character of the community remained constant, but occupational patterns had changed. Now, a full 70 percent of the male household heads were in executive and managerial positions, or worked at a profession. The major shift came in the introduction, on the south side, of midlevel managerial employees—bankers who were neither vice presidents nor young clerks, but somewhere in between, stockbrokers employed by a firm, even a small number of bookkeepers, stenographers, and agents. A few families headed by men in these occupations moved to the north side (5 percent), but most were on the south side, where they made up about 19 percent of the male household heads.

In their occupations and economic status, the men of Overbrook Farms illustrate the patterns of change delineated in the last chapter. By 1910 this community was filled with men who worked for salaries, and for very good ones. They lived in a suburb, where they rented more often than they owned. Business owners, like their Victorian forbears, continued to prefer ownership to renting, as did independent professionals. But the executives and managers, fully 65 percent of them, chose to rent (see table 4.2). Although what these men did for a living was different from the earlier residents, it was not less remunerative. These families certainly enjoyed such trappings of success as live-in domestic help. Nine-tenths of the families continued to have at least one live-in servant, and for the majority that still meant one or two young black or Irish women.[18]

In the last chapter, I argued that changing occupational patterns on the part of men was an important factor in the creation of a favorable climate for marital togetherness, but also that it was necessary to

Table 4.2. House Ownership According to Occupation, Male Household Heads, Overbrook Farms, 1910

OCCUPATION	NO.	PERCENT OWNERS
Business owners	63	65
Professionals	45	80
Executives, managers	53	38
White collar employees	27	34
Retired, no occupation	24	67
Total	212	

Source: Manuscript Census Data, 1910.
Note: Percentages are rounded, and are a function of the number of men in each category who owned houses.

construct a particular kind of domestic and community "space" in which families could engage in joint pursuits. One of the elements of that space was its physical separation from influences considered antagonistic to the achievement of domestic harmony and togetherness. Home ownership was less relevant to that goal than it had been to the aims of an earlier generation of American suburbanites. Neighborhood exclusivity, however, had become extremely important.[19] And Overbrook Farms was almost a model of a homogeneous community, insulated from the poor, the working class, and the ethnic. The suburb overwhelmingly attracted the native born and the Protestant.

The dimensions of this religious and ethnic uniformity may have surprised Wendell and Smith, who promoted economic but not religious exclusion; in fact they advertised in the German language *Demokrat* and in some Catholic publications.[20] But only 9 percent of the residents in 1900 were foreign born and most of them were from England, although there was a sprinkling of German households. There were some Irish Catholics here, too, but as servants, not householders. The same was true of blacks, and there were no families from among the so-called new immigrants. Regardless of what the developers intended—and the catholicity of their advertisements suggests that they believed that suburbanites were ready to ignore *some* differences of ethnicity and religion as long as the residents were of the same social class—the actual residents of Overbrook Farms were white, upper middle-class, native-born Protestants, who had small families and kept live-in help. These families selected themselves for this new community, and they created a community life that reflected both their homogeneity and their domestic aspirations.[21]

This community life included a large measure of family activities. The men of Overbrook Farms had a relatively short commute to and from their offices downtown, which would allow them to spend time with their families. A twenty-minute train ride brought them home, where they engaged in leisure pursuits with their wives and children. Some of that leisure was organized. One resident estimated that at least a third of the families were deeply involved in organized community activities, while others participated more irregularly.[22] First, the community established a small tennis club in the mid-nineties, and by 1898 the families were eager for more space and more kinds of outdoor recreation. They leased land and built an athletic field, with facilities for tennis, cricket, quoits, and croquet. Heavily used by children as well as adults of both sexes, the athletic field sparked a desire for a golf club. The golf club was built in 1900 and women as well as men could take to the links, often in husband-wife pairs.[23] But as popular as golf and the field sports were, bicycling outstripped them all at the turn of the century. According to the community's memoirist, the Wheel Club attracted nearly "all of the men and many of the women" in Overbrook Farms. And in the winter, when bicycling was difficult, whole families went sledding and ice-skating together after supper, then "gathered afterwards at the different houses, and sipped hot chocolate, while thawing out before the open fires." Overbrook Farms residents found these shared activities, involving entire families, very appealing.[24]

Men and women also worked together to form the community's religious institutions. The Episcopal church's organizing committee, for example, consisted of six men and three women, with one of the women as an officer. This is not to say that "togetherness" pervaded every aspect of the community. Overbrook Farms had a men's club and two women's clubs: a Civic Club and a branch of the Needlework Guild of America. The men's club, which opened its membership to all male residents (that is, unlike some civic organizations, one did not have to be invited to join) interested itself in such things as the quality of local schools and the beautification of the community. It was the men's club, for example, that made sure that the trees and hedges of the suburb were well cared for, and that lobbied successfully for "ornamental street signs." The men's club also interested itself in zoning laws, police protection, and street lighting. What these men were doing was not precisely what Abby Diaz had in mind in 1875 when she suggested that men's clubs ought to redirect their efforts toward helping their members become good fathers; nevertheless, they were taking a serious interest in education and in the appearance of their houses and yards.[25]

Like the Overbrook Farms men's club, but unlike the city-wide Civic Club of which it was a part, the Thirty-Fourth Ward Branch of the Civic Club was open to any woman who wanted to join. The club was created and dominated by Overbrook Farms women, although a few members lived outside the suburb. Its leaders were women in their thirties, mothers of small families, who were married to professional men. The first two presidents were lawyers' wives. The Civic Club sent poor children to summer camp and engaged in other charitable activities; within its own borders it lobbied for zoning restrictions, traffic lights, and better police protection. While the Civic Club took an interest in the political doings that affected its community as well as more broadly based charitable activities, the Needlework Guild, the other major women's organization in Overbrook Farms, was more specifically a charitable society. The Needlework Guild was a national organization which had been transplanted to the United States from England in 1865. Its mission was to provide new clothes for needy children, and its slogan was, "Old garments pauperize; new garments equalize." Although men could (and sometimes did) become members of the Needlework Guild, only women could be "directors," which meant that women coordinated all the actual work of the society.[26]

The Overbrook Branch of the Needlework Guild was founded by Overbrook Farms women in 1897. Its leaders were married women whose husbands were a physician, a bank president, and a lawyer. The Guild attracted wide support in the community, which subscribed heavily to its clothing drives. Although in the early years the female members of the Needlework Guild of America had actually sewed new clothes for poor children, by the time the organization came to Overbrook Farms the emphasis was on buying the clothes and distributing them to the "worthy poor." In 1909 the Needlework Guild of America joined the General Federation of Women's Clubs, formalizing their participation in the massive women's club movement of the period.[27]

The existence of women's clubs and men's clubs does not negate the idea that the suburbs promoted family togetherness. Particularly for women, the club movement was perhaps the single most important organizational phenomenon in the late nineteenth and early twentieth centuries. Men's clubs had an even longer history and had been at the heart of masculine associational life in the mid-nineteenth century. Sex-segregated social life did not entirely cease among either women or men; however, the new domestic ideal both changed the meaning of single-sex associational life and blurred the lines separating men's from women's roles. As we can see from the activities of the men's Overbrook Farms Club and the women's Civic Club, their interests and behavior converged, even when they met separately. Of course, Overbrook Farms men sometimes belonged to other clubs that were not so focused on home and community, and women went together to matinees at the city's Academy of Music after lunching at the downtown department stores. Husbands and wives still had some separate interests. What is significant, however, is that they had fewer of them than the previous generation.[28]

Overbrook Farms children, like their parents, had both a family life and what we might call a life among their peers, although the term "youth culture" would not be applicable. Most of the Overbrook Farms children attended private schools. For the girls, that meant Miss Sayward's School. Born in Maine in 1855, Janet Sayward had attended Normal School in Vermont, and had taught in Maine and Maryland before coming to Philadelphia. A career woman, unlike those whose daughters she taught, Sayward opened her school in Overbrook Farms in 1893, the first year of the community's existence, with twelve students. She prospered; within two years she needed more room, and Wendell and Smith gave her a new building. By the early twentieth century Miss Sayward's School offered both primary and secondary education for girls, who could take a college preparatory course in addition to studying "domestic science [and] domestic art." The boys did not attend Miss Sayward's School, nor did the developers build a boys' school in the suburb. Instead, the boys traveled downtown or to the town of Haverford, where there was a private school of some considerable repute. In either case, the boys commuted to school on the train.[29]

As for what the girls and their brothers did after school, there is only a sketchy record. I discovered no evidence of a boy scout troop in Overbrook Farms, nor of any other organized boys' or girls' clubs. In the Overbrook Farms Community Center, however, children of both sexes endured dancing classes. The athletic field was also open to children, although the degree to which children used it unaccompanied by their parents is not clear. In the winter, cold evenings found the children ice-skating, often with their parents, while on the snowy ones they were out sledding, with parents and other adults hovering nearby. Summer found the children displaying their athletic prowess for their parents and neighbors, as well as playing ball among themselves. This is all we know for sure. Beyond that, we must speculate. The fact that Overbrook Farms families educated their daughters locally, while the boys were allowed to range far afield, might mean diametrically opposite things. On the one hand, we might argue that although parents wanted their daughters close to home, they were willing to give their sons more freedom. That would indicate that girls faced greater restrictions on their independence. On the other hand, parents may have felt that there were good schools available for their sons, but nothing comparable for the girls. Hence a new school, and Miss Sayward did, after all, offer college preparation and not simply a "finishing school" education. Either explanation is plausible. The former is compatible with an argument that the urban environment was more threatening to girls than to boys, the latter with the idea that girls were entitled to an education that fitted them both for careers and to be companions to educated men.[30]

One of the problems of attempting to untangle various kinds of prescriptive evidence and then to see how those prescriptions work themselves into the fabric of the daily lives of real people is that there can never be a perfect fit. That is true partly because for actual people the data is always incomplete. As historians we come upon partial lives, and so much is missing—words unexpressed in a diary, commonplaces never mentioned in newspapers because they are part of the routine of life, dreams or fears that never arise to the level of consciousness. So it is not astonishing that we come up with an imperfect fit when we compare an actual suburb with the new suburban ideal. It is not the extent to which Overbrook Farms departs from the vision of the new suburbia that is remarkable, but the extent to which it conforms. Wendell and Smith created a highly successful marketing strategy—to promote Overbrook Farms as an exclusive upper middle-class suburban enclave that would provide residents with an instant community consciousness. With the developers' help, and with the physical structures either in place or planned, the residents institutionalized their domestic priorities in a community setting. The men, both in their families and in the organized men's club, concerned themselves with the beauty of their surroundings in much the same way that their wives did. And the fact that the clubs were open to all who were interested rather than only to invitees suggests that the creators of those clubs were confident enough of shared styles of living and values among potential members. All in all, the families, in their impromptu ice-skating parties and their more formalized recreational clubs, sought both a sense of community and family togetherness. If the new domestic ideal had not entirely replaced the gender and age separation of the patriarchal family, it had eroded it considerably in Overbrook Farms.

HADDONFIELD: MIDDLE-CLASS FAMILIES AND "THE AIR OF DOMESTICITY"

Overbrook Farms, one might argue, was unique in some ways; an upper middle-class suburb sheltering like-minded families, it was the kind of place where family and community coherence might readily be found. Other suburbs, perhaps, would not reveal the same kinds of patterns. Haddonfield, New Jersey, the second Philadelphia suburb considered here, was in many ways different from Overbrook Farms, yet its residents held similar beliefs about togetherness and community. Haddonfield went so far as to advertise its "domesticity" in promotional literature. Unlike Overbrook Farms, Haddonfield was not a planned suburb. Established as a village in the late seventeenth century by English Quaker Elizabeth Haddon, by the middle of the nineteenth century it had become a thriving town that served as a regional center for the surrounding rural communities. Its suburbanization was made possible by the advent of the commuter railroad, although so flat a statement seems to suggest that the railroad arrived, and suburbanization began immediately thereafter. Actually, it was not nearly so simple.

In the 1850s, a group of forward-looking investors, bankers and others with financial ties to the Pennsylvania Railroad, believed that Haddonfield was destined to become a suburb of Philadelphia. This was at a time when the city itself had barely begun to suburbanize. These investors, together with Haddonfield land baron J. L. Rowand, determined to create a planned suburb that would cover much of what is now the town, as well as some land beyond its borders. They called themselves the Haddonfield Ready Villa Association, and they intended to turn the community into an elite Philadelphia suburb. It is particularly interesting to come across their plans, laid at a time when the only planned suburb in existence was Llewellyn Park, and it makes the historian wonder how many failed suburban plans lie buried in local historical societies, or if this one was an isolated attempt.[31]

For in the end this was a failed plan. The extension of rail service to Haddonfield notwithstanding, the suburban demand was not there. Still, it is interesting to see what the developers planned, and to explore the differences between their promotional literature and that of Overbrook Farms more than forty years later. The creators of the Ready Villas appealed to the rural ideal, harkened back to a vision of the virtuous republic, and proclaimed the value of property ownership, all important elements of the mid-nineteenth century suburban ideal. They envisioned

> an immense park with lakes, fountains, streams and cascades, and dotted over with hundreds of neat cottages of every size, form, and hue, the happy abodes of intelligent and interesting families, who literally grow up among the flowers of the meadow, and beneath the shade of the forest trees, secluded in rural solitude, yet in close proximity of [sic] hundreds of estimable neighbors, and within the sound of the steam engine, which in the space of a few minutes, transfers them . . . to [Philadelphia,] one of the most beautiful cities of the world.[32]

These men were not frivolous dreamers. The seriousness of the venture may be gauged by the fact that the developers hired Samuel Sloan, one of the most prominent architects in Philadelphia, to design the houses. With land, each house would cost from $1,300 to upwards of $2,600. Sloan at first intended for the houses to be "twins," in keeping with the affection of Philadelphians for attached houses, even in the suburbs. But residents could choose to have each design built as a detached house instead of a twin. As the architect's drawings show, the houses were typical of the domestic architecture of the period and were inspired, as was most American suburban architecture in the mid nineteenth century, by Andrew Jackson Downing.

The investors wished to construct an entire community. Much of Haddonfield itself was still undeveloped, so they intended to build a separate waterworks for the Ready Villas, in order to provide indoor plumbing. And they planned for two schools, a girls' school first, a boys' school to follow. They did not, however, mean to risk large amounts of their own money on the Ready Villas. Instead, they announced their plan to begin construction as soon as the association acquired three hundred "subscribers." Subscribers were future residents who had paid up half the cost of their property. Those three hundred families did not materialize, and the Ready Villas became just another speculative land scheme that failed. It was too soon to suburbanize Haddonfield: In 1854, the newly consolidated city of Philadelphia itself was still dotted with villages. The creators of the Ready Villa Association may have convinced themselves when they insisted that Germantown, then the only important middle-class suburb of Philadelphia, was "filling up." But they could not convince their intended buyers. Philadelphians in the 1850s, seeing plenty of possibilities within the city itself, were not yet plagued with fears that they would soon be driven to look for houses in New Jersey.[33]

By 1900, the situation was different. Collingswood and Merchantville, within a few miles of Haddonfield, had been developed successfully as suburbs during the last third of the nineteenth century—Collingswood by sugar baron E. C. Knight.[34] Although Haddonfield itself still possessed some of the hallmarks of its former status as an important county town, its tanneries and mills had disappeared, and only a few farms were left. The West Haddonfield Land Company was busily subdividing with far greater success than had the Ready Villa Association, and the Pennsylvania Railroad now owned the New Jersey rail lines that provided convenient commuter service. Some 2,776 people made their home in Haddonfield in 1900, and within a decade the number swelled to 4,142. If the Ready Villa Association had succeeded, Haddonfield might have been an earlier version of Overbrook Farms. As it was, Haddonfield in 1900 was on the cusp of its transition from small town to suburb. At the turn of the twentieth century, it had become dominated by the middle class, although there remained an admixture of the service workers and laborers needed to keep the community in working order.[35]

When the census of 1900 was taken, just over 60 percent of

Haddonfield's male household heads were middle class or above. Unlike the families of Overbrook Farms, however, this middle-class population ran the gamut from white-collar workers to a sprinkling of corporate executives and those who referred to themselves as "capitalists." Haddonfield at the turn of the century was a solidly middle-class community, weighted toward the respectable middle of the middle classes, with a few very well-to-do families. In 1910, when the population of the town had grown by 50 percent as a result of the successful efforts of land developers, it had become definitively suburban in character and hence more heavily middle class; the proportion of unskilled and semiskilled workers, only 11 percent in 1900, declined dramatically, and that of managers, executives, and white-collar workers increased.[36]

Haddonfield had become a residential suburb, with grand houses along the descriptively named Mansion Avenue and somewhat more modest ones on streets with less stately appellations. Because its families extended over a larger range of the middle class than those of Overbrook Farms, they were not all so uniformly affluent. For example, fewer Haddonfield families had live-in servants. Just about 30 percent of them, compared to the 90 percent of the Overbrook Farms families, had a live-in domestic. In 1910, that figure was down to about one fourth of the town's families, showing Haddonfield's congruence with the national decline in live-in service. The reader should not, however, conjure up an image of middle-class wives doing the laundry or scrubbing the floors. If resident domestics did not abound here, servants by the day were fairly common. As Ruth Schwartz Cowan has pointed out for the United States as a whole, most middle-class housewives enjoyed some sort of part-time domestic help.[37] In 1900, some of these household workers were able to live as well as work in Haddonfield. At least one member of some 9 percent of the families worked as domestics, mostly doing "days work," as it is still called among the women who do it, or working as laundresses. Some of them were Irish, but most were black, living in the town's predominantly black section, a small community that nevertheless was able to support a church and a full-time minister. But by 1910, only 2 percent of Haddonfield's households included women who worked in domestic service; housing for the working class became much more difficult to find within the town itself as suburbanization became pervasive. But that did not mean that the town's middle-class women were deprived of help. Across the border of the town in one direction was a working-class area, and about a mile away in another was the community then known as Snow Hill, a predominantly black unincorporated district that later became the town of Lawnside.[38]

Between 1900 and 1910 the West Haddonfield Land Company

sold lots all around the railroad station, while Henry Moore, a businessman and land developer, who perhaps not coincidentally was Haddonfield's wealthiest citizen, platted lots and sold them throughout the town. Moore and other developers had successfully marketed Haddonfield to the families of the men who worked in Camden and Philadelphia. Local industries had disappeared by 1900, and by 1910, very few of the unskilled could afford to make their homes here. By the early 1920s, indeed, the "majority of the male population of Haddonfield [was] composed of business and professional men of Camden and Philadelphia," but even before World War I such men and their families had come to dominate the town. The mayor in the early twentieth century, for example, was a Philadelphia businessman. Camden, an industrial satellite of Philadelphia, was a ten-minute train ride away. To commute to Philadelphia took just twenty-five minutes, counting the ferry ride across the Delaware. Passengers also had the choice of taking the route that crossed the railroad bridge at Delair, thereby eliminating the ferry ride altogether. There was also trolley service to the ferryhouse in Camden, which was cheaper, but more crowded and slower. By most accounts, at least until the 1920s, residents preferred the train for commuting.[39] Good commuter service helped to make Haddonfield, in the first decade of the twentieth century, an appealing location.

Houses in Haddonfield were more expensive than those in Collingswood or Merchantville, its nearest rivals for potential suburbanites in New Jersey, but housing costs were somewhat lower here than in comparable Philadelphia suburbs on the Pennsylvania side of the Delaware River. To buy a house in Haddonfield cost an average of $4,000; to rent cost between $15.00 and $25.00 per month. To that, of course, must be added the costs of commuting. Fourteen trains picked up commuters at the two Haddonfield stations every morning, and returned them in the evening, for a monthly fare of $4.85. Although it cost less to rent or buy a house here than in Overbrook Farms, Haddonfield remained what the real estate agents would call a desirable location.[40]

As in Overbrook Farms, when the decision to rent or to purchase came up in Haddonfield, the answer was similar. In 1900, only about 40 percent of the residents of Haddonfield owned the houses in which they lived. In 1910, Haddonfield's ownership rate was somewhat closer to that of Overbrook Farms, when 53 percent of the houses were owned.[41] Neither of these communities had the high rates of ownership that historians have found among working-class Americans during this period. A rate of just over 50 percent comes nowhere near the 70 percent ownership levels that Roger Simon discovered for turn-of-the-century, skilled workers in Milwaukee, or that Olivier Zunz found for Detroit's working class. The idea that for many suburbanites, place was more important than ownership was as true in Haddonfield and Overbrook Farms as it was in suburban Detroit.

We are not talking about families who could not afford to buy a house. Although the self-amortizing mortgage had not come into use, various mortgage options were available. Look at the example of young Americus Underdown, Jr., son of a prominent Haddonfield resident, who, like his father, worked in the family haberdashery business in Philadelphia. Underdown and his family lived in a rented house, but they did not disdain property ownership, purchasing a similar house in the same neighborhood and renting it to others.[42]

Haddonfield was not an "instant" suburb, but a community that reflected—at the same time—generations of building and a new suburban boom. Its churches, for example, had stood for decades, and simply grew larger, or were rebuilt on larger sites. There was a school system in place. And modern suburban houses were added to an existing housing stock. When the new suburban houses went up, however, they reflected the new architectural ideal, with their more open floor plans. In Haddonfield, the houses of the 1880s and early 1890s had possessed that hallmark of the Victorian house, interior separation, although by the 1890s pocket doors had become increasingly common. By the first decade of the twentieth century, interiors were much more open, and the most common floor plans featured an entrance hall opening into a living room on one side and a dining room on the other. In exterior design, Haddonfield residents preferred the Colonial Revival or the "Foursquare." A few bungalows were built here in the pre–World War I years, but that style was not very common.[43]

In some ways, Haddonfield residents—men and women alike—appear to have been more progressive than those who lived in Overbrook Farms. For one thing, Haddonfield took pride in its public school system, and many parents were actively interested in education, demanding that the high school offer courses in college preparation for both boys and girls. Furthermore, Haddonfield had attracted a group of talented women active in social reform and teaching. As single women, they did not face the same strictures as their married counterparts, and their presence in the town, and in community organizations, offered the next generation a different set of role models besides their mothers and their mothers' friends.

Among these women was Margaret Bancroft, founder of the well-known Haddonfield School for Backward Children. Her staff, which included several women, also lived at the school. St. Agnes Episcopal School for Girls, a boarding school that closed in the early 1900s, also had a female staff. In addition, Haddonfield had a very successful woman physician, "Mrs. Dr." Lavinia Clement, as the townspeople called her, a graduate of Women's Medical College in

Philadelphia who was in practice with her husband and who specialized in the diseases of women and children.[44]

Most Haddonfield women, however, did not have careers. Their energies went into domestic and community life. Much of that community life consisted of club activity, both with other women and, to an even greater extent, with their husbands. Haddonfield had a number of clubs open to both men and women. Perhaps the two most important were the Debating Society and the Natural Science Club, both of which came into existence around the turn of the century. The Debating Society, which had a membership of about a hundred men and women, met regularly in the high school, and engaged in debates on important public issues. Other Haddonfield residents turned out to hear the debaters, many of whom were couples who had joined the club together. Women took as energetic a role in the Society as men, and lest the debating club be construed as a club of feminists and their spouses, we should remember that one of the club's liveliest members, Mary Bergen, was a vigorous member of the New Jersey Association Opposed to Woman Suffrage.[45]

Like the Debating Society, the Natural Science Club consisted of men and women, many of them husbands and wives. This group studied nature together as educated amateurs. Each year, the club put together a program for which members prepared papers on various themes—one year astronomy, another South America. In 1914, for example, when the Natural Science Club organized its program around the Delaware River, Gertrude Smith talked about geology while Samuel Rhoads talked about the culture of the native people.[46]

Another club that encouraged husbands and wives to join together was the Penn Literary Society. Its name notwithstanding, this was not a club that met to discuss works of literature; instead, some twenty to forty people got together at one another's houses to talk about their travels, discuss local history, and listen to visiting speakers. Like the other clubs that men and women joined together, the Penn Literary Society was a success.[47] This does not mean that men and women had abandoned single-sex activities altogether. The men of the Natural Science Club, for example, occasionally took hunting or camping trips without their wives. The town also boasted a "gun club" in the first two decades of the century. This was not a hunting club, but one for target shooting. Interestingly, and perhaps not irrelevantly, the programs that the club had printed for the target-shooting events remind the modern reader of nothing so much as a women's club program. Beyond these few examples, there was not a great deal of separate male activity in Haddonfield. There was, in the early twentieth century, an attempt to institute a civic club for men only, but that attempt failed.[48]

Like the men, women also had some single-sex activities; the most important was the Haddonfield Fortnightly, a civic and social organization very much like the women's club of Overbrook Farms. Inspired by Philadelphia's New Century Club, Haddonfield women started the Fortnightly in 1893. In the early twentieth century it was divided into five sections, for art, civics, reading, study, and "mothers." In 1901 the mothers were investigating "Parents' Mistakes" as well as studying children's nutrition and exercise. The Fortnightly was the most successful women's club; Haddonfield had, in addition, chapters of the Daughters of the American Revolution and the Colonial Dames.[49]

The Fortnightly flourished, but the most traditionally oriented women's club in the community—the Haddonfield Sewing Society, which had been in existence since 1867—disbanded in 1903. The Sewing Society had been in some ways like the Needlework Guild in its earliest years. The women of the Sewing Society still sewed clothes for distribution to charity, as well as solicited donations of clothes from merchants. Recipients of their largesse included orphanages in nearby Camden, The Vineland Training School for the Feeble Minded, about forty miles away, and institutions in states as distant as Missouri and Kansas. At their meetings, the women of the sewing society chatted while they cut out cloth, or one of them read aloud to the others. By 1897, when as few as four women might turn out to a meeting, the group could no longer ignore its decline. This little band held on for six more years, then disbanded, "owing," as they put it, to "changed circumstance."[50]

The Sewing Society had atrophied, a Young Men's Literary Society failed to attract much in the way of membership, and the Men's Civic Club died aborning; but the Debating Society, the Natural Science Club, and the Penn Literary Society were very successful. So too, were athletic clubs in which the whole family participated. As in Overbrook Farms, the suburbanites of Haddonfield became quite athletic and the town had both a country club, where families played golf and socialized, and a "field club," devoted to tennis. The field club accepted both male and female members as active players as well as social members. Neither the social members of either sex could vote, nor could the female players. Still, women and men played tennis together, and took their children to the courts.[51] Men and women, whether the activity at hand was athletic or sedentary, wanted to belong to groups together in Haddonfield, perhaps even to a greater extent than they had at Overbrook Farms. Men did go on camping trips occasionally without their wives, and wives spent time in activities with other women, to be sure. But men and women seem to have spent a lot of their leisure time together.

They also spent time with their children and worried about how best to rear them. One of the five sections of the most important women's club in town dealt solely with parental questions, and when these women took their concerns to the wider community by forming the Mothers and Teachers Club, the fathers expressed such interest that the group decided to reschedule two of the eight meetings of the year in the evening so that men could attend. Parents also brought their children along to the athletic clubs. The Haddon Field Club was for families, and it encouraged the children of members to remain in the club as young adults by establishing preferential membership for them. There was also a boys' baseball team, managed by fathers, somewhat like the later little league. Family scrapbooks offer evidence of leisurely family vacations, to Maine or to the beaches of New Jersey, for periods of a couple of weeks or more than a month.[52] Intimate recollections of family life that remain in these scrapbooks show the same kinds of family activities as in Overbrook Farms.

Husbands and wives in Haddonfield took most of their recreation together, and they involved their children as well. Still, there is also evidence that adolescents (a term just gaining currency) had a significant number of interests which, although they did not exclude the family altogether, were primarily for their own amusement. There were school parties, sports (basketball for the girls, much more for the boys, including baseball, track, and football), and the debating club, school paper, and theatricals for both sexes. And girl graduates in Haddonfield were more likely than those in Overbrook Farms to repudiate the idea that young women, after finishing high school, ought to stay at home until marriage. Of the fifteen young women who graduated from Haddonfield High School in 1912, only six were without some occupation; four had jobs (all in Philadelphia), and five were at college. The growing independence of young men and women did not contradict the idea of family togetherness, but it does suggest that adolescents were beginning to detach themselves from their families in spite of their parents' best intentions. Giving this period of life a new name of its own showed a need to come to terms with it. And there was a spate of new books that dealt with parental anxieties about teenaged children that were just beginning to appear in the second decade of the twentieth century.[53]

In both Overbrook Farms and Haddonfield, husbands and wives spent their leisure together. Although in both communities there was a great deal of family recreation that included both parents and children, in Haddonfield one also notices that parents spent some of their leisure with each other and other adults, without the children. These two communities—different in origin as they were—developed in a remarkably similar manner in the early twentieth century and illuminate on the intimate stage of daily life a cultural model of the new suburban domesticity. What would have happened to the new suburban ideal under ordinary circumstances, and how the barely showing hint of middle-class, youthful restiveness would have affected family togetherness, we will never know, because World War I interrupted the processes of suburban development. The impact of the war, and its aftermath, on the patterns of middle-class suburban family life is the subject of the next chapters.

Commuters and others wait at the Haddonfield train station in the 1880s. Courtesy of the Historical Society of Haddonfield.

House in Haddonfield, New Jersey, built in the late 1880s or early 1890s. By the nineties, Haddonfield had become a thriving railroad suburb of Philadelphia. Courtesy of the Historical Society of Haddonfield.

A block of new houses in early twentieth-century Haddonfield. These houses were built by a prominent local developer. Courtesy of the Historical Society of Haddonfield.

In Haddonfield, the tennis clubs of the early twentieth century catered to players of both sexes and all ages. Courtesy of Haddonfield Public Library.

The "Foursquare" was a popular design, not only in Haddonfield, but in surrounding New Jersey suburban towns in the early twentieth century. This one was constructed by local builder William Capern. Courtesy of the Historical Society of Haddonfield.

This Design Has the Feeling of an English Country House of Brick or Plaster, with Small Windows

A Plaster or Brick Design. The Hip-Roof Combined with the Arches Gives It an Italian Feeling

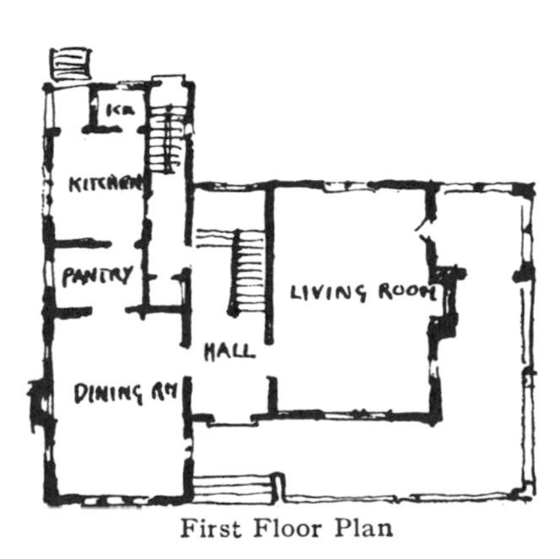

First Floor Plan

Just as they do today, some architects and builders in the early twentieth century standardized interiors while allowing for varying exterior styles. From *Modern American Homes,* 1912.

Colonial Type of House with Hip-Roof. This May Be Executed in Wood, Plaster, or Brick

An English Type of House. Plaster or Brick Would Be Suitable Materials for This Design

A Colonial Design with Gable Ends—Brick Material

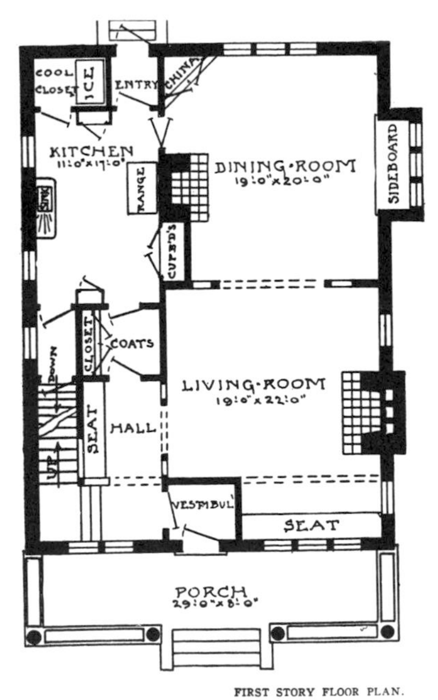

FIRST STORY FLOOR PLAN.

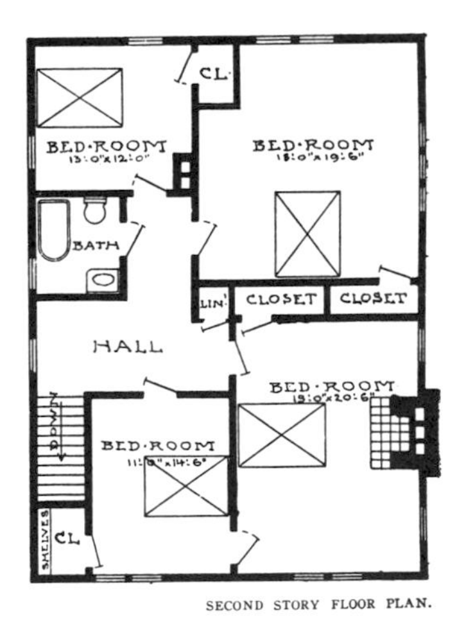

SECOND STORY FLOOR PLAN.

This "comfortable and convenient suburban house" first appeared in the *Craftsman* in 1907. From Gustav Stickley, *Craftsman Homes*, 1909.

By 1896 the developers of Overbrook Farms were advertising not only its convenient location, pure water, and modern heating and electricity, but also its "Established Stores, School, Churches and Stable." Courtesy of Jane Smith Taylor.

OVERBROOK FARMS...

34th Ward, Philadelphia

STEAM HEAT FROM A CENTRAL PLANT

PURE WATER | **ELECTRIC LIGHT** | **PERFECT DRAINAGE**

A Desirable Home Place

Suburban Living at its Best | **Houses and Ground For Sale**

14 Minutes / 5 Miles / 10 Cents } **From Broad Street Station, Penna. R. R.**

30 Minutes / 5 Cents } **From Broad and Arch Streets, by Trolley**

WENDELL & SMITH, Managers

6092 Drexel Road, Station W, Phila.

THAT OVER A MILLION DOLLARS WORTH OF SALES
have been made at OVERBROOK FARMS in less than three years to the most critical buyers, shows that the transformation from a grazing farm to an ideal home-place made perfect by the liberal expenditure of money and the best thoughts architects and builders could devise, has not only been appreciated, but has been a SUCCESS.

THE REASONS ARE NOT HARD TO FIND

PRICES ARE LOW
compared with other portions of Philadelphia, lacking the good points of Overbrook Farms.

MATERIAL AND WORKMANSHIP ARE THE BEST
Made possible by the magnitude of the purchases and work.

CONVENIENCE OF ACCESS
to Philadelphia is another factor: Overbrook Farms being but 14 minutes by P. R. R., trains at half-hour intervals from Broad Street Station for 6½ cents a ride to those using 180 trips in three months: and 30 minutes from Broad and Arch Streets by Trolley for 5 cents.

THE GROUND IS HIGH
The lowest point being 140 feet higher than Broad and Market Streets; and there are a number of grand old SHADE TREES.

PURE CLEAN WATER drawn from deep bored wells—cold even in summer.

ELECTRIC LIGHT
for houses and streets at three-fourths the price charged by city companies; no bad smelling gas anywhere.

STEAM HEAT FROM A CENTRAL PLANT. No dust, no ashes and little trouble.

CEMENTED SIDEWALKS, BROAD AND WELL MACADAMIZED ROADS

PERFECT DRAINAGE by ample sewers, connected with city system.

Established Stores, School, Churches and Stable

WENDELL & SMITH, Managers,

6092 Drexel Road, Station W, Philadelphia

This Overbrook Farms house, from the late 1890s, exhibits some of the influences of the arts and crafts movement. From *The Scientific American Building Edition*, 26, 1898. Note the relative openness of the first-floor plan. Courtesy of the Athenaeum of Philadelphia.

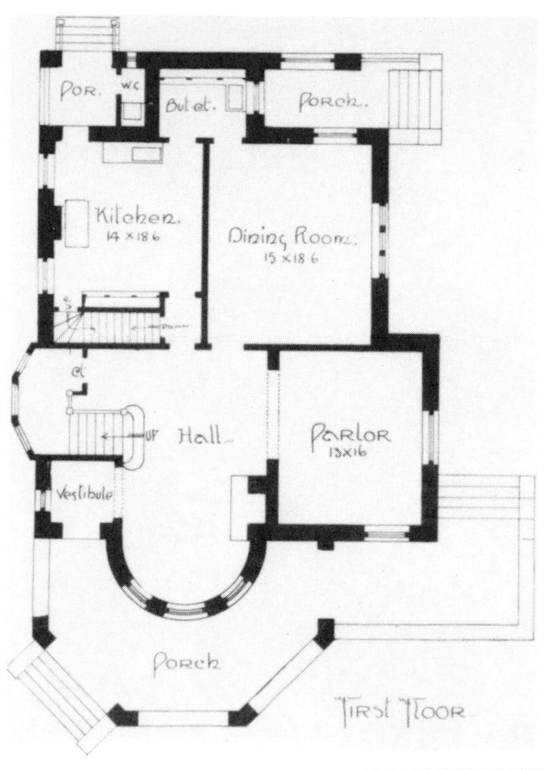
Por.
WC
But. ct.
Porch.
Kitchen.
14 × 18 6
Dining Room.
15 × 18 6
Hall
Parlor
13 × 16
Vestibule
Porch
First Floor

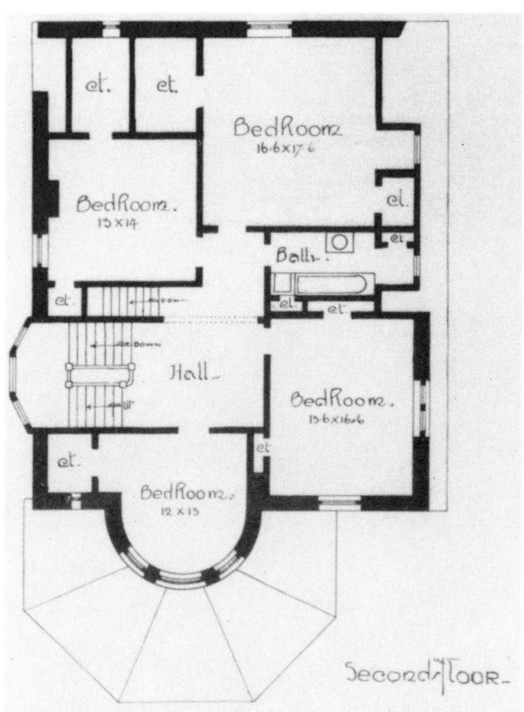
ct.
ct.
BedRoom
16.6 × 17.6
ct.
BedRoom.
13 × 14
Bath.
ct.
ct.
ct.
ct.
Hall
BedRoom.
13.6 × 16.6
ct.
BedRoom.
12 × 13
Second Floor

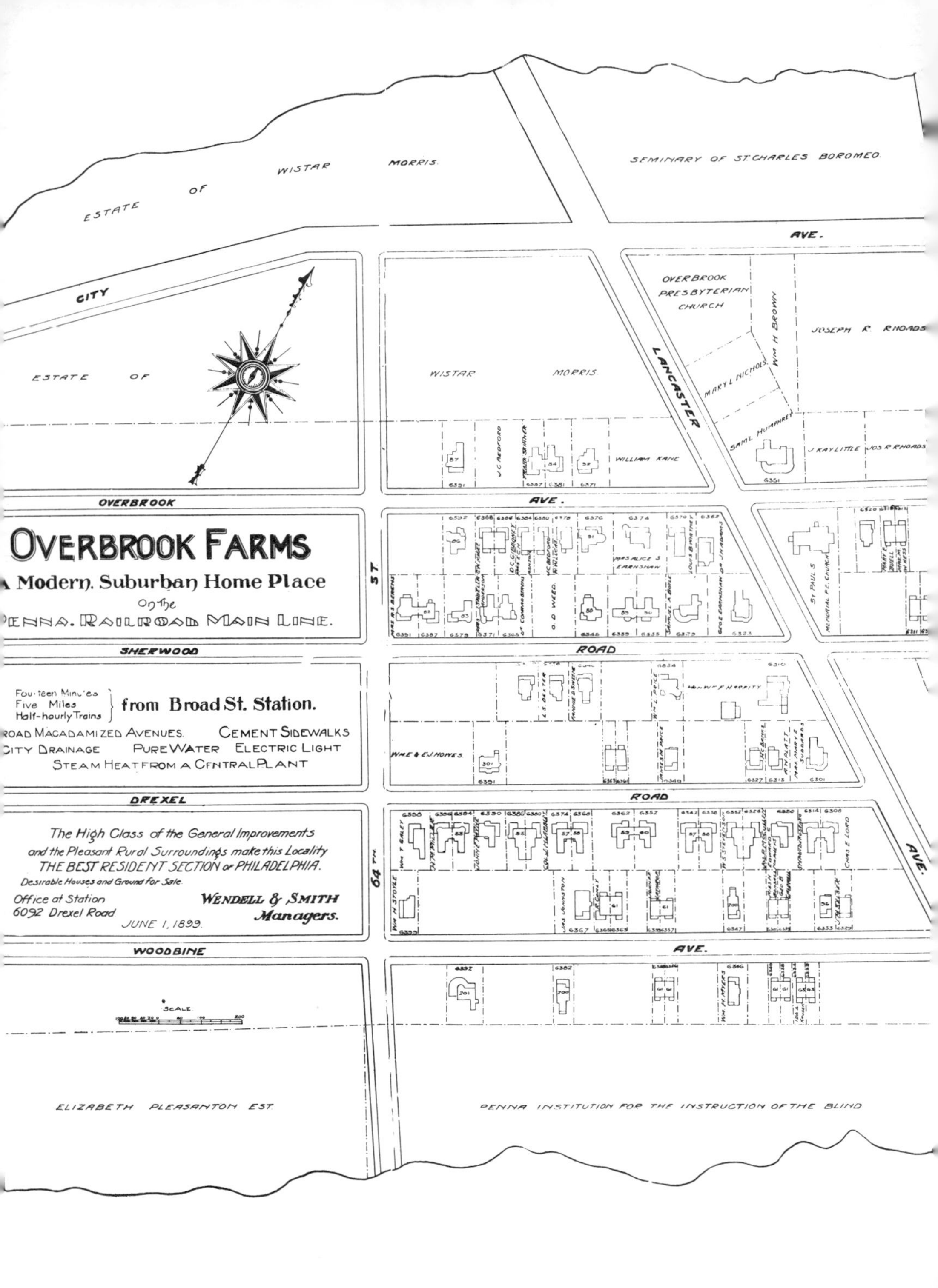

Overbrook Farms in 1899. Courtesy of Jane Smith Taylor.

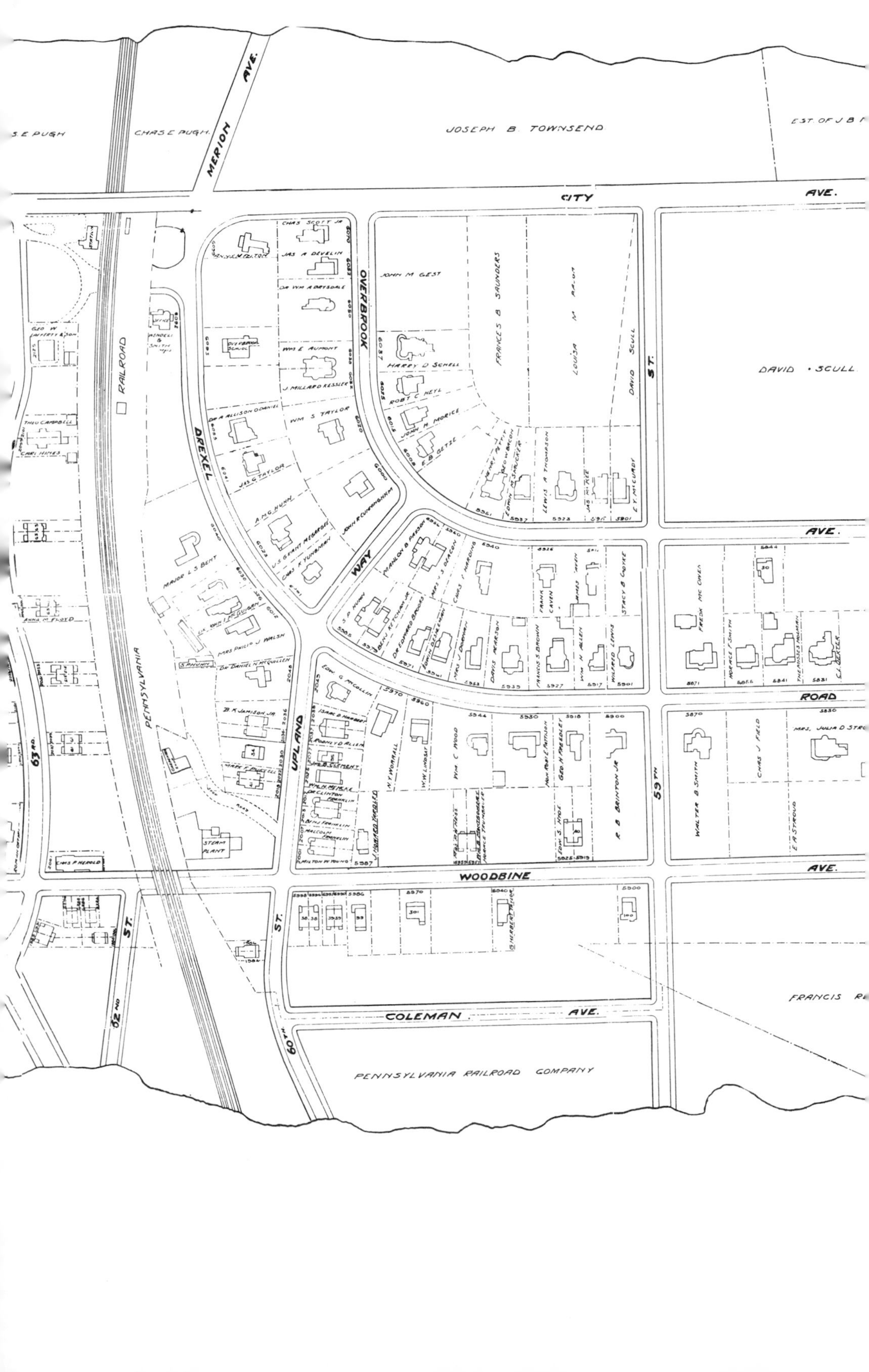

S. E. PUGH
CHAS E PUGH.
MERION AVE.
JOSEPH B. TOWNSEND
EST. OF J B
CITY AVE.
OVERBROOK
DREXEL
WAY
RAILROAD
PENNSYLVANIA
CHAS SCOTT JR
JAS A DEVELIN
DR WM A DRYSDALE
WM E AUMONT
J. MILLARD KESSLER
WM S TAYLOR
JAS G TAYLOR
A M G HUHN
U.S. GRANT MCGARGEL
CHAS K YUNGMAN
JOHN E CUNNINGHAM
OVERBROOK SCHOOL
JOHN M GEST
HARRY D SCHELL
ROBT C HEYL
JOHN H MORICE
E B GETZE
FRANCES B SAUNDERS
LOUISA M
DAVID SCULL
LEWIS A THOMPSON
E Y MCCURDY
ST.
DAVID SCULL
AVE.
MAJOR L S BENT
MRS PHILIP J WALSH
DR DANIEL H MCQUILLEN
B K JAMISON JR.
UPLAND
STEAM PLANT
CHAS P HEROLD
GEO W
THEO CAMPBELL
CARL HINES
ANNA M FLOYD
63 RD.
MAHLON B PAXSON
CHAS I HARDING
FRANK CAVEN
STACY B COYKE
S P HUHN
BENJ KETCHAM JR
DR EDWARD BROOKS
DAVIS PEARSON
FRANCIS S BROWN
WM H ALLEN
WILFRED LEWIS
FREDK MC OWEN
HORACE F SMITH
C L DEXTER
ROAD
EDW. G MCCOLLIN
ISAAC D HARBERT
RODNEY D ALLEN
MRS B CLEMENT
DR CLINTON FRANKLIN
BENJ FRANKLIN
MALCOLM FRANKLIN
MILTON W YOUNG
N Y WORRALL
W W LINDSAY
WM C WOOD
GEO H PRESDLEY
R B BRINTON JR
59TH
WALTER B SMITH
CHAS J FIELD
MRS. JULIA D STR
E A STROUD
WOODBINE AVE.
ST.
62 ND
ST.
FRANCIS R
COLEMAN AVE.
60TH
PENNSYLVANIA RAILROAD COMPANY

PHOTOGRAPH BY WILLIAM T. CLARK

These four suburban interiors were part of an ongoing feature in *The Ladies Home Journal* in 1902, called "Inside a Hundred Suburban Homes." The illustrations here appeared in the November issue.

PHOTOGRAPH BY HENRY FUERMANN

PART *Three*

SUBURBAN PROSPERITY AND DEPRESSION

CHAPTER FIVE

A Version of America

And they come on like scenery mingled with darkness
The damp plains, overgrown suburbs,
Places of known civic pride, of civil obscurity.
These are connected to my version of America.

JOHN ASHBERY,
"THE ONE THING THAT CAN SAVE AMERICA"

The suburban vision that took shape at the turn of the twentieth century had altered both the conventional conception of the ideology of domesticity and the notion of suburbia as a political substitute for the pastoral ideal. It retained the former's insistence on the primacy of the family as the nation's most important cultural institution, but now required husbands as well as wives to preserve and protect family values. And instead of a pastoral ideal based on property ownership, it emphasized the political significance of choosing a suburban location. A blend of domestic, pastoral, and democratic values, the new suburban ideal carried such weight because of the increasing belief among the American, protestant middle class that the cities imperiled both the family and the polity. It had emerged gradually during the last two decades of the nineteenth century and the early years of the twentieth, and manifested itself in the daily lives of the families who chose the suburbs as well as in advice literature and social commentary. Exactly how it would have continued to develop under ordinary circumstances must remain a mystery, however, because World War I intervened. This chapter is about the impact of the war and its aftermath on the new suburban ideal. Many of the elements that will go into it—home ownership, the reprivatization of women's lives, and the popularity of planned communities—have been dealt with by other historians; however, they have usually been treated as discrete phenomena, or as new experiences. My purpose is to illuminate their connection to the suburban values delineated earlier, to explore the continuities as well as understand the breaks from the past.[1]

In the aftermath of the war came a suburban boom outdistancing anything that went before it, accompanied by a dramatic return of the idea that home ownership and good citizenship were inextricably connected. In two obvious material ways, the war contributed to that boom. First, the wartime housing shortage meant both that there was less housing available overall and that people could not effectively choose their neighbors. The housing shortage had begun in 1914, when the war in Europe started and changed the investment climate in the United States. Building costs had been rising, which made residential construction a less attractive investment. And as Sam Bass Warner has observed, "more lucrative opportunities for investment elsewhere had driven capital away from new construction, so that a housing shortage existed even prior to our entry into the war in 1917." Nevertheless, American entry into the war intensified the shortage dramatically, so that just at the time when more Americans than ever were moving to urban areas—both city and suburb—because of war-induced economic changes, housing choices had narrowed. Residential construction nearly ground to a halt.[2]

More than simple overcrowding was at stake. In the cities themselves, racial tensions increased as some communities were forced to accept black neighbors who had moved from the South in search of industrial jobs. In two residential neighborhoods of Philadelphia, for example, a few black families had joined the white clerks and skilled workers who already lived there. These families were mostly long-term Philadelphians, many of whom had moved out of the historic black community in South Philadelphia in order to escape identification with southern blacks who had begun to settle there. These "old Philadelphians" moved to residential neighborhoods in West Philadelphia, where they initially appeared to have little difficulty renting or buying houses. Then came the war, and with it a concerted effort by white residents to stem the influx of blacks.[3]

Ultimately, whites were unsuccessful in keeping out black residents in these communities and communities like them. When the war was over, and the construction boom of the postwar years began, whites moved into more outlying areas. Many of those who could afford it went to the suburbs. Although the war did not create racial and ethnic hostility—the Progressive Era, after all, witnessed considerable racism and nativist hatred—the hiatus in residential construction that it did cause built up an enormous demand for new housing. And when builders and middle-class buyers made decisions about where they wanted these new houses to be, they chose the suburbs.[4]

The second way in which the war exercised an influence on postwar ideas about housing would not come to fruition until the New Deal, but wartime experiments in housing workers did have more immediate effects. Here again, it is not a matter of new ideas springing into consciousness as the war began, but rather the wartime situation allowing for greater experimentation with the use of governmental authority. The ideas of the Progressive Era still had considerable influence, particularly in the altered form that had lent such patriotic fervor to the war effort. Progressives, after all, had been interested in using the might of governmental power—local, state, and federal—to promote societal goals. The war gave them a chance to mobilize federal power for those goals. War housing had been one such effort. Communities in Bridgeport, Connecticut, and Camden, New Jersey, were two important federal efforts. And although the federal government, for the short run, got out of the housing business as soon as the war was over, the long-term effects continued to influence American housing.[5]

THE IMPACT OF THE WAR ON THE SUBURBAN IDEAL

In 1919, Woodrow Wilson's secretary of the interior, Franklin K. Lane, urged the president to make suburban housing a governmental priority. "Somewhere and sometime," insisted Lane:

> [A] new system must be devised to disperse the people of great cities on the vacant land surrounding them, to give the masses a real hold upon the soil, and to replace the apartment house with a home in a garden. . . . I put first among the constructive things which may be done by the exercise of the Government's power of supervision and direction, this matter of providing suburban homes for our millions of wage-earners.[6]

Taking up Lane's proposal, housing reformer William Smythe pressed the government to make suburbanization a national priority. Smythe favored the creation of literal garden cities, where each household grew its vegetables and fruits on a half-acre to an acre of ground, where the family kept poultry and goats, and where parents and children could gain some freedom from dependence on wages and salaries to earn their living. The scope of the task, he insisted, required that the national government take charge of building such "garden communities."[7] Smythe did not call for a "back to the land" movement, but argued for a new combination of urban and rural environments that would connect the agrarian dreams of Jeffersonian democracy to the culture and civility of ideal urban life. His "message," was "designed for the country-minded who desire to satisfy their passion for the soil without sacrificing any of the good things they are now getting in their urban experience, including their hold upon the payroll."[8]

Smythe's proposals are interesting for two reasons: First, he prefigured the national institutionalization of the suburban ideal, and second, he insisted that home ownership (and not simply suburban life) was a requisite for creating the new peacetime America. Responding specifically to the challenge of the Bolshevik revolution, he revived the argument that property ownership preserved self-government. Housing reformers of the early twentieth century had claimed that home ownership was a cure for radical tendencies among the masses; ironically, as the reader knows from the last chapters, immigrants and working-class Americans indeed had a higher rate of ownership than middle-class, native whites. But Smythe was not talking about working-class immigrants. He spoke directly to the middle classes, and he was worried about the inability of salaried men to save enough money to provide for their families. Noting that 82 percent of American men left no "income producing estate" for their widows and children, he went on to argue: "[These men] are unable to provide for their nearest and dearest, as the net result of their lifetime labor! . . . Really, is it any wonder that among our hundred millions there are some who openly declare for Social Revolution? A great New York banker, on returning from a trip to Russia, remarked: 'We would all be Bolshevists if we were hungry enough.'"

Smythe was no conservative. He often quoted approvingly the words of the anarchist Peter Kropotkin and the anarchist-leaning Bolton Hall. Still, he believed that individual ownership of small parcels of land was at the center of democracy, and his aim was to find a way to accommodate that goal to an industrial and corporate society. Although "there is no holier place on earth than the home; no more sacred altar than the family hearthstone," the preservation of that holy place now depended, according to Smythe, on the federal government: "To make millions of such homes would be the proudest achievement of statesmanship."[9] Although the specific advice of Franklin Lane and William Smythe went unheeded—neither the executive nor the legislative branches of government showed any interest in subsidizing a modernized version of the Jeffersonian yeoman farmer—their words reflect a change of emphasis in suburban advocacy. No longer was the suburban vision a congeries of localized hopes and fears. It was on the way to becoming a national goal. Further, both men reflect a return to the idea that property ownership and democracy were somehow linked; although it had not been the case in the first decade and a half of the twentieth century, by the 1920s the suburban ideal became once again tied to home ownership.

After the war, ever larger numbers of middle-class Americans wanted a house in the suburbs. As Mark Foster has pointed out, "while demographers cannot pinpoint the years when more Americans actually left than entered the inner city, they are virtually unanimous in the view that the process intensified in the 1920s."[10] Until 1920, the urban fringe had grown at a slower rate than the central cities. But in the twenties, the pattern reversed: the fringe areas of America's cities grew at a rate of 33.2 percent; the inner core at 24.2 percent.[11]

In the 1920s, unlike the prewar years, the growth of middle-class suburbanization was accompanied by an increase in home ownership. Overall, home ownership increased by more than 2.4 percent. (The comparable rate of growth for the previous decade was less than 1 percent.) This may not seem like an enormous jump, but in terms of numbers it meant that 3,231,770 more families were home owners in 1930 than had been in 1920. Housing starts were up by an annual average of 9.75 percent during the 1920s. By 1930 48 percent of American families owned their houses, and the average value of a single-family house was around $5,700.[12] Typically, these houses were financed through a savings and loan association, rather than through the traditional mutual savings bank. Mutual savings institutions had been traditionally associated with working-class home ownership. Middle-class home buyers preferred the more impersonal form of lending.[13]

Working-class Americans in the 1920s began to find themselves priced out of the housing market. In the early years of the twentieth century, these families frequently rejected such things as street lighting, sewer hookups, and paving in their neighborhoods in order to save on taxes so that they could afford to buy their houses. Often they built those houses themselves, because they could not pay a builder. Zoning regulations and buildings codes made such choices increasingly difficult. If working-class families found such obstacles in the cities, they existed with more force in the suburbs, where even small houses were hard to find for under $6,000.[14] The average American family had an income of $2,000. The advice about whether that family could afford to buy a house, and hold a mortgage on it, was roughly the same given to families now—not to buy a house with a price greater than two and a half times annual income. In addition, the family needed to come up with a substantial down payment, and had to be prepared to meet a stiff monthly mortgage.[15]

A family did not need training in higher mathematics to know that a $2,000 income could buy a $5,000 house and that few such houses could be had in a middle-class suburb. It would take what home economists called a "moderate" income of $2,500 (considered the floor for the middle-class) to buy in a middle-class suburb. Families in which the breadwinner held a managerial position or had a profession had annual average incomes of $4,310, and these were the families most able to buy or to build one of the $8,000–$17,000 houses pictured in many of the home magazines.[16]

The reasons for the dramatic shift to a preference for home ownership are not immediately self-evident. In the first decade and a half of the century, readers of chapters three and four will recall, it was important for a middle-class family to be in the suburbs, not necessarily to own a house. (For working-class families, on the other hand, ownership had been the important thing.) One reason, no doubt, had to do with the general climate for investment. In the first decade of the twentieth century, property ownership was a reasonable and respectable source of income, and those who bought residential real estate rented out that real estate; other middle-class families preferred to invest elsewhere rather than tie up money in a house. There was no stigma attached to renting. Now, there was a change in the entire cultural climate as a result of both the war and the fears of revolution engendered by the Bolsheviks; ownership was once again considered to be a sign of good citizenship.[17]

WOMEN, THE WAR, AND DOMESTICITY

When Americans entered World War I, many women's rights women, schooled to the idea of service, viewed American involvement as a chance for women to participate actively. (Then too, the pragmatic politicians of the suffrage movement saw the war to make the world safe for democracy, and women's service to that war, as an opportunity to press ever more strongly to have that democracy extended to them.) Further, some women reformers thought that the war effort might enable them to direct the energies of young women. Historians have shown that in the prewar years, in cities like New York and Chicago, rebellious young men and women were daringly casting aside the conventions of their parents. In Greenwich Village, in its imitators in the "bohemias" of other cities, feminism and youthful rebellion made a heady combination. Not all older suffragists were pleased, and the war offered an opportunity for them to try to redirect youthful energy toward an ideal of service and away from what they viewed as a hedonistic focus on the self. (It did not work, of course; what resulted was a return to the home combined with the ideal of a romantic, and erotic, marriage.)

Margaret Slattery's *The American Girl and Her Community,* published in 1918, was representative of this genre. A mixture of analysis and advocacy, Slattery's book defended young women (for her, as for others who referred to "the girl," the term meant a young woman from sixteen to twenty-two) from those who denounced their independence and desire for excitement. She blamed parents for deprecating the former and for failing to channel the latter in an appropriate direction. Before the war, she claimed, it did appear that adolescent girls had been "dominated by the pronoun *I,*" but the war was changing all that. The spectacle of girls seeking fulfillment in a career, in sports, in sexuality, which had been evident in the past decade, would be subsumed in a new ideal of service: "The new American girl . . . will live in a world where 'they' is of as great importance as 'I'."[18]

Slattery considered herself a women's rights woman. She insisted that every young woman, even one who did not expect to "'earn her own livelihood', must be taught that duty and self-respect demand that her life shall be in some fashion a real contribution to the welfare of the human race." And she argued that the war might result in the loss of the lives of many young men, so that women might find it impossible to marry. Those women, she said, must be trained for careers. Most, however, would marry, and Slattery never suggested that married women might consider having a career as well. "The new American girl . . . will accept the duties of the home as they come to her without fear or dread. I believe she will desire, to a far greater degree than have the girls of the previous generation, to share with the man she loves the joys and responsibilities of parenthood . . . aware of the fact that the earth's richest treasure . . . is a child."[19]

Slattery combined suffragism, patriotism, and domesticity in this book, designed both to reassure parents and to guide young women. But after the war, the ideals of service that had motivated the social feminists seemed less important to the next generation of women. And some of their elders began to wonder, in the words of the title of one book, *What's Wrong with our Girls?* The answer, as author Beatrice Hale and others became convinced, was urban life. "More than half America's population is now urban," she remarked, and "only today is it true here in America that more than half the race has left the soil. The transition is too abrupt for sanity. . . . All our racial habits have been destroyed in one or two brief generations."[20] Hale's attitude reflected a growing fear on the part of middle-class Americans that the new suburban domestic ideal of the Progressive Era had not succeeded in reaching enough Americans and therefore had not stabilized family life. Many progressives, who had initially viewed the war as the climax of their reformist crusade, now witnessed a ravaged western world. Domestic reformers, likewise, who had looked to the war effort to bring about a new wave of commitment to national service, found that instead the signs of youthful pleasure-seeking, already evident in some cities before the war, would make the new domestic ideal even more difficult of fulfillment.

After the war was over, and woman suffrage was won, and the nation settled down to "normalcy," middle-class young women seemed little interested in reform or in fighting what they considered to be old battles. Many believed that suffrage had brought political equality; now women could enjoy the fruits of their victory. And the new psychology, whether Freudian—at least as it was popularized in the United States—or behaviorist, insisted that women seek fulfillment through a romantic, sexually satisfying marriage. It was not so much that women became antifeminist as that they became "postfeminist," to use a current phrase. Young women were attending college in growing numbers in the 1920s; their entrance into the professions had reached substantial proportions (who was to know that those proportions would not be reached again until 1980?); and once out of college, women generally worked until marriage and often until the first child was born. Women could make choices, it seemed, and young, middle-class women of the 1920s would have grown up, after all, in households where their parents held the values described in the last two chapters. It is easy to see how they could have deceived themselves that equality had been won.[21]

We now know how wrong they were. Such young women, if they decided to embark on a professional career rather than one of the office "jobs" that employers encouraged them to take, found that equality was a chimera. Professional advancement invariably required them to forgo family life. Women scientists, professors, and physicians found that if they married, their careers suffered irretrievable losses. That it was necessary to choose seemed inescapable, even to most who called themselves feminists.[22] Young college women were encouraged, sometimes by the women who taught them, to choose marriage and a family over a career. In their home economics courses, they learned that while a career was appropriate for a few women, it was a mistake for most of them.

Mary Hinman Abel's widely used textbook, for example, strongly asserted the values of suburban home ownership, the importance of women serving as full-time housewives and mothers, and family privacy. Citing official-sounding statistics, Abel and other home economists "proved" that the ideal home was a single-family house in a neighborhood of "whole blocks of two-story houses," where the "chief pleasure" of everyone was "the home itself." And the perfect family consisted of husband, wife, two children, and a "grandmother," living in the suburbs. Here they have their small vegetable garden; they find their pleasures in the family itself, the husband doing carpentry for pleasure and home improvement, the mother, who is "intelligent, sensible . . . does all housework except washing, much canning, and all the sewing" with the help of grandmother. Although Abel reluctantly made exceptions of highly trained or highly talented women, to exempt them from the day-to-day demands of housework and childrearing, "the average woman whose husband is receiving a moderate income," should stay at home and care for her own children, have a garden, preserve food, and sew.[23]

Popular magazines offered women the same advice. They did not deny the achievements of women, but they did convey a powerful sense that a woman remained unfulfilled without a happy marriage and children. Women received a somewhat mixed, but not literally contradictory message, which ran something like this: The suffrage movement was victorious, and now women possess the same freedom as men. However, if they want to be truly fulfilled as women, they will use that freedom to marry, have children, and keep a home. As Nancy Cott superbly summarized it: "[W]omen's household status and heterosexual service were now defended—even aggressively marketed—in terms of women's choice, freedom, and rationality. . . . Feminist intents and rhetoric were not ignored but appropriated."[24]

THE REIFICATION OF SUBURBAN DOMESTICITY

In the 1920s the suburban domestic ideal, having been promulgated and set in place by a self-conscious middle class in the quarter century before World War I, became a mass-produced commodity. This is not to say that all white Americans could, or wished to, become suburbanites; however, it does mean that the suburban vision jumped out at readers of home magazines, took hold of the women who leafed through *Good Housekeeping,* lured parents who poured over child-rearing literature, and even made it to the front pages of the newspapers that covered national politics. The new suburban advocacy was built on the prewar themes of family togetherness and physical separation from urban life, but there was one very important difference. Before the war, there was genuine emphasis on marital togetherness, and on the responsibilities of men to make that togetherness a reality. Now, not only did the burden of maintaining marital intimacy shift back to women, but there was also much more stress on the suburb as the proper place to rear children.

If we look first at the advice literature on children, we see a shift from what Kate Wiggin called at the turn of the century "children's rights," to an aggressive insistence that parents ought to organize their lives around what was best for their offspring. And what was best, according to most authors, was a suburban environment. Prominent educator Jessica Cosgrove, for example, urged her readers to abandon the city for the sake of their children. If they did not, she suggested, dire consequences would result. She contrasted the stories of "two young mothers of equal wealth and position, [each with] four children. One had realized that city conditions would make it almost impossible to give her children the simple bringing up that she desired for them." This devoted young mother moved her family out of the city: "She and her husband were normal young people and probably would have had a rushing social life themselves if they had remained in the city, but the enforced leisure of the country gave them an opportunity to discuss the problems connected with the children as they arose and to plan for them carefully and thoughtfully." Cosgrove was not very sanguine about the future of the children of the other mother however, who had "said positively, when I urged my doctrine of simplification, that it could not be done, [and] that she had decided to float with the tide."[25]

Other advice-givers, not all of them so dogmatic as Cosgrove, shared her assumptions about the dangers of urban life for children. One writer condemned "the limitations and artificialities of the city home," stating flatly, "The city flat-dweller is an outcast from her inheritance of life's sweet things." Warnings about the city were not confined to the professed advice-givers. The young heroines of *Good Housekeeping*'s romances always went to the city first, where they met wickedness and deceit, before returning home to marry the boys they left behind.[26] Readers of such advice, whether propounded didactically or in the guise of romantic fiction, did not wish to escape the benefits of urbanity and modernity. After all, newspapers, magazines, and the radio all brought urban culture, speech, and fashion even to those beyond the suburbs and to the small towns and farms of rural America. *Good Housekeeping* had a fashion shopping service designed to provide rural women with urban styles. What the advice-givers hoped was that suburbanites could escape the constant need for vigilance; in the suburbs children could play in the yard rather than in the streets or a distant park.[27]

A new anxiety crept into middle-class childrearing; women, even those fortunate enough to have domestic help, began to feel compelled to become the sole caretakers of their children. There was a reluctance to hand over the care of children to the nursery school or to nursemaids. In some measure this was the logical outcome of the partial acceptance of the so-called "scientific childrearing" of the Progressive Era. But in that earlier period there had been a spirited debate on the meaning of that term. Charlotte Perkins Gilman and her supporters had insisted that the best way to rear children was to hire specially trained teachers, while her opponents had argued that mothers should become their own experts. The 1920s witnessed the amalgam of the two views—women relied on experts for advice, but felt it necessary to do the actual childrearing themselves.[28]

Such a change had important implications as well for masculine domesticity. Although it did not disappear entirely, there is a sense that men seemed to draw back from the commitment to family life the previous generation had made. On the one hand, in a natural outgrowth of the marital togetherness of the prewar period, husbands and wives in the suburban havens of the 1920s expected romance and excitement from their marriages. On the other hand, the pressure was mostly on the wife to stay young, to keep her husband interested, to make sure that her housekeeping met the standards of the neighborhood so as not to disgrace him professionally. Advertisements in this decade, far more than in previous years, were designed to make women feel guilty. In the Progressive Era, women held men responsible for being good husbands and fathers. Now, if a husband strayed, it was his wife's poor sexual, childrearing, or housekeeping skills, chapped hands, dry skin, or unpleasant breath that was the cause.[29]

Magazine fiction reinforced the advertisements. Men, the stories claimed, lost promotions because of nagging wives, or refused to settle down because women displayed the mistaken idea that they had as much right to achievement in the larger society as men did. (As the fiction in the magazines made clear, if a women wanted to keep her man, keeping her looks and sexual interest while at the same time being a devoted mother and skilled homemaker was the way to do it.) Many of the stories were about young women who resisted the proposals of sober young professionals or executives, and who fled their parents' houses for office jobs in the big city. They found, predictably, that the sophisticated men they met in the city wanted to use and manipulate them, and that they had rejected true love because it had not seemed very glamorous. At the end of the stories these young women discovered that their sober and steady young men were the ones they really wanted, that true romance was found in marriage, and that motherhood offered all the scope they needed for their talents.[30]

There were some voices that continued to speak to men and to insist that not all success in family life was dependent upon women. For example, Philip Howard's *Father and Son,* published in 1922, exhorted every man to "allow a large section of time in his life program for fatherhood." Howard went on:

> In one home where there are two little boys, one of three and the other less than two years of age, the father, a young man of twenty-six, in charge of a growing and very engrossing business, takes time to tell the little chaps their good-night stories, and to read aloud to the busy mother chapters from Henry Clay Trumbull's "Hints on Child Training." And his face lighted . . . as he told a visitor about the twenty-five books on child training he had already gathered. He has given time to . . . arranging . . . the pictures for the nursery; he gives time to the little boys themselves.[31]

Howard spent the next few pages on similar stories of fathers: busy men with important jobs who nevertheless considered fatherhood to demand active participation. Yet these fathers, he complained, were exceptions: "Most men are too individualistic, too pre-occupied with the drive of ambition . . . to come sufficiently into partnership with motherhood." As a result, "[f]ar too much responsibility is shifted to the mother."[32]

Some women pushed Howard's argument further. Dorothy Dunbar Bromley, for example, argued in the pages of *Good Housekeeping* that marriages succeeded only when couples understood each other and possessed similar values. That sounds like homely and commonplace advice, except that her successful couples included, in addition to traditional unions, one in which the husband and his wife were both "ardent feminists"; and another with three children, both parents having careers, the husband sharing the housework. One wife had a career before her first child was born, but left it because it was expected that a mother would stay at home. She was unhappy at home; her husband encouraged her to resume her work and shared childcare and housecleaning chores. Bromley was at pains to point out that there was no "right" way to be married, but she clearly favored shared domesticity, and a woman's right to choose to have, or not have, a career. A woman's career, however, required a husband not only sympathetic but also willing to take on some of the chores.[33]

Philip Howard saw the domestic men he wrote about as exceptions, and the advice of Dorothy Bromley went unheeded because it was considered too radical, even for those few who agreed that exceptionally talented women should be able to work, whether mothers or not. Although Helena Huntington Smith stated crisply (in 1928) that "children . . . are quite as well off . . . in a modern home where both parents have an outside occupation than under the best of old-fashioned, twenty-four hour maternal care," she did not suggest that fathers become involved in running the household. Her solution to the childcare problem was a nursery school, to which the "business mamma" (never the business daddy) took her children every day, plus "a good maid or nurse." There is no mention of husbandly involvement with the chores. It was not that Smith took for granted that the men would take part; she expected no help from father. Instead, she argued that women who worked outside the home should be paid by their husbands for the housework. Smith explained one couple's daily routine:

> Mr. Jones has an unhurried breakfast, tucks his newspaper under his arm, and proceeds to his law office . . . where he arrives about ten o'clock with a mind unencumbered by trivial concerns. Mrs. Jones arrives at her office also at ten o'clock. But before getting there she has . . . ordered the food for dinner, and typed a note to the laundry. . . . Then she dashes to the office, and for the next three hours, concentrates on the details of business. But during her luncheon interval she has to get in some shopping for the children. At the end of the day Mr. Jones comes home, relaxes in a comfortable chair, and plays with the children. Mrs. Jones, too, makes a point of being with the children at this time, but before dressing [to go out], she writes notes and pays a flock of bills. And so it goes.[34]

Smith did not suggest that Mr. Jones order dinner, pay the bills, or do anything other than play with the children; instead she suggested that Mr. Jones pay Mrs. Jones for her extra work. Since a wife who works outside the home "is still personally responsible for many of a woman's traditional duties, [she] ought to be allowed a definite salary for the work she does at home . . . at least as much as a housekeeper receives."[35]

Not Smith, not Mary Hinman Abel, not marketing writer Christine Frederick—indeed no one with the exception of Bromley among those women who wrote for a mass audience—suggested that men ought to do any of the daily chores of housework. Abel tortured economic statistics to show that married women, with certain exceptions, should not take outside jobs because it was not cost-efficient for them to do so. When women did work outside the home, she assumed that another woman, maid or housekeeper, would do the household chores. Christine Frederick was contradictory on the subject of jobholding wives—sometimes referring to it as dangerous, at other times accepting its inevitability, especially before children were born—but her solution, as one might expect from the doyenne of household efficiency through consumerism, was more household appliances, not husbandly help.[36]

By the 1920s, those promising indications of the early twentieth century that men might finally become fully integrated into the daily life of the household were hardly in evidence; still, some elements of masculine domesticity had become part of the fatherly role. Men were expected to spend time with their children, and the emotional duties of fatherhood were no longer in question. And yet those duties seemed strangely divorced from the husband-wife relation itself. That is not to say that fathers disappeared from family life; however, masculine domesticity in the Progressive Era had meant that a man took on a genuine proportion of the responsibility for sustaining a companionate relationship with his wife. Companionate marriage was more important than ever, but now wives were responsible for maintaining it.

Just as the new suburban houses of the pre–World War I years had reflected a specific set of values—the open first-floor plan emphasized family unity, the private space for husband and wife upstairs reflected marital togetherness—so too the houses for middle-class suburbanites in the 1920s met the needs of their families. Two things were going on here: One was the consolidation of the design trends first developed around the turn of the twentieth century, and the second was the reflection of the primacy of children in suburbia.

The houses middle-class families bought or had built in the suburbs were, as the architects of the period might have put it, traditional in inspiration, but modern in execution. Most domestic architects of the 1920s who catered to middle-class buyers favored houses of ersatz colonial design. In the pages of the average home magazine, Frank Lloyd Wright no longer had much influence. And it was not until the early 1930s that magazines like *The American Home* began to notice the modern architectual styles imported from Europe. The typical suburban house claimed colonial inspiration, although there was some leaning among the upper-middle class toward what became known as "Stockbroker Tudor." Actually, fidelity to any particular historical period was rare. Details were intended to suggest a period: A center hall evoked the Georgian; a sloping roof recalled the eighteenth-century Pennsylvania farmhouse; green shutters were reminiscent of a New England village. Often houses contained more than one such referent. For example, one design, its architect claimed, combined "the distinctive quality of the early Pennsylvania farmhouse and the appeal of the provincial New England home." Stuccoed, with a center hall and a dormered second story, it recalls for the modern observer nothing more clearly than the American suburb of the 1920s and 1930s. Architects offered these houses of mix-and-match character without apology, proclaiming that "the most praiseworthy architecture of the day is that which ackowledges precedent, but does not imitate or copy." Those who built for America's suburbs aimed for a nostalgic visual impression rather than historical fidelity: A good house "recalls the colonial tradition," but remains nonetheless "entirely modern."[37]

This blatant appeal to nostalgia is interesting. Odd as it may seem in the decade often characterized as devoted to a hedonistic pursuit of pleasure on the part of middle-class youth, when those youths married and started families they wanted to begin life in a house that recalled this country's colonial antecedents. Should the breadwinner become successful, his thoughts turned farther backward, toward Henry VIII or the Norman conquest, and he eyed with pleasure the stuccoed and beamed fronts of what real estate agents called Tudor or Norman houses.[38]

Inside, suburban houses continued the trend toward open floor plans that had become so prominent in the first decade of the twentieth century (see table 5.1). Also, the trend toward the abolition of segregated living spaces observed around the turn of the century was even more evident at the close of the 1920s. Less than 25 percent of the designs included two or more first-floor living spaces by this date. In part, the reasons for a more open design were economic. Suburban life had become accessible to a wider portion of the middle class, and many houses were smaller. Such houses needed to have fewer rooms in order to give an illusion of greater space. As architectural writer Howard Eberlein noted, "It is a mistake to imagine that the small interior can be stretched farther by cutting it up into small pieces." Still, writers and architects found moral significance in the

Table 5.1. Use of Interior Space in Suburban Houses, 1920s

	NO.	%
1 story	88	26
$1\frac{1}{2}$ and 2 story	254	74
Entrance halls	135	39
Kitchens		
First floor	342	100
Dining rooms		
Basement	0	0
First floor	280	82
No separate d.r.	62	18
No. of first-floor living areas		
1	263	77
2	79	23
3 or more	0	0
Living areas on second floor	6	2
Bedrooms		
1–2	138	40
3	166	49
4	31	9
5–6	7	2
$1\frac{1}{2}$ or 2 story houses w. first fl. bedrooms	46	13
Bathrooms		
1	256	75
1 plus w.c.	25	7
2 or more	61	18

Sources: Marcia Mead, *Homes of Character* (New York, 1926). This is a book of plans from the Architects' Small House Bureau. *American Home* (1928–1932).

Notes: N = 342; percentages are rounded.

decline of the parlor, lauding nostalgically the "return" of the living room, "the heart of the household, a room where the family gathered and from which its many interests radiated." Ideology was as important as economics in creating the floor plans of the 1920s, plans to which (in varying degrees) traditionalists and modernists both adhered. Some modern designs, such as those advocated by the American disciples of the Bauhaus group, were at least equally, and probably more, economical than the ersatz colonials favored by a majority of suburbanites. Yet by and large these suburbanites of the 1920s rejected the architecture of modernism. But they did not return to the nineteenth-century architecture of separation. What these buyers wanted was not authenticity but nostalgia.[39]

The popularity of the false fireplace graphically demonstrates the importance of nostalgia and the primacy of symbol over substance. In the 1890s, architect E. C. Gardner expressed a commonly held belief when he declared: "A fireplace is a sacred thing. To pretend to have one when you have not is like pretending to be pious when you know you are wicked; it is stealing the livery of a warm, gracious, kindly hospitality to serve you in making a cold, heartless *pretense* of welcome." By the late 1920s, however, image had triumphed over reality. As etiquette writer Emily Post noted, with obvious pleasure: "A woman of notable taste has just put into [her] dining room . . . a mantel and chimney-breast and fireplace complete—all but a chimney! . . . It is arranged with logs with kindling and paper and even ashes carried from the real fireplace in another room. It can, of course, never be lighted, but it *does* complete the room."[40]

Some of the open floor plans, mostly in smaller houses, even eliminated the dining room. The family ate in the kitchen (now largely servantless), in a small alcove adjacent to the kitchen, or in a combination living-dining area, for which home magazines provided advice on appropriate furnishings. Kitchens had become part of the family's preserve, no longer a place to be avoided by all but the domestic help. Most middle-class housewives no longer had servants; wives cleaned the bathrooms and modern kitchens themselves. Electricity and gas had arrived in suburban houses by the 1920s, eliminating the heat and fumes of the Progressive Era kitchen. Wives spent a great deal of time in that kitchen, the breezy appliance ads notwithstanding. Florence Brobeck stated what most builders acted on, that "the kitchen of today is the result of a deliberate attempt to make the kitchen an attractive workshop for the woman who must plan meals and cook them and then carry on with dishpans, mops, and soaps after the last truffle has been consumed."[41] Having at least the family meals there made the tasks of setting up and cleaning up somewhat easier for the housewife.

The 1920s also witnessed the virtual elimination of the entrance halls in many houses, thereby making the entire first floor open to family, friends, and casual callers alike. (With the advent of the telephone, however, families may have faced less danger of surprise in-person callers.) If the first floor had become accessible to everyone, the second had become, by contrast, more privatized; one popular domestic architect even inveighed against center hall staircases: "Why should the stair go up from the hall? Actually, from a social standpoint there is every reason why it should not. The second story is the 'sanctum sanctorum' of the family. The stranger who comes to the door certainly is not expected to go up the stairs, and even a view to the second floor hall from the front door is undesirable."[42] Bedrooms on the second floor were fewer and smaller, three bedrooms rather than four becoming the norm. Although the number, and size, of bedrooms had decreased, middle-class houses did have more bathrooms; a sizeable minority, about 25 percent, of new suburban designs now had more than one.

The above description seems to suggest that there was almost nothing different about these houses from those of the previous generation, except perhaps their smaller size and more sophisticated technology, both of which were to be expected. But there was at least one very significant change. What is remarkable about the suburban house designs of the 1920s, in the final analysis, has less to do with size or number of bathrooms than with the emotional content of family life. As article after article in the home magazines insisted, children were now the most important members of the household. An environment conducive to children's learning and emotional growth was considered essential. In order to accomplish that purpose, some writers urged parents to provide playrooms, apart from bedrooms, for the children; however, most parents living in suburban houses built during the 1920s would have found that almost impossible. That meant that the house had to revolve around the children; advice-writers insisted on the importance of making sure that children had virtually indestructable play spaces because it was essential to their development that they be able to play "without constant admonitions." As one expert said, "A child must have a life based on his own needs and readiness—one day at a time.[43]

Parents could raise their children properly, such advice implied, only by planning the whole house around the children. Architects and builders quickly followed with plans for such houses. One of the most popular was the "Everyman's House," misnamed because it was really not a house for "every man" but one designed for rearing children: "[A] house built around mother and her baby. . . . [It] was designed, built, furnished, and exhibited to nearly twenty thousand people as a modest cost plan of comfort and convenience for a mother of several children, including a baby." Child expert Pauline Duff agreed; parents should adapt the house entirely to their children's needs. Extra space was children's space, to be used as play areas. Further, the arrangement of closets, bathrooms, and even the laundry area was planned with children in mind. There were practical as well as ideological reasons for such a change; without household help, a woman needed to be able to keep an eye on youngsters while doing her household chores.[44]

In order to gain some respite from the unremitting task of personally doing all the work of her children with "a life based on [their] own needs," some women opted for nursery schools to give their children the untrammeled yet supervised play the experts said they needed. Nursery schools, to which mothers typically sent the children for a half day, grew in popularity in the late 1920s for middle-class children. Yet, in general they were not seen as a means to allow women to have careers. Nursery school advocates insisted that such schools were not in business to give mothers freedom from their children, but to allow children "to live more fully."[45]

Advice-givers, social scientists (particularly the childrearing and marriage "experts"), designers and decorators of suburban houses, writers of domestic fiction in women's magazines—all marched together urging middle-class women to fulfill their individualism through wifehood and motherhood. Indeed, as Nancy Cott has recently demonstrated, "the sexual pattern advanced in social science (and popular culture) of the 1920s confirmed bourgeois marriage as women's destination." But there was more pressure to come. As we saw in the beginning of this chapter, the experience of federal involvement in war housing led some to conclude that there was a place for governmental involvement in middle-class housing. But the demand, not very powerful to begin with, was transient; and postwar, middle-class prosperity laid it temporarily to rest. Nevertheless, political concerns helped to fuel the suburban boom.

THE POLITICS OF SUBURBAN DOMESTICITY

Politics played a role in each wave of suburban advocacy. Its earliest proponents were men who believed that republican values prevailed "within the ring fence of a *country residence*," and that a suburban house was above all the "home of the virtuous citizen."[46] And those who believed in the suburban domestic ideal of the early twentieth century insisted on the importance of suburban life to the polity. In neither of their arguments, however, was a belief in political exclusion the guiding force. It is true that the upper middle-class suburbanites of the Progressive Era deliberately barred those not like themselves from their own communities; however, they also promoted suburbanization (in different suburbs of course) as the cure for the problems of the working classes. Now, by the end of the 1920s, there was an offensive odor of political sanctimoniousness in much suburban advocacy.

First, there was the claim that husbands and wives who chose to live in the suburbs were both more patriotic and more devoted to their children than those who lived in the city. *The American Home* insisted that good citizens owned their homes. Its editor pontificated:

> At the the back and beginning of [patriotism] is the home. Pride of home, reverence for home, affection for home, loyalty to home lie at the very foundation of true patriotism. The home-making propaganda is the best training in national pride that the child or the adult can have. Homeless people make poor citizens. Nomads are seldom patriots. Give us a nation of homes, with each family loving and beautifying and developing its own, and there will be small need for teaching patriotism.[47]

The 1928 Republican candidate for president could not have agreed more. In his acceptance speech for his nomination, Herbert Hoover exulted, "Home ownership has grown," and went on to "rejoice" in the "improvement of the American home . . . the sanctuary of our loftiest ideals, the source of the spiritual energy of our people."[48]

We might dismiss the editorial in *American Home* as self-serving, the words of candidate Hoover as political rhetoric. There was more than a touch of partisan politics in suburban advocacy, since as secretary of commerce during two Republican administrations before his own candidacy for president, Hoover endorsed government sponsorship of business and community groups interested in suburban home ownership. As Gwendolyn Wright has noted, while serving Presidents Harding and Coolidge, "Hoover supported the 'Own Your Home' campaign, launched by the Department of Labor to encourage homeownership; this included the sale of federally financed housing for war workers through local realtors." Further, Wright concluded, "it was private builders and middle-class suburbanites who won the [1928] election for Hoover."[49]

This line of reasoning has merit. The middle-class suburbanites of the 1920s grew ever more insistent on turning their communities into exclusionary havens, and they drew on the power of government, particularly local and state, to assist them. One of the things that this kind of publicly sponsored privatization led to was a greater reliance on home ownership as a neighborhood protective strategy. In the late 1920s, home owners listed their principal reasons for buying a house as "a duty toward the children and their greater comfort and safety, personal privacy and freedom, a sense of achievement in gaining a definite . . . standing, the pride of ownership, and . . . freedom from the dictation of a landlord." Some listed economic reasons, too:

"savings, the building up of an investment, the getting to a tangible return for money spent," but the noneconomic reasons outweighed these.[50]

Not just in *American Home* and the pages of similar magazines, but in the writings of home economists and social observers, home ownership began to be viewed as the hallmark of middle-class "arrival" in society. In fact, editorials in such magazines implied, not to own a house seemed almost to shut a family out of traditional pleasures. John Haynes Holmes insisted that in order to have a "real Christmas" one needed "A home! A child! A loving heart!" The celebration of Christian traditions, he argued, very nearly demanded a single-family house, owned and not rented. According to Holmes, "What does [Christmas] mean if not that life itself, must found itself upon the home, center itself in the child and crown itself with love?" Now, people who did not own suburban homes could be seen as antitraditional as well as unpatriotic.[51]

The political strategy of Hoover, first as commerce secretary and then as president, was to forge links between business and government so that government would, mostly through rhetorical and symbolic gestures, rather than outright subsidy, support national prosperity. (A prosperity, let us remember, that left out about 40 percent of the nation's families, even while white-collar, business, and professional earners profited from it.) Business was the engine that drove the partnership, and business had considerable help from the new specialty of advertising. We saw earlier how advertising influenced the housewife, but marketing strategists also set out to influence the polity.[52]

Christine Frederick, who made it her business to understand how America bought in order to advise companies how to sell even more goods, also advised them how best to get families into suburban houses so that they would need more consumer goods. Frederick viewed the arrival of the first child as the event that sent couples to the suburbs. Her solution to the "problem" of women working after marriage to save for the down payment on a suburban house was for banks to finance young, middle-class, married couples as if the family were a small industrial concern. Frederick urged "the 'industrial banking' corporations" to

> make special provision and special contracts for the loan of money to be used in the financing of new homes. A couple which could qualify as steady and serious intentioned would be able to secure a house, complete furnishings, even radio and automobile, and the best labor-saving equipment, without being required to pay more than a very small initial sum. This burden would be amortized over a period of years, and possibly the credit risk shared by

> parents or friends as endorsers of the "paper." . . . [T]he method should not be looked upon as an "instalment" [sic] method at all; it should be looked upon as *capitalization of a new home*, and have . . . prestige and dignity.[53]

If her plan were not adopted, she insisted, "evils" would result, including "living in small apartments, or rooms rather than homes," as well as "the temptation to have the wife continue at work." Far better, said Frederick, to make "suburban homes" available "at the beginning of marriage." The result would be, in her view, "a more normal and efficient home life begun immediately upon marriage."[54]

Frederick's endorsement of suburban life was cynically manipulative, designed to please the companies that she advised, and was not based on conviction. Expressing her contempt for those consumers whose spending habits made her wealthy, she sneered that suburbs were only for the "general run of people." For "the more sophisticated and individual types," like herself and her husband, she argued in an article for *Outlook Magazine*, suburban life was "a snare and a delusion." Condemning suburban architecture as "sugary and commonplace," she damned suburban life as a mode of existence that "flatten[ed] out . . . personal individuality." The Fredericks enjoyed a house in the country, and a city apartment. ("Our own social life is in the big city, where I go once a week.") She felt no need to live in the suburbs for the sake of her children, since she sent them to boarding schools. Here Frederick made most of the antisuburban criticisms that would appear in greater volume in the 1950s. For herself, an urban sophisticate, suburbs were dull, unbeautiful, and filled with boring people.[55] Still, it was politically and economically expedient for her to devise more ways to get more of those people into them.

Frederick's cynicism did not, any more than did the Republican party's platitudes, force families into the suburbs. Still, there is an element of popular manipulation in the 1920s that was, if not absent in earlier years, at least nowhere nearly so widespread. On the other side of the issue, however, the vast majority of suburbanites seemed happy with their choice. According to one team of sociologists headed by George Lundberg, which studied New York's Westchester County, most suburban families found numerous "satisfactions" in their choice of a community. They particularly expressed their "deep attachment to neighborhood and domestic life and the traditional family pattern."[56] Elsewhwere, suburbanite Ethel Longworth Swift angrily responded to Christine Frederick's attack on the suburbs in a subsequent issue of *Outlook*. Swift, having lived the earlier part of her married life in apartments in "two European capitals and the two largest cities of America," chose to move to a suburb. "We moved because (dare I say it in the presence of those who turn up their sophisticated noses at the suburb) we liked the country, because we believed that our small children would find there a more normal, healthy environment than the city was providing, and because we ourselves wanted a certain material spaciousness." If her children were one reason she chose the suburb, country life within commuting distance for her husband was another. Swift concluded:

> Those whose eyes light to see a swirl of dry leaves in the street in the autumn, whose hearts lift at the crunch of hard snow under their feet in the winter, who watch for the first furry signals of the pussy willow in the springtime, and who, on hot lazy summer afternoons, hear contentedly the locust and the crickets singing their interminable chorus, thank that enterprising realtor, Babbit, for the suburb.[57]

A survey of three hundred suburban commuters confirmed what Smith had argued. Having to commute was more than balanced, as one respondent claimed, by being "enable[d] to bring up [our] daughter in [a] healthy and clean atmosphere, without undesirable associations and contacts in [the] city." And after all, others mentioned, even uptown New Yorkers have to commute if they work downtown, and trains were a lot more comfortable than the subway.[58]

These traditional suburbanites, who had only their families in mind, found themselves joined, toward the close of the decade, by some entrenched urban reformers who had decided that their best chance to transform the urban environment lay outside the city. Planners, who had hoped in the years before World War I that the city, beautified and purged of its corruption, would represent the promise of American life (to use the words of Herbert Croly, who numbered architectural criticism among his many talents), began to turn to the suburbs. By their very nature, planners like to work with as large a canvas as possible—to arrange, rearrange, to have control over architecture, street layout, and landscaping is their profession and their delight. To be given half a city block when one longs for areas measured in square miles is a disappointment indeed. And by the 1920s, open space in cities was measured in half blocks.[59]

There were those who doubted that the suburbs could be reshaped. Lewis Mumford, who would go on to a long career of criticizing the ways in which Americans chose to live, called the suburbs a "wilderness" in 1921, and fretted, "Having failed to create a common life in our modern cities, we have builded Suburbia, which is a common refuge from life, and the remedy is an aggravation of the disease!" And some planners, such as Catherine Bauer, wanted to tear down much that was in both city and suburb and replace it with communities designed in the international style. Other planners agreed with Bauer on what they would like, but knew that to tear down whole cities was unfeasible. There was more land, more space, in the suburbs. And there was less governmental regulation. More than a hundred American cities had planning commissions in the early 1920s, and seventy-five of them had official city plans. The problem was that the commissions had little legal authority to implement those plans, and when they had some time free from their generally fruitless attempts to secure enabling legislation, they had their very survival to worry about. No wonder the comparative open space of the suburbs looked inviting.[60]

As Mark Foster has observed, "the overwhelming majority of urban planners gave up their visions of reconstructing urban cores in the 1920s, opting instead to exercise their creativity by shaping suburban environments." Part of the reason was the sheer enormity of the prospect of making major changes in the city, but part of it as well was the opportunity to make a genuine difference in the way the suburbs of the future would look. Foster again: "By the end of the 1920s, the great majority of American planners endorsed decentralization as a positive social objective."[61]

Some of this country's foremost planners were organized in the Regional Planning Association of America. Their vision was decentralist, but they were also critical of existing suburbs. Their idea was to create environments that would be "aesthetically pleasing, stable and harmonious." Of necessity, most of their work would have to be outside the core cities. Henry Wright and Clarence Stein, advocates of comprehensive planning and believers in Ebenezer Howard's garden city idea as a major component of such planning, were responsible for Radburn, New Jersey, which was perhaps the first attempt to put garden city principles into operation.[62]

Radburn was a planned suburban community outside New York City. And although it was not perhaps a typical upper middle-class suburb, it was upper-middle class nonetheless. In 1928, the first year of development, houses sold for between $7,900 and $18,200, and the families who moved into them were headed by managers, salespeople, engineers, lawyers, and other professionals and executives. Its upper middle-class character reminds us that even the most modern planned community shared the demographic characteristics of conventional suburbs. Nevertheless, in many ways it epitomized the best of the planners' designs for a new suburban America. Its developers intended specifically to create, in the words of the community's historian, "a physical and social landscape that would focus on the family, and especially the child." The houses fronted walkways or parkland, and cars were accommodated on the periphery. Housing critic Catherine Bauer praised Radburn as "the first American attempt to build a complete pre-planned community on English Garden City principles."[63]

What is especially interesting about Radburn is that it demonstrates clearly that planners, even those who considered themselves "advanced," not only abetted the popular urge toward decentralization, but also, in their designs, illustrated how powerful the concept of the centrality of the child had become. Earlier we saw that significance in terms of the individual house. Now, the entire community was to be planned around children. Radburn's first residents chose to live there, in fact, because of the children. As one of them said, "If you want to own a lot of . . . private property, then Radburn isn't the answer. But if you like a place which is at the same time busy and safe for children . . . and where you have beautiful parks and great public amenities, then it's dandy." Others agreed: "My wife was pregnant and we wanted to start a family in that kind of environment rather than the city streets."[64]

The community went to great lengths to provide for its children—there were tennis courts, baseball fields, basketball courts, playgrounds, tot lots, and various other sport and craft activities. The community hired professionals to staff its recreation centers. In the summer there was day camp. Radburn also had nursery schools. The intent was to keep the children close to home, not to free mothers from childcare. Since the houses faced the park, children could always be kept in view. If mothers were using the system to free themselves from the unrelenting duty of childcare, they did not admit it.[65]

There are some important differences between the business-oriented Republicans who advocated suburbanization and the reformers who planned Radburn. The former espoused family privatism and focused on the individual house while the latter wished to build community both aesthetically and culturally. And yet in both suburban visions there was an intense focus on the child as the center of suburban life, on home ownership, and on rejection of the city as an appropriate place to develop family life. What would have happened to Radburn, and whether it would have sparked similar developments, can never be known of course, because the depression intervened. The entire housing industry collapsed.

THE SUBURBS AND THE GREAT DEPRESSION

In the first year or so of the Great Depression, middle-income Americans did not suffer to the same extent as working-class families. In Radburn, for example, houses continued to sell at a brisk clip into 1930, although across the nation housing starts had begun to decline in 1929. Between 1929 and 1933, when the housing industry bottomed out, construction of new houses dropped at an average annual rate of 34 percent. When the housing industry began to recover, it did so slowly. Since the war intervened, it was not until 1948 that new construction surpassed the 1928 level.[66]

The depression took the home magazine industry, just as it did nearly everyone else, by surprise. At first, it was thought to be a temporary "period of readjustment," but that turned out to be a chimera. House designs in such magazines as the *American Home* became more modest. There were houses for $8,000, $7,500, and by 1932, even one for $5,000. But even before *American Home* bowed to the inevitable and admitted that Americans were not buying or building houses, it offered suggestions on how to build a small house designed for expansion so that a family, as the magazine so delicately phrased it, could "make . . . additions to it to take care of their changing needs." The interior design articles began to change as well, emphasizing inexpensive furniture and accessories that would look more expensive than they were. For the middle class, keeping up appearances was still important, and the magazines were there to help them do so.[67]

By the fall of 1931, the depression could no longer be ignored, and middle-class Americans were exhorted to hold fast to traditional values. As one editor insisted, "[I]t so happens that when there comes the testing-time of storm and stress, it is the home makers who stand up against the gales, steadfast because of the roots of home and the life-giving flow beneath them." The editor even claimed, although he must have been self-delusive, that "beneath the loud wailings of the pessimists, one with an ear to hear can detect busy sounds of hammer, saw, and chisel—America building." But building was what America was not doing.[68]

Herbert Hoover, who believed in suburban home ownership, but not in federal subsidies for it, called together a housing committee in December, 1931. He reminded those present that "our people . . . never sing songs about a pile of rent receipts. To own one's home is a physical expression of individualism, of enterprise, of independence, and of the freedom of spirit." Given the president's reliance on voluntarism, even though he was willing to use the federal government to assist that voluntarism, it was not surprising that his committee recommended that building and loan societies lend out more money, and that manufacturers of building supplies develop more extensive financing plans. Even the staunchly supportive *American Home* called the report of Hoover's committee "ultra-conservative."[69]

Despite the unrealistic expectations of President Hoover that private enterprise could solve America's housing problems, his view that Americans ought to live in their own houses, outside the city, would be shared by the Roosevelt administration as well. Of course, there were people who hoped that the new administration would finally let the planners create environments for all Americans, and not simply the upper-middle class, which would allow for community building and comfort. Among them was Catherine Bauer. An American advocate of the newly emerging Bauhaus movement, and important critic of this country's housing practices, Bauer insisted that "there is a better way to do things. That the justling small builders and the front-foot lots and the miserable straggling suburbs and the ideology of individual Home Ownership must go."[70] But Bauer's vision was not to be.

Frank Lloyd Wright, in contrast to European-inspired architects, continued building suburban houses in the 1930s, and had grown increasingly aware of the housing needs of the lower-middle classes. In his "curious mixture" of idealism and reaction, he attempted to meet the needs of less affluent Americans during the depression by designing stripped-down versions of his prairie houses. He called them Usonian (borrowed from Samuel Butler's use of the word Usonia for USA), and he considered these houses to be at least a partial solution to the hard times of ordinary Americans. But even a stripped-down Wright house was out of reach for most. Nevertheless, Wright's decentralist views were more in accord with the popular taste than Bauer's, even if most Americans could not afford his houses.[71]

Within the Roosevelt administration, Rexford Tugwell was the architect of much of the administration's housing policy, and he believed firmly in urban deconcentration. Congress demonstrated its willingness to go along by the nature of the legislation it passed for mortgage insurance and for highway construction. Soon after his inauguration, during the famous Hundred Days, Roosevelt asked Congress to legislate to protect the home owner from mortgage foreclosure. The resulting act set up the Home Owners Loan Corporation (HOLC). Immediately, the HOLC supplied over three billion dollars for mortgages, but it also had more lasting effects. As Kenneth Jackson has noted, "the HOLC is important to history because it introduced, perfected, and proved in practice the feasibility of the long-term, self-amortizing mortgage with uniform payments spread over the whole life of the debt." In the 1920s, home buyers usually carried two mortgages, and had to refinance every five years. Longer term mortgages with equal payments offered much more security. When the HOLC proved their workability, they became a standard practice.[72]

But the HOLC also initiated another practice that would eventually make it difficult for families to choose to stay in the cities, even if they wanted to. HOLC invented "redlining." To do this agency justice, it did not use its racist appraisal system to deny mortgages to people living in "less desirable areas." As Jackson argues, "the damage caused by HOLC came not through its own actions, but through the influence of its appraisal system on the financial decision of other institutions." The HOLC made its appraisal system and its maps available to private lending institutions. And when the National Housing Act created the Federal Housing Administration in June, 1934, the FHA adopted that system, and probably acquired the maps themselves.[73]

FHA-guaranteed mortgages might mean that it would be cheaper to buy than to rent. And as a result, the construction industry slowly began to recover. But the inner cities suffered. The best FHA terms went to the construction of single-family houses, there were few and only short-term loans for house repair (so it would be cheaper to move than to fix up), and the FHA openly refused to lend money for housing in black, integrated, or inner city communities. So if a white family wanted to benefit from the FHA guarantees, and there was even in the 1930s a lot of benefit to be had, it would almost have to move to the suburbs and buy a new house.[74]

The federal government facilitated commuter travel, as well. As Mark Foster has pointed out, "a variety of federal agencies poured millions of dollars into street and highway projects." Spending on such projects was politically popular. The WPA put people to work; and rural, urban, and suburban dwellers all wanted better roads. To add to the message that decentralization was best, under Rexford Tugwell's guidance, the government even sponsored three suburban towns, incorporating the traditional values of the importance of the nuclear family and a wife who stayed at home. Although there were only three greenbelt towns, and Congress declined to authorize more, their very existence came about because Tugwell and the President both believed that families ought to live away from the cities, and they managed to persuade the congress to at least partial agreement.[75] The policies of the national government during the New Deal—its spending for highway building, its mortgage guarantees, and the greenbelt communities—institutionalized the process of suburbanization for middle-class, white Americans.

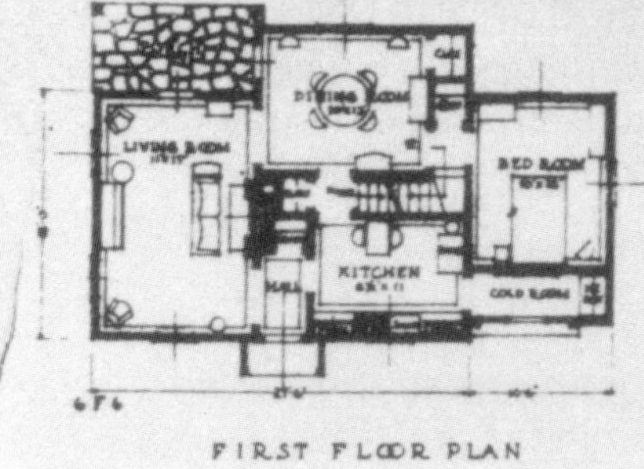

FIRST FLOOR PLAN

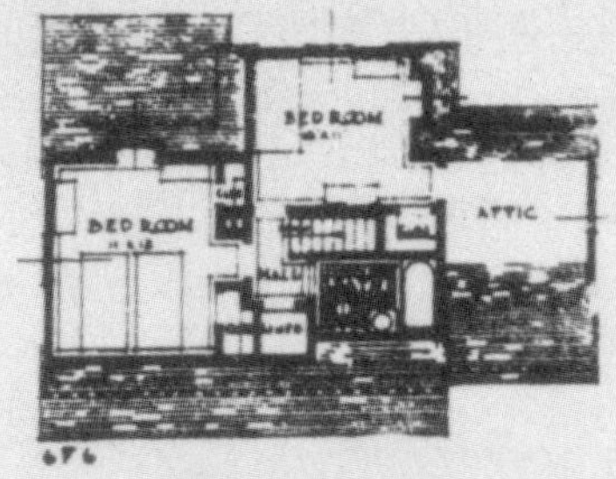

SECOND FLOOR PLAN

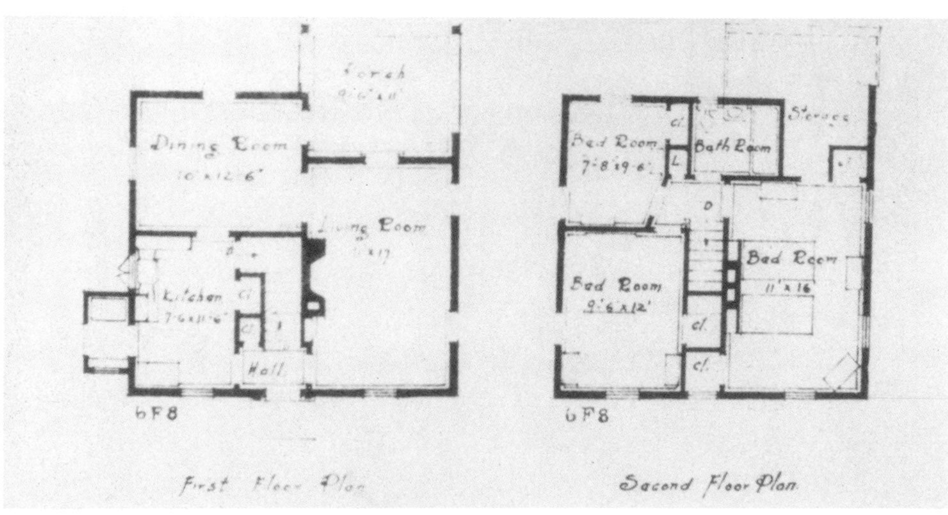

Designers of suburban houses in the twenties built upon the open floor plans of the Progressive Era. Exteriors manifested a blatant nostalgic urge. From Marcia Mead, *Homes of Character*, 1926.

Altadena
Woodlands

Rigali & Veselich
Subdividers ~ Realtors

Vaillancourt

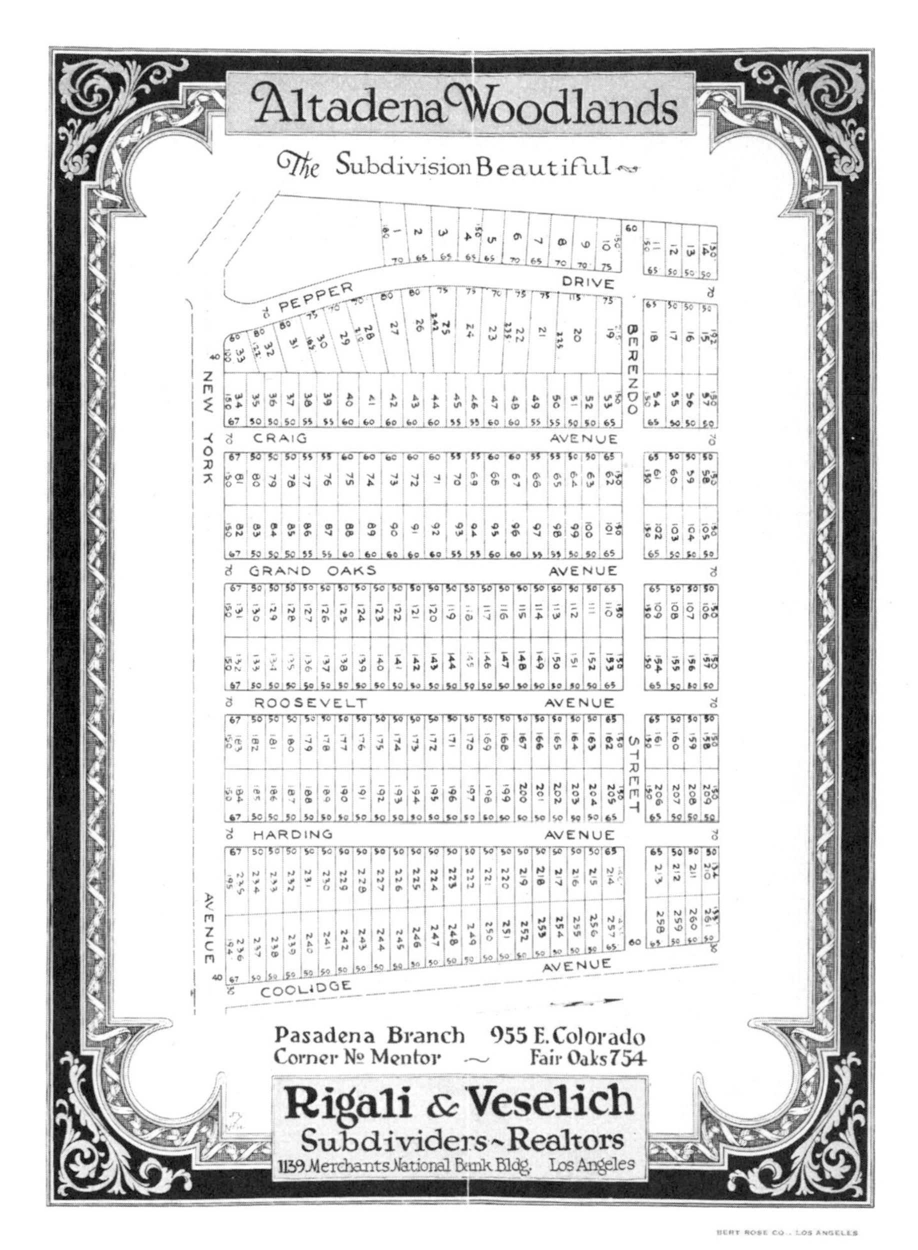

The developers of Altadena Woodlands, in suburban Los Angeles, presented a bucolic and pastoral image in the cover for this advertisement. The plot plan, however, unlike the evocative drawing, showed an unimaginative grid without provision for parks or orange groves. Courtesy of the Huntington Library, San Marino, California.

A new suburban development in Los Angeles County in the late 1920s. Courtesy of the Huntington Library, San Marino, California.

The developers of Palos Verdes Estates had the advantage of a spectacular site upon which to create their vision of an ideal suburban community. From *The Palos Verdes of Today,* 1926. Courtesy of the Huntington Library, San Marino, California.

1. *The East facade of a lovely home which overlooks Malaga Cove Plaza.*
2. *A veritable bit of Old Spain.*
3. *Native stones have been used to good effect in the approach to this home on Via Ramon.*
4. *An old California type house on Rosita Place, looking north toward Santa Monica Bay.*
5. *Facing the sunset sky—one of the earlier homes on the heights of Montemalaga.*
6. *A thousand-square-mile view from this charming residence on Via del Monte.*
7. *A sunken garden one year old in a Malaga Cove home.*
8. *"Quiet seclusion of walled patio." Architecturally true to the old Spanish-California type.*
9. *Reminiscent of the romance of a bygone day.*

Potential Palos Verdes residents had to have their plans approved by the community's Art Jury, to insure architectural harmony. Courtesy of the Huntington Library, San Marino, California.

As a community, Palos Verdes Estates possessed a distinctive appearance. Inside many of the houses, however, was an interior plan typical of suburban America in the 1920s. Courtesy of the Huntington Library, San Marino, California.

· PERSPECTIVE ·

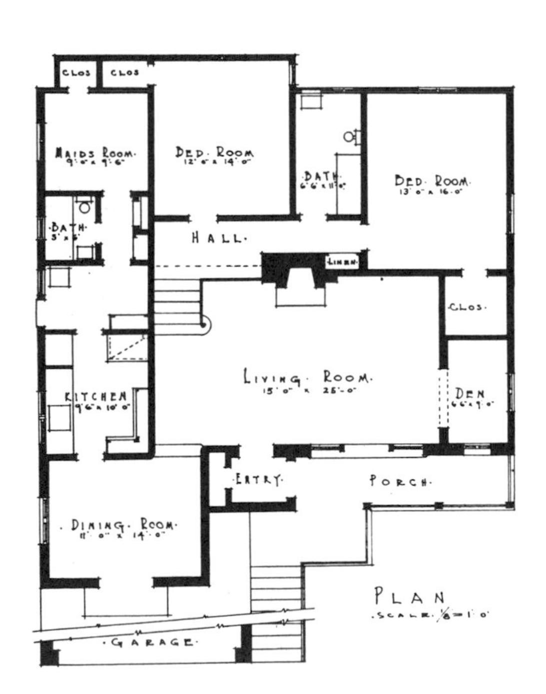

The nursery play school at Palos Verdes provided "supervised play in the sunshine, . . . [and] lessons in French, music, and rhythm" for children between the ages of three and six, every weekday morning. Courtesy of the Huntington Library, San Marino, California.

CHAPTER SIX

The Suburban City Beautiful

[We have] set out to create the Suburban City Beautiful. . . . Palos Verdes, City of Dreams Come True, beckons you to a life of Health, Happiness, Contentment.

THE PALOS VERDES OF TODAY, 1926

Perhaps it will seem to readers to be a dizzying trip from the railroad suburbs of turn-of-the-century Philadelphia to the automobile suburbs of 1920s Los Angeles, with scarcely a refueling stop in the middle of the country, or a detour to the South. But our destination was not arbitrarily chosen. If we want to understand twentieth-century suburban life, we must go to Los Angeles, the archetype of the twentieth-century American metropolis. The white, middle-class, midwestern Protestants who wrested Los Angeles from its original settlers had the opportunity to create the kind of city that they believed represented the hopes and dreams of people like themselves. Their world view, which in the words of one historian "everywhere dominated the layout of greater Los Angeles," was suburban. Other cities that developed in the same period—Detroit and Minneapolis are two good examples—looked more like the older cities of the East and Midwest, but the City of the Angels began its life as an Anglo-American city decentralized and deconcentrated. As early as the 1880s, when Los Angeles grew from a town of eleven thousand to a thriving small city of over fifty thousand, its residents conceived of their community as a new kind of environment, one that would combine the culture, civility, and business opportunities of an urban center with the single-family houses, gardens, and sense of community of the suburb. By 1930, when the Los Angeles metropolitan district totalled 2.3 million people, they still retained that vision.[1]

In 1880 Los Angeles had been an isolated pueblo, but by the middle of the decade two things had happened that would change the sleepy town irrevocably—the transcontinental railroad arrived, and the technology became available to irrigate the arid land. Almost immediately there was a spectacular land boom, setting off a frenzy of subdividing and speculation. Right from the beginning, the settlers and speculators capitalized on the suburban vision. Whether the subdivisions were within the existing city limits or beyond them, developers advertised them as suburban. Land dealers in the Malabar Tract, some five miles from the town center in 1886, sold a suburban philosophy as well as a house lot: Malabar, they said, "combines the advantage of city with the healthfulness, lovely scenery, and low taxation of country property, and it may safely be predicted that the neighborhood in which it is situated will become very shortly the favorite spot for suburban residences." And in 1887 an auction broadside for Alhambra called it, in capital letters, "the GARDEN SUBURB of Los Angeles."[2]

Even as the auctioneers brought their gavels down in Alhambra, the first great land boom was on the verge of collapse. Many of the buyers were themselves speculators, hoping to turn their purchases over for a quick profit. Seeing the warning signs, some developers attempted to distinguish their offerings from those of the land schemers. The owners of the Moran Tract, for example, insisted in very large print, that the lots "are being rapidly SOLD TO ACTUAL SETTLERS." Others combined appeals to investors and potential home owners. Orangedale's subdividers promised buyers: "Your lots will resell in sixty days," at the same time declaring that "the place to build your home is ORANGEDALE."[3] The subdividers saw no incongruity in presenting a tract for sale both to speculators and potential residents; such a pairing of what may appear to be incompatible, or at least disparate, goals continued well into the 1920s. In this as in so many other ways Los Angelenos began to do things and have ideas that later spread to the rest of the country. Since World War II, it has become customary for Americans to consider their houses as "investments," for which they expect to turn a profit. Although this notion was not exactly *invented* in Los Angeles, land developers here did bring a heightened emphasis to the idea of buying a house for future profit, rather than for security.

The boom of the 1880s collapsed in 1887, but Los Angeles continued to grow, and to grow in the path its citizens and land speculators laid out for it in the 1880s. By the mid-1890s its citizenry had recovered confidence. By 1900 more than a hundred thousand people made Los Angeles their home, and the land use patterns of the city and surrounding county had become what they were to remain—deconcentrated, decentralized, and dispersed. The transit system grew to accommodate the way the city had developed, and not the other way around. The "big, red cars" of the Pacific Electric interurban railway system served the entire metropolitan area well into the 1920s. It was a mass transit system that excelled those of the older cities. Transit magnate Henry Huntington actually made his fortune in the land he sold for subdivision and the water companies he controlled that made the land habitable, and not in his transit ventures themselves, which sometimes turned a very small profit, sometimes broke even, and mostly lost money.[4]

Dana Bartlett, social gospel minister and progressive reformer in the early twentieth century, proclaimed Los Angeles "the better city" because its low density development, he believed, "would prevent this city from experiencing the horrors of congestion, particularly for the poor," that plagued the eastern cities. Bartlett, like most social observers, equated the single-family house with the virtuous family. Los Angeles, he believed, should come to serve as a model for the restructuring of all American cities. Bartlett suggested that the city's low density was responsible for its comparative prosperity, not recognizing that what he saw was a city whose anglo population mostly consisted of relatively prosperous settlers from the Midwest. There were almost no immigrants from southern and eastern Europe, and the city's native Mexican population was shunted aside by the newcomers. Although the logic was faulty, other observers who saw the same residential dispersion reached the same conclusion. Even a railroad guide to southern California sounded the same theme, informing the tourists: "There is no huddling of people in the residence parts of the city," and then adding, in the particularly stilted exuberance that marked such publications: "The suburbs of Los Angeles are not less pleasant than the city itself, and possess individual excellences that are ample argument for their existence."[5]

Housing reformer William Smythe agreed. Los Angeles and cities that would follow in her footsteps, he insisted, "will naturally spread over a vast area—the vaster the better. They should spread until they meet the country, and until beautiful forms of urban life blend almost imperceptibly into beautiful forms of rural life." Los Angelenos created a suburbanized city from the beginning, unhampered by an urban form inherited from a mercantile or industrial past. They possessed the means, in the form of modern transportation technology. They had the desire, in the form of a citizenry composed of settlers from the East and Midwest who desired to recreate a small town atmosphere with the advantages of urban life. Their intent was not to deny urbanity, but to recreate it in a new, decentralist form, reflecting the new suburban domestic ideal. As Elaine Tyler May noted perceptively, middle-class Los Angelenos in the early twentieth century created an intense family life in suburban environments that they hoped would both protect the family from the dangers of urban life and allow its members to enjoy its material blessings.[6]

They succeeded, to a remarkable degree. If by the 1960s that success had become the city's undoing, in the 1920s it served as a model for the rest of the United States. As historian Robert Fogelson has noted, "[M]ost American metropolises have duplicated, to a remarkable degree, the pattern of Los Angeles' landscape, transportation, community, politics, and planning." Los Angeles in the 1920s had become this country's prototypical city.

PALOS VERDES: THE "QUINTESSENCE OF LOS ANGELES"

To an easterner, no suburb of Los Angeles seems representative. Some, like certain sections of Pasadena, are early-twentieth century havens of craftsman bungalows; others could have housed nineteenth-century royalty; and some of the earliest suburbs look as if they might have been transplanted whole from pre-Frank Lloyd Wright Oak Park, Illinois. And yet, taken altogether, there seems to be a clear pattern, at least by the 1920s—in the suburbs housing the prospering middle classes, the builders, now called "developers," attempted to create architectural harmony and to exclude any heterogeneity of race or class. Although no one suburb exactly typifies the Los Angeles of the decade following World War I, "Palos Verdes Estates," in the words of the principal historian of the city, Robert Fogelson, "most clearly illustrated the pattern prevailing by the 1920s." Fogelson called Palos Verdes "the quintessence of Los Angeles," and Robert Fishman some twenty years later situated it in a long tradition of planned communities, beginning with Llewellyn Park in New Jersey in the 1850s, and extending through Riverside, Illinois, in the post–Civil War era. "The Palos Verdes design," Fishman noted, "was a synthesis of the Riverside idea of community and the Llewellyn Park concept of the dramatic picturesque." Conceived by speculators, laid out by the son of the great planner Frederick Law Olmsted, Palos Verdes was transformed by its residents into a community not only emblematic of suburban Los Angeles, but exemplifying suburban America itself in the years before the depression.[7]

The Palos Verdes peninsula faces the Pacific Ocean, and in the early twentieth century was almost entirely undeveloped. About 17,000 acres belonged to sheep rancher George Bixby, who sold 16,000 to developers in 1913. Two of those developers went bankrupt in quick succession, the beneficiary of the bankruptcies being the banker, Frank Vanderlip, who became the owner in 1914. Vanderlip's initial idea was to develop all 16,000 acres as country estates for the wealthy. He built his own house there, and planned to engage Frederick Law Olmsted, Jr., to plan the rest of the community. The war intervened, and for several years Vanderlip's house stood in solitary grandeur. It is not clear what changed Vanderlip's mind, but after the war he decided against his original plan, and allowed real estate promoter E. G. Lewis to take an option on all but the land surrounding his own house.[8]

E. G. Lewis intended to develop the entire acreage, and to finance the venture through what Robert Sherwood has called "an involved profit sharing plan that was radical for its day." Although Lewis's ideas generated considerable enthusiasm, he was not able to raise the money. His option lapsed, and in 1923 Frank Vanderlip once again took over the task of development. He decided to begin with developing only 3,200 acres, to be called, in a nostalgic glance backwards at his original intentions, Palos Verdes Estates. Frederick Law Olmsted Jr. was still interested; he, Myron Hunt, and Charles H. Cheney took charge of the planning. Although they soon removed Lewis from the project, the men who took over shared his commitment to the idea of planning. Like the earlier Forest Hills Gardens in New York, like Roland Park in Baltimore, and like the proposed Ready Villas in Haddonfield and Overbrook Farms, Palos Verdes was to be a planned community.[9]

When the developers designed and promoted Palos Verdes Estates, their initial marketing techniques were very similar to those used in Overbrook Farms, modified by the changes in middle-class family life that had occurred in the first decade and a half of the twentieth century. Responding to the trend toward greater husband-wife togetherness in the prewar years, advertising brochures for Palos Verdes Estates emphasized the activities that couples could enjoy together; since this was southern California, they also stressed the outdoor life. There were to be bridle paths, beaches, parks, a golf club, and tennis courts. The earliest promotional literature took the recreational idea very far; the community's advertising slogan was: "Palos Verdes: Where Your Home is Your Playground." Its illustrations showed page after page of couples on horseback, on the golf course, and on the beach admiring the views. For the facilities for this outdoor recreation, Vanderlip and Olmsted set aside 25 percent of the land.[10]

Perhaps somewhat fearful that the idea of home as playground had too hedonistic a sound, the developers combined it with the idea that the planned outdoor facilities not only promised fun for the couples who chose to live here, but also good health. Photographs of the water company share space in the brochures with those of other amenities. One might argue that in Los Angeles, where water was a problem, prospective residents would seek assurance that the community had water; such illustrations, however, had their symbolic uses as well. The promotional material for Overbrook Farms had incorporated similar imagery, including pictures of the wells and the heating plant. In these two suburbs, thirty years and a continent apart, there were some commonalities. One early Palos Verdes prospectus, indeed, pledged its residents "health, happiness, and contentment."[11]

The emphasis of the developers on their commitment to creating a planned and protected residential environment was reminiscent of the prewar suburbs as well, but it also mirrored the new exclusionary virulence of the 1920s. More was at stake than architectural harmony and enforced socioeconomic homogeneity; such a commitment had come to include specific residential covenants formalizing the exclusion of blacks and other unwanted racial and ethnic groups.[12] Some restrictions were specifically intended to ensure that Palos Verdes Estates would remain a community of single-family houses. Ninety percent of the buildable land was restricted to single-family detached housing. Business, apartments, and "house courts" were relegated to a strictly defined, and confined, 10 percent of the land: "No flats, apartments, duplexes, house courts, or stores are permitted in the single family neighborhoods, but only at very limited convenient centers where they have been designed to be as much out of the way of the strictly home neighborhoods as possible." The developers planned four clusters of stores and service stations with the multifamily dwellings, located in each of the "communities" that comprised Palos Verdes Estates—Malaga Cove, Lunada Bay, Valmonte, and Miraleste. In addition, the developers planned for smaller clusters of "local store building groups" about a mile apart, for convenience.[13]

Vanderlip and his associates, in their "constant effort . . . to build . . . an ideal garden suburb and residence park, with all the advantages of the city, in the country," made it clear that one of the most important things they had to sell was status. In language almost identical to Wendell and Smith's promises to potential residents of Overbrook Farms at the turn of the century, the developers of Palos Verdes insisted that "every purchaser . . . will feel secure in knowing that his home can never be damaged by any unsightly or undesirable structure either upon adjoining lots or in any part of Palos Verdes Estates."[14]

Racial covenants kept out specific ethnic groups; cost restrictions kept the unprosperous from buying a homesite. Frederick Law Olmsted, Jr., confessed that he designed the community "predominantly for fairly prosperous people." Although the restrictions varied by section, no one could build a house here with construction costs of less than $4,000, exclusive of the cost of the lot itself. On some of the grander building sites, minimum construction costs exceeded $20,000. One section of Lunada Bay, for example, had construction costs ranging from $6,000 on the smaller lots to $25,000 on large lots with spectacular views. On most of the lots in this section, home owners could expect to spend between $6,000 and $12,000. Not all sections were as expensive, however. In one section, one could have bought a small lot—about a sixth of an acre—and built a $4,000 house on it. Most lots, however, required building cost minimums of $6,000. Assuming $2,000 for a moderately sized lot, one could have a house at Palos Verdes for $6,000 to $10,000, a not unreasonable cost for professionals and corporate managers.[15]

The bankers, lawyers, engineers, salesmen, and businessmen who moved their families to Palos Verdes, some from the Los Angeles area, others from various parts of the country, not only accepted but endorsed the restrictive covenants imposed by the developers, in spite of the fact that to some extent they limited both individual liberty and full self-government. Palos Verdes Estates, because it was in unincorporated Los Angeles County, did not have a local government. As a result, the Palos Verdes Homes Association conducted all the political business of the community. In the association, each *building site* had one vote. Before the community had very many residents, the developers by this means controlled most of the votes. Later, as the estates filled up, only the home owners could vote—tenants in single-family houses owned by absent residents, people who lived in the house courts or the apartments, as well as domestic servants were effectively disenfranchised in the local community. There were far more owners than renters, and these owners never questioned the idea that property holding was the most legitimate basis on which to allocate political power; consequently they endorsed the association's practice of assigning voting rights by site ownership. In words much like those appearing in such magazines as *American Home,* or in the speeches of Herbert Hoover, the *Palos Verdes Bulletin* noted, "it . . . makes better citizens of people to own their own homes. It gives them stability . . . and it gives them . . . a field of daily exercise and recreation which keeps them young and entertains them better than any game which cannot result in real achievement."[16]

For suburbanites here as elsewhere it was an article of faith that home owners were "better citizens." In 1923, one of the early investors in Palos Verdes Estates, *Los Angeles Evening Express* publisher F. W. Kellogg, equated investing in this land scheme with the patriotic fervor that had led him to buy liberty bonds during the late war. Palos Verdes, insisted Kellogg, "typif[ied] American citizenship, [and] . . . American patriotism." A few years later, the editors of the *Palos Verdes Bulletin* took up the same theme. In an essay in honor of the birthdays of Presidents Washington and Lincoln the *Bulletin* averred, "Our greatest presidents, Washington and Lincoln, to whom our thoughts turn naturally this month, could have accomplished nothing without that great power back of them, the American home . . . [the] irresistible force [that] founded our nation."[17] The suburbs had come full circle. Ownership once more, as it had not since the nineteenth century, determined who had a right to control community development.

The Homes Association served as a form of general self-government, at least for the home owners. And the Art Jury scrutinized every house plan—rejecting, accepting, or modifying as they saw fit. The Art Jury had the final say on any house built in the estates. With the exception of the few areas in which the American colonial- and tudor-inspired designs held sway, the architecture was what has come to be called Californian, a 1920s' interpretation of Spanish-style, domestic architecture. The structures were low, of one or at most two stories; their roofs were of red tile, and their exteriors most often stuccoed. Because the land was irregular, some of the houses were built into the hillsides. The roads curved through the development, opening up views of houses and the Pacific Ocean. Olmsted's house, one of the first to be built, replicated a classic hacienda, surrounded by pepper and eucalyptus trees. Most of the houses, however, were not reproductions but evocations of a particular style. The Spanish inspiration was to southern California in the 1920s what the American colonial or Tudor was to suburbs in the eastern United States during the same period.[18]

Initially, prospective residents hired their own architects, who submitted their plans to the Art Jury. But by 1927 they could choose plans selected from a group of designs made available by the community. The new designs were very similar to those already in place, they required less supervision by the home owner, and the Art Jury had already approved them. The interiors of most of the houses in Palos Verdes, with the exception of grander haciendas in the exclusive sections, were very similar to suburban houses built everywhere in the United States during the 1920s, allowing for the greater number of terraces and verandas that the climate encouraged. The plans were open, with the living room dominating, and the dining room defined by archways rather than doors. Even when residents strove for originality, they did so in a predictable way. The Gartz family, for example, in order to be unusual, decided on a circular dining room, and earned a photograph in the *Palos Verdes Bulletin*. But it is not its uniqueness that strikes the modern observer, it is rather the way in which the placement of the room and the general organization of space conforms to the typical house of the 1920s, opening to the rest of the living area by means of a wide arch. Most of the houses in Palos Verdes had similar interiors, and they usually also had three bedrooms, although there were some much larger dwellings. In short, although the houses of Palos Verdes were unusual in their harmony, their site placement, and their owners' willingness to be guided in their landscaping by Olmsted and his coworkers, they did not break any new architectural ground. As Robert Fishman noted, the Art Jury "never discriminated against banality, especially when it came clad in stucco and a red tile roof."[19]

How ironic! Palos Verdes excluded Mexican-Americans, who, as of the 1930 census, had been reclassified from white to non-white, from living in the estates, yet Mexican-inspired architecture was mandated in most of the area. (A few sections, the largest of which was called Margate, allowed "colonial architecture or the English type steep-roofed building" so that people "who could not be happy with the transition to mediterranean architecture" might build houses in which they could be happy.) With those few exceptions, the Spanish designs, now renamed "Californian" to take away the distasteful ethnic implications, prevailed.[20]

Although the Art Jury insisted on an architecture of nostalgia, in one respect it was entirely modern. Palos Verdes was designed and built as an automobile suburb. As the developers noted, "nearly every lot must be provided with a private garage," and therefore "special attention has been given to the prevention of unsightly garages." Most designs incorporated the garage into the house, a solution that became commonplace in American design. "Architects and builders," they suggested, "have learned that the garage can very agreeably be made a part of most dwellings." The family car had become a part of the family.[21]

The men who had conceived of the idea of Palos Verdes Estates envisioned a community in which upper middle-class families could own their own homes in a restricted and protected environment, where they would spend their leisure hours on the golf course, the bridle paths, or the beach. Although they gave a great deal of thought to architecture and recreational facilities, they paid little attention to the development of community institutions. And unlike the planners of Radburn, who a few years later would design the entire community around the needs of children, they did not appear to consider the place of children here. In the beautiful and richly photographed magazines that initially served as promotional literature for Palos Verdes, there were no pictures of children. Men and women were everywhere doing things together, but even a photograph of the school was without children. It almost seemed as if the developers took literally their marketing slogan, "where your home is your playground." There were similarly no provisions for donating land to churches; indeed, the promotional literature did not even mention any nearby opportunities for religious observances.[22]

FROM ADULT PLAYGROUND TO CHILD-CENTERED COMMUNITY

When the families actually arrived, they restructured many of the developers' ideas. One of the first things that the residents discarded was the original marketing slogan. Parents of young children, they did not like the frivolous implications of the playground-for-adults motif. Instead, the community motto became "Palos Verdes for the Joy of Living." And in the community's monthly bulletin, unlike the earlier promotional material put out by the developers, children abounded—at school, at play, on patios, on the beach, in the park. In their concentration on their children, the residents of Palos Verdes were representative suburbanites, no different from the Westchester County (New York) commuter who asserted, "We came out to the suburbs for a home life and we don't want anything else."[23]

The residents of Palos Verdes expressed their family-oriented ideas to the outside world by giving considerable public attention to their children's education. The school received enormous coverage in the *Bulletin*. No activity was too small to be reported, whether it was a photo of the birdhouses built by the boys or tree planting on Arbor Day. There was only one school, for grades one through eight, although a second one was completed in 1930. The first, the Malaga Cove School, was well-staffed, and enjoyed the supplement of private funds from the parents and raised by the women's club. Its teachers all held baccalaureate degrees, rather than normal school certificates, and most had considerable post-graduate training. At least one had a master's degree. Palos Verdes parents sat on the school board and had considerable influence on the curriculum. In addition to the standard academic subjects, the Malaga Cove school had a manual training department for the boys (staffed by women teachers), and a domestic science department for the girls. The boys made the usual benches and birdhouses, while the girls sewed and cooked. The school also had a student government, intended to inculcate "democratic principles" in order to lay "the foundation for good citizenship."[24]

It was the women of the community who accomplished the change in emphasis. George Gibbs may have been responsible for the new community motto, but it was his wife and the other women who founded the Palos Verdes Women's Club in 1926 who transformed the image of the community into a child-centered one. In common with women's clubs of the 1920s in general, this one deemphasized the political and civic interests that had preoccupied women's clubs in the earlier years. Although the club claimed to "devote itself to the social and civic welfare of the community," its real interest, besides organizing social life, was its own children's education. The club's first projects included a resolution to the board of education in favor of "school gardens" for the children, and to the Palos Verdes Homes Association requesting that the developers speedily finish the tennis courts.[25]

The women's club was the principal group in Palos Verdes that attempted to focus the use of leisure time around the family and community. A woman had to live in the estates in order to belong, but the club was not in any further ways exclusionary. It "cordially welcomed" new residents as members, and publicized its doings extensively. (Exclusive clubs, as Carol O'Connor has shown for Scarsdale, eschewed publicity and kept a very low profile.) Women's clubs during this period were organized into "departments" or committees, and a club's committees offered a pretty good indication of the kinds of activities in which it was interested. In the beginning, this club had three committees—art, education, and entertainment. By 1930 it had altered its structure to include men in some activities and to increase the emphases on children and on socializing. Five departments replaced the earlier three. There were garden, art, and child-study groups, plus a "tea cups section," which met solely for conversation, and which was apparently one of the best subscribed groups. These four groups met during the day, but a fifth group, for "public affairs," met in the evening, and husbands attended as well.[26]

At first, all of the events sponsored by the club had to be held in individual houses, because there were no community buildings. The Olmsteds, for example, hosted the club's "community dinner" in June. In August 1926 the Malaga Cove school auditorium was completed, and the club then had the space to hold large dances, which it proceeded to do almost monthly. It was not until the library was completed in 1930 that the club started to hold some of its meetings there, but most of the sections continued to meet in individual houses. There was no neat shift from homes to public spaces, either for the women's club or other kinds of community activities.[27]

Although the women's club was the most important organization attempting to build a community consciousness around family life, there were more informal mechanisms as well. One was the communal observance of Christmas Eve. The ways that this observance changed tells us much about the development of the community. The earliest reference to this Christmas event was in 1925. Adapting what the residents believed to be a Mexican tradition, the families of Palos Verdes walked in procession to the Olmsted house, which was a replica of a Mexican hacienda. Two children, dressed as Mary and Joseph, knocked successively on the doors, where they were told there was no room. Eventually, they were let in, and a children's choir sang carols. For the finale, the children engaged in the custom of striking the piñata, which was filled with gifts, for which they scrambled. Afterward, families went home to their own observances.[28]

The modern reader might find it puzzling that the residents of Palos Verdes, who abhorred the Mexican-Americans with whom they shared the city of Los Angeles, not only adopted Mexican domestic architecture but also their holiday customs. Although the irony seems to have escaped them, perhaps they sensed the contradiction; nevertheless, anglo southern Californians did not address that contradiction by becoming more tolerant. Instead, they excised the Mexican connotations from both their architecture and their celebrations. They called the architecture "Californian" and by 1926 they called their Christmas Eve ritual a "Spanish" rather than Mexican custom. That year, many of the residents dressed in "Spanish costume," with two children once again playing Mary and Joseph. The ritual of knocking at the door and being denied entrance was repeated, followed this time by a New Testament reading. The exuberant custom of striking the piñata was eliminated; instead a "grab-bag" was passed around. By 1927, the ritual had become briefer and less important to the community, as attention shifted to the school Christmas play and a community dance under the sponsorship of the women's club. By 1929 the Olmsted observance had become "the usual brief Christmas fête"; and by 1930 it had ceased to be, because the Olmsteds had pulled up stakes and returned to Brookline, Massachusetts.[29] In that year the Christmas observance was held in the school auditorium, before Christmas Eve, and all Mexican or Spanish references had disappeared entirely. The "theme" was "Jesus, the light of the world," and it consisted of New Testament readings and carols. Some members of the community wanted to retain some Christmas Eve tradition, so candles were passed out to the residents to take home and light if they wanted carolers to sing at their house.[30]

Changes in the Christmas observance marked changes in the way Palos Verdes displayed its community consciousness. In the earliest years, when everyone knew the neighbors, the suburb did indeed seem to be much like a small town. Meetings and community gatherings took place in people's houses. But as the community grew, residents knew each other less intimately. Activities were more likely to be events where people grew to know each other rather than the gathering of small groups of friends. But something else was going on as well. The residents, while they continued for the most part to build houses in the "California" style, had departed from any idea of their community as uniquely connected to California's Mexican heritage. As if to emphasize its sense of Palos Verdes as an American suburb like any other, the women's club in 1927 started an annual "Colonial Ball," and it was not the conquistadores that they commemorated. A couple dressed as George and Martha Washington presided, and the ball was such a success that it remained an annual tradition.[31]

Even in ostensibly adult events like the colonial ball, the children of Palos Verdes were not excluded; at the ball, they danced the "children's minuet." And at Christmas they presented holiday plays for the women's club. It was the women's club that arranged for the children to participate. Indeed, the club devoted the bulk of its energy to child-related projects. Women's clubs had traditionally cared deeply about childrearing; after all, the "expert mothers" of the early twentieth century often became experts in their women's club study groups. Nevertheless, the interest of the earlier generation of clubwomen in children differed in that it included children of the entire society as well as their own children.[32]

In the Progressive Era, women's clubs tended to be political—either overtly or under the guise of humanitarian concerns. In Los

Angeles and its suburbs during that earlier period, the Friday Morning Club was the preeminent women's club, and its members involved themselves directly in civic and political concerns. They served on the city's Playground Commission, Housing Commission, Juvenile Court, League of Justice, and the boards of the Children's Hospital and the Orphan's Home. Married clubwomen considered their club activities as auxiliary to their roles as wives and mothers. As one of them said, "Instead of interrupting home life, [the women's club] promotes it at its best."[33]

In the Friday Morning Club, involvement with progressive political and civic issues continued into the war years; but such involvement, particularly in areas regarding women's rights, had become increasingly controversial. And by the 1920s the Friday Morning Club was able to applaud the Italian fascist Santa Borghese, who was on tour in America, when she told them that Benito Mussolini was "a self-made man, finely-made and cultured." By then, the reformers had become a minority. In 1924, after a bitter battle for the club's presidency, political and social conservative Florence Kriedler rather easily defeated an opponent considered "modern in her ideas and very progressive."[34]

Political controversy did not disappear entirely from the Friday Morning Club—its members could still listen to a lecture on birth control, and Roger Baldwin of the American Civil Liberties Union spoke, once, to them—but something had changed. The zeal for social justice had eroded. The members became immersed in club politics and ignored national issues. They turned their energies to planning fashion shows of mid-nineteenth-century garments, or mounting vaudeville shows. The club also created a "Junior Division" for young married women that appeared to focus solely on social events: They rode horses, played tennis, swam, held dances, put on amateur musical reviews, and learned fancy cookery. Whatever lingering hold the Progressive Era reforming clubwomen had on the Friday Morning Club as a whole in the 1920s, it was not apparent among the Juniors. Even the depression did not rouse the club. As late as the spring of 1931 it had not had a single program on current American economic conditions.[35]

If the Friday Morning Club, which had been noted for its civic consciousness, had lost so much of its political energy, suburbanites out in Palos Verdes could not have been expected to be any different. Their major focus throughout the 1920s and early 1930s continued to be their children. The women's club did the fund raising for the school cafeteria, and its members sat on the board of education. Outside of the school, it was the clubwomen who decided that Palos Verdes needed a Boy Scout troop. Under its sponsorship, a committee of local men supervised the troop, and a teacher in a nearby military school became scoutmaster. And the "children's dances" were also the creation of the club.[36]

Although they did not do so directly under the auspices of the club, it was also women's club members who founded the nursery play school. For children aged three to six, the nursery school, like those described in chapter five, did not exist to free mothers from the constant demands of childrearing; rather, the mothers created it, they said, because their small children were too isolated from others their own age. Mothers took their children every weekday from 8:45 to 11:30, and the children had "supervised play in the sunshine . . . [and] lessons in French, music, and rhythm." The play school was private, not because the women were adverse to having their young children in public school, but because the state board of education would not allow Palos Verdes to create a public kindergarten. For a time, the president of the women's club directed the play school, but there was also a paid staff.[37]

Finally, the members of the women's club were responsible for bringing regular religious instruction, in the form of a Sunday school, to the children of Palos Verdes. It may seem surprising to realize that Palos Verdes did not have a single church during the 1920s and early 1930s, and although there were occasional attempts to have church services in the school auditorium, such efforts occurred only sporadically. A lack of interest in organized religion was fairly common in the suburbs of the 1920s, however. In suburban Westchester County, New York, for example, only about 40 percent of the men in executive and professional positions ever went to church, even irregularly. Among the women in the same survey, only half ever attended church services. Some of those who never attended church belonged to church-sponsored women's clubs. One sociological study suggested that the higher the income of a family, the less likely its members were to attend church. Palos Verdes adults appear to have fit this pattern. They do not seem to have been regular churchgoers—at least not to the point that it concerned them to have a church within their own community.[38]

The lack of adult interest in church services for themselves did not deter the Sunday school founders, who created an all-woman Sunday school committee. The committee secured three teachers, two of them clubwomen and the third a woman religious studies student from a nearby college, and opened the school at the Gibbs's house in May 1926. The Sunday school was nondenominational, but obviously Protestant, and grew large enough to be moved to the school auditorium in September, with attendance at twenty-three in September and up to thirty-six by December of that same year.[39]

Palos Verdes women, in the club and on their own, took pains to see that their children's lives were filled with organized activities. Not all of them were sponsored directly by the club or its members, but the women supported the school's provision of swimming lessons and a long list of extra-curricular activities ranging from an aviation club to nature study, books, and current events. The riding club offered lessons. There were tennis tournaments. And besides the Boy Scouts, there were Boy Rangers and Campfire Girls. The pattern is similar to the one at Radburn. There, the planners themselves had tried deliberately to build an environment for children. At Palos Verdes, the developers had had different ideas, but the residents recreated the community so that children had a very large place in it. The mothers of Palos Verdes, like the mothers of Radburn, left no evidence that they viewed the nursery school, the riding lessons, the Boy Scout troops, and all the rest of the things that children did under the supervision of others, as a way for them to gain a few moments of time to themselves. Rather, they served as an indication of the way the community built itself around the activities of the children.[40]

THE ROLE OF MEN

Women took the lead in organizing children's leisure, but men were not entirely absent parents. Along with their wives, they had transformed the developers' vision of Palos Verdes from one in which the couple was the focus of the community to one in which the family dominated. The developers had fully intended to create a suburb that resembled a resort. Although they did build a school, their promotional literature was obviously directed at young adults. Its photographs showed couples, not families, enjoying the outdoors—on their patios, the horseback riding trails, and the golf course. Perhaps the developers were ahead of their time; it was in southern California that the adult-centered communities designed for leisure blossomed some forty years later. But the Palos Verdes residents of the 1920s desired primarily to spend their energy on directing the lives of their children. If the youngsters at Palos Verdes actually did a quarter of what the women's club, their teachers, and their parents organized for them, they would never have had time to sneak into the city and sample its forbidden pleasures. It is impossible to say, because the record is not there, whether these children were organized so intensely because the adults thought it was fun for them or because they wanted to keep them busy and out of trouble. What is evident is the intense interest in what the children were doing.

But if the men were not absent or unimportant in all of this, they seemed more passive than Progressive Era suburban fathers. Both fathers and mothers served on the community's board of education, and fathers, at the behest of their wives but without reluctance, volunteered their services for the Boy Scouts and the Boy Rangers. They also participated in the social calendars created by the women's club, attending dances, accompanying their wives to parties and the regular meetings of the "public affairs" department of the club. And finally, like the suburbanites of Westchester County studied by the Lundberg group, they chose to spend their leisure with their families. As early as 1925 the manager of the Palos Verdes Golf Club complained that the course got little use from the men of the community, although travelling golfers went out of their way to play the course. The trouble was that the men were more interested in staying at home with their wives and children on weekends. "Bring your families," urged the manager. The wives could read or play cards in "the delightful sun room" of the clubhouse, and the children could play on the beach or ride the horses at the nearby stables. Golfing, the manager felt compelled to point out directly, need not sunder a man from his family.[41]

This was not the masculine domesticity of the suburbs of the Progressive Era, when men had taken on as considerable a share of the responsibility for marital togetherness as their wives, and when there had seemed to be a genuine advance in the direct involvement of men in the home. In Palos Verdes, home life was the responsibility of women, although men went along to social activities and spent much of their leisure with their children. What was different from the past was that men took the initiative in family life much less often. Historians have noted that in the 1920s women shouldered their duties as wives and mothers, expecting that they were chiefly responsible for keeping the marriage fulfilled and the family happy.[42] Men could relax. The masculine domesticity of the Progressive Era had turned into the equally sweeping, but more woman-intensive, idea of focusing the family around the children.

If Palos Verdes was, in Robert Fogelson's words, the quintessence of Los Angeles, it was also the quintessence of upper middle-class suburbia during the years before the Great Depression. Its architecture was superficially different from that of Scarsdale or Radburn, but it was nevertheless nostalgic; inside, the houses were very similar to their eastern and midwestern counterparts. Its family-centered organizational life was almost exactly like that of Scarsdale or Radburn. And in its emphasis on home ownership, on racial and economic homogeneity, and on enforcing such homogeneity through the use of zoning and restrictive covenants, Palos Verdes was part of a national trend. Its Art Jury was atypical, but other communities expanded zoning restrictions in order to achieve the same ungenerous and restrictive purposes. Although Palos Verdes Estates was more beautifully planned and designed than many other suburbs, the hope of being able to plan a complete community occupied the dreams of many a member of the Regional Planning Association across the country.

The depression halted the growth of Palos Verdes just as it had cut short the promise of Radburn. Lots were left unsold, construction ground down, and some of the original residents, led by Olmsted himself, left the community. After the war, the peninsula grew rapidly, and other suburban communities joined the estates. The red-roofed houses are still there, looking out over the spectacular bluffs, and Palos Verdes Estates is still an expensive and exclusive community. But it was never completed along the lines envisioned by the planners and developers who had wanted to create a planned and ordered suburban America. In the 1920s, people like Olmsted had hoped that Palos Verdes would stand as a model of what planning could accomplish, just as Los Angeles itself stood as an exemplar of a metropolis that united urban opportunity with suburban values. The decade of the 1920s was perhaps the last historical moment that such a hope could come close to being achievable.

Epilogue: The Mystique of Fulfillment

The suburban housewife—she . . . was healthy, beautiful, educated, concerned only about her husband, her children, her home. She had found true feminine fulfillment. . . . In the fifteen years after World War II, this mystique of feminine fulfillment became the cherished and self-perpetuating core of contemporary American culture.

BETTY FRIEDAN
THE FEMININE MYSTIQUE, 1963

In the preceding chapters I have undertaken two tasks: First, to understand the nature of some of the ideas that influenced middle-class Americans to choose suburban life (and how those ideas changed over time); and second, to explore the lives of suburban families in communities exemplifying middle-class suburban America during the early pivotal periods of suburban development. Throughout, I have not bound myself to a rigid geopolitical definition of suburbia, although I have tried not to forget either geography or politics. My goal was to balance the spatial and the cultural, the physical and the metaphorical, in order to begin to figure out what it meant, to residents themselves, to live in the suburbs. Out of the original suburban ideal—created principally by men, centered on questions of property ownership, beset by the dilemma of reconciling participation in the urban economy with the retention of the values of the agrarian republic, and holding out the vision of a residential ideal that required spatial separation from the city—a new suburban domestic ideal emerged at the turn of the twentieth century, one that incorporated the ideology of domesticity.

Animated by vast socioeconomic and technological changes, which included new gender roles and new attitudes toward childrearing, upper middle-class women and men alike looked to the suburbs as the appropriate place to develop a new kind of family life. In the years before the United States' involvement in World War I, middle-class suburbanites took up the idea of marital togetherness, husbands became intensely involved in the day-to-day domestic lives of their families, and both parents interested themselves in childrearing. For many of the suburbanites themselves, suburban life did seem almost idyllic. But the idyll was costly to others, and the price of suburbia was the exclusion of heterogeneity. In the Progressive Era, this exclusion had not yet become bitter and hateful; suburban advocates wanted every family to have the opportunity to move to its own class-based suburb. If families insisted on homogeneity, they balanced that insistence with support for universal suburbanization. Once made, this connection between suburban life and the preservation of family togetherness could not be severed. During the 1920s, as middle-class suburbs boomed, suburbanization and domesticity had become seemingly inseparable.

By the end of the 1920s there had developed an image of suburbia that was to remain fixed in the landscape of the American mind for decades to come. The owner-occupied, single-family house, set in a community of similar houses, where children were the central focus of family life, and from which families considered "undesirable" were excluded, had become, not the norm for all families, but very nearly the standard by which one's middle-class credentials were judged. The depression dashed the plans of many intended suburbanites, but a number of the programs of the Roosevelt administration explicitly embodied suburban values. It may not go too far to say that the New Deal institutionalized the suburban vision. Its programs, including the highway subsidies but more importantly the Home Owners Loan Corporation and the Federal Housing Administration, provided the government's imprimatur to a way of life that much of the middle class had already espoused.

FROM SUBURBAN DOMESTICITY TO THE FEMININE MYSTIQUE

One purpose of this book has been to trace the ways in which the suburban ideal and the ideology of domesticity became inextricably interconnected, and to understand how the family—specifically the child—came to be at the center of suburban life. All the strands to weave that particular suburban tapestry were in place by the time Herbert Hoover was inaugurated in 1929. The depression might have resulted in the destruction of it, or its profound alteration, but it did not. The policies of the national government during the New Deal insured—in the literal as well as the figurative sense of the word—the suburban vision as it had become fixed in the 1920s.

To explain how that happened, and what it did to suburban family life, would require another book; however, to complete this story, a brief look at the fate of the suburban domestic ideal in the postwar period seems in order. Initially, during the New Deal and then the war, the full effects of legislation benefitting suburban growth was blunted by the greater economic priorities of recovery and then war production. Housing starts, for example, during those years, had not risen above an average of a hundred thousand a year. By the time the war was over, the pressure was enormous—during the war marriage rates had risen dramatically, and the birth rate had also begun to climb. The Federal Housing Administration's policy of favoring new construction over rehabilitation, the periphery over the central city, and segregation over integration was replicated by the Veterans Administration's housing plan for returning servicemen. By 1948 housing starts for the first time surpassed the 1928 figure, and continued to climb. Most of these new houses were in the suburbs. Easy financing, combined with the advent of assembly-line construction, pioneered by the Levitt brothers and adapted by other builders, meant that for the young, white, middle-class family, owning had become cheaper than renting.[1]

The suburban boom of the postwar United States was the fulfillment, for white Americans, of the visions of the upper middle-class couples who at the turn of the century moved their children to the suburbs in quest of a new domestic ideal. Before World War I, only prospering middle-class families had the financial ability to achieve the suburban domestic ideal. By the 1920s the numbers of suburbanites were considerably larger within the American middle class, and the focus of family life had subtly shifted. In the years before World War I, suburban men and women took pride in the primacy of the husband-wife bond and their mutual interest in the children. Their vision embodied masculine domesticity, marital togetherness, and the integration of family and community life in a physical setting that emphasized the residents' shared values. But by the 1920s, women took on the responsibility for keeping romance alive in the marriage, and family life had become more noticeably centered around the demands of childrearing; the integration of family and community had developed into a routine involvement with local clubs; and the idea that residents would have shared values (which had always had overtones of racism and ethnocentrism) had degenerated into the exclusionary covenant.

Masculine domesticity had also, readers will recall, begun to degenerate. If in the early twentieth century it had appeared to be a genuine—if inherently inadequate—male response to the demands for equality pressed by wives, by the 1920s women were responsible for organizing the events in which their husbands took part. Men were not absent, but there are some suggestions that they might be losing interest. The popular press of the times gave considerable attention to men's fears of female domination.[2]

During the 1930s, the marriage rate dropped, the chorus of voices inveighing against career-minded women grew louder, and the unsettled economic situation made the desire for a traditional family life understandable, albeit often impractical. In various ways, the federal government, private corporations, and others made clear that the nuclear family, with a male breadwinner and female homemaker, ought to be considered the "normal" type of family. All three greenbelt towns, for example, excluded all families with wives employed outside the home; banks, schools, and insurance companies all across the country began to bar the employment of married women, and the women's magazines urged married women with jobs to quit so that men could take their places. But the numbers of wives in the labor force increased anyway, to 17 percent by 1940. World War II would increase the participation of married women to more than 25 percent in 1944. Many of these women did not wish to leave paid employment once the war was over.[3]

Although most of the married women in the paid work force in the late 1920s through World War II were not the wives of the physicians, lawyers, bankers, brokers, and managers who lived with their families in the middle- and upper middle-class suburbs described in this book, the increasing number of working wives did result in lamentations over the "decline" of traditional womanly behavior. In the 1940s, the authors of *Modern Woman: the Lost Sex* insisted that because women had abandoned the traditional subordinate position in marriage they had thereby emasculated their husbands and prevented their sons from growing up. Urging women to "recapture" the domestic functions of their grandmothers—by baking the family's bread, canning its food, and decorating the house with handicrafts—Ferdinand Lundberg and Marynia Farnham decried what they viewed as the "masculinization" of women as a result of misplaced notions about sexual equality. They were not alone in their view; as Betty Friedan remarked, *Modern Woman: The Lost Sex,* was "paraphrased ad nauseum in the magazines and in marriage courses, until most of its statements became a part of the conventional, accepted truth of our time." American society in general had only grudgingly tolerated as a temporary necessity the idea of women taking on wartime employment and enjoying wages nearly equal to those of men, but most people never accepted the idea that women's place might change permanently. At war's end, if women refused to leave their jobs, employers forced them out; and there was a flurry of films, books, and articles expressing fears of deleterious long-term effects of women's wartime employment. As the new suburbs filled with growing families the traditionalists felt that they could breathe a collective sigh of relief.[4]

The suburban vision of the early 1950s was less a new expression of the domestic ideal than a feverish—and in the long run unsuccessful—attempt to erase the depression and the war and return to the 1920s. The architecture of the new suburbs was nostalgic; ersatz colonial and "cape cod" styles abounded, styles that Frank Lloyd Wright had once lumped together as "codfish colonials." Even the newer ranch house designs were not really new, but had been lifted from the California suburbs of the 1920s. Although some well-to-do Americans favored the international style, or the dramatic visions of Wright's later work, they were a minority. Inside, the floor plans of the majority of houses continued the openness of the earlier generation. Many of the houses were smaller, and there were sometimes basement recreation rooms; on the whole, however, the interior designs would not have seemed unfamiliar to the earlier suburbanites.[5]

Suburban families of the 1950s, like their counterparts in the Progressive Era and in the 1920s, espoused the idea of togetherness. By now, indeed, the word itself had become a clichéd description of suburban marriages. It seemed so characteristic of the couples observed by social commentators that some of them mistakenly viewed it as a new phenomenon, rather than as an attempt to reclaim the past. The "togetherness" of the 1950s, as seen through the eyes of journalists and critics, included male participation in playing with the children, some husbandly "help" around the house in the form of lawn mowing, taking out the trash, and cleaning the garage, and a social life in which couples went out together. However, we are not talking about a revival of the masculine domesticity of the early twentieth century, but an ersatz version. Husbands were heard to say that togetherness made them feel "trapped." And for many women, as Betty Friedan pithily noted, "togetherness was a poor substitute for equality."[6]

In many ways the suburbs of the 1950s seemed very much like those of a quarter- to a half-century before, but they were about to become quite different. First, there were more of them, and although individual suburbs retained their socioeconomic homogeneity, suburban life itself had become accessible to greater numbers of families, including those of the best paid of the skilled, white working class. Second, to pay for these houses, to buy the washer and dryer, to acquire a second car so that the children could be driven to the Girl Scouts or baseball games, women continued to hold down jobs outside the home. In 1950, five years after the war had ended, a quarter of married women were still in the paid work force, and the number kept growing. In 1953, *Glamour* magazine attributed the rise in home ownership in the fifties to the employment of wives, insisting that "the two paycheck family has helped to bring about a revolution in home ownership."[7]

Suburban wives found jobs in the shopping centers and banks that had moved out to the suburbs, and they became clerical workers in the new corporations that in increasing numbers had begun to move to the periphery. Banks had been among the first to recognize the untapped resource of housewives willing to work for low wages as part-time tellers and bookkeepers. As early as 1953, the U.S. Labor Department noticed, women in the work force were older, married, and had children; one of its studies noted that for many of these women, "the work has . . . given them a new outlook and interest, as well as permitted them to add to the family income." As the 1950s became the 1960s, more and more women held jobs. In Forest Park, Ohio, a new middle-class suburb built in the 1950s, a quarter of the wives held jobs outside the home in 1960, at a time when the overall participation of wives in the work force was just 5 percent above that. In the ensuing decade, such participation only increased. In 1970 in Forest Park, nearly 36 percent of the wives held jobs outside the home, still just 5 percent under the national average for all married women.[8]

Wives holding jobs outside the home did not constitute the only change for suburbia. The very outmigration of jobs wrought a major change in the physical configuration of the metropolitan area itself. Beginning in the 1960s, and continuing into the 1970s and 1980s, some suburbs became so urbanized themselves as to make the core city almost seem superfluous. Kenneth Jackson has referred to this phenomenon as the "suburbanization of the United States." Another historian, Robert Fishman, goes further, calling it "the creation of a radically new kind of city that differs so fundamentally from both English and American suburbs of the past that the new city should not be called 'suburban' at all." According to Fishman, "the most important feature of postwar American development has been the simultaneous decentralization of housing, industry, specialized services, and office jobs. . . . This phenomenon, as remarkable as it is unique, is not suburbanization but a *new city.*" Using the term "technoburb" to describe this new city, Fishman is the first historian (albeit not the first scholar) to envision contemporary suburbs not merely as the culmination of a long-term process but as the beginning of a new era.[9]

American suburbs are no longer homogeneous enclaves of white, middle-class families. The suburban domestic ideal, which developed from the marriage of the male concept of suburb as stronghold of the new republic and the female-based ideology of domesticity, no longer holds sway. From its appearance in the late nineteenth century to its peak of influence in the middle of the 1950s, white American middle-class families (and the skilled working class as well after World War II), held to the belief that suburban life somehow offered the keys to successful marriage and childrearing. By the 1960s and 1970s, as many Americans again recognized the great strengths and virtues of the city, as the suburbs themselves came to take on many of the demographic qualities heretofore seen as characteristic of urban life, and as the feminist movement sparked a repudiation of the idea that a woman's most important roles ought to be as wife and mother, suburbia lost its image of "exceptionalism" as an environment. In 1980 40 percent of Americans lived in the suburbs, more people than lived either in cities or rural areas. The country has indeed become suburbanized, but in doing so, the concept of what a suburb is has changed dramatically.[10]

The middle-class residential suburb, the physical expression of a set of ideas about the nature of marriage and family life, has become an historical artifact. Here and there it still exists, overwhelmed by the massive growth of the new suburbia. Recently a museum administrator remarked to colleagues at a workshop, more or less in jest, that it would not be long before she and her colleagues would be turning their attention to the first Levittown: They would seek a house from which they could strip away the "improvements," and restore it to its original 1947 condition. Guides would give tours, dressed in period costumes, and museum educators would design "living history" tableaux. A few people laughed, and most dismissed the idea as at the most fanciful, at the least very premature. But within weeks of this workshop Hofstra University, which is located on Long Island near that same Levittown, marked the suburb's fortieth anniversary with a conference. As scholars and policymakers gathered to analyze the suburbs of post–World War II America, a local museum official confessed to a desire to restore one of the early Levittown houses. No one smiled; the idea seemed perfectly credible. It is not farfetched to think that Levittown, or a community like it, might become the Colonial Williamsburg of the twenty-second century.[11]

To think of Levittown, one of the principal symbols of postwar suburbanization, in the same category as a place like Williamsburg is to underscore the artifactual quality of any particular suburb at a single point in time. Americans have moved to the suburbs since the early nineteenth century, but living in the suburbs meant something different in each period of suburban growth. The very nature of both suburban form and the suburban ideal has undergone profound changes. From the fringe communities of the early nineteenth century to the "technoburbs" of the late twentieth, the relationship of the city and suburb has been changing, not constant. The economic and political dimensions of suburban transformations have received a great deal of attention, but it is equally important to an understanding of both the changes and the continuities of suburban life for historians to analyze the ways in which families functioned in their communities—structurally, spatially, and culturally. In important ways, as American suburbs become increasingly disconnected to the cities that gave birth to them, we are witnessing the end of an age. The residential suburbs of the 1950s, which sheltered nuclear families with young children in racially homogeneous enclaves, were the culmination of more than a century of the creation of a set of political and cultural beliefs. That era is over. Suburbanization as a process has not ended, but the nature of the urban-suburban connection has altered dramatically. This book has been one historian's attempt to explore the dimensions of a vision of family and community that created twentieth-century suburbia, and that was, ultimately, inadequate to sustain it.

NOTES

Introduction

1. Frederick Lewis Allen, "The Big Change in Suburbia," *Harper's* (June 1954): 25; see Stuart Ewen and Elizabeth Ewen, *Channels of Desire* (New York, 1982), esp. 236, for an interpretation of 1950s television that connects it with suburbanization in a way different from my own.

2. Classic suburban studies of the decade include John Seely et al., *Crestwood Heights* (New York, 1956); and Robert Wood, *Suburbia: Its People and Its Politics* (Boston, 1959).

3. The definitive recent work on suburbanization is Kenneth Jackson, *Crabgrass Frontier* (New York, 1985). Other important studies include Robert Fishman, *Bourgeois Utopias: The Rise and Fall of Suburbia* (New York, 1987); Clifford E. Clark, Jr., *The American Family Home* (Chapel Hill, N.C., 1986); and Henry Binford, *The First Suburbs* (Chicago, 1985).

4. Among those we might consider architectural determinists, the work of Delores Hayden is perhaps the most compelling. Her books include *Seven American Utopias* (Cambridge, Mass., 1976), *The Grand Domestic Revolution: A History of Feminist Designs for American Homes, Neighborhoods, and Cities* (Cambridge, Mass., 1981), and *Redesigning the American Dream* (New York, 1984). Gwendolyn Wright has been an important voice in warning planners and architects of the futility of placing too much reliance on the ability of architecture to change behavior, particularly in her excellent *Moralism and the Model Home* (Chicago, 1980), and her survey *Building the Dream: A Social History of Housing in America* (New York, 1981).

Prologue: Homes of the Virtuous

1. One of the best introductions to the early history of urban America is in the first three chapters of Charles N. Glaab and A. Theodore Brown, *A History of Urban America*, 2d ed. (New York, 1976). Urbanization figures are taken from 21–22.

2. Kenneth Jackson, *Crabgrass Frontier* (New York, 1985); see also the special issue on "Technology and the City," *Journal of Urban History* 5 (May 1979); Peter Moore, "Public Services and Residential Development in a Toronto Neighborhood, 1880–1915," *Journal of Urban History* 9 (August 1983), 445–471.

3. Jackson, *Crabgrass*, 29.

4. Jackson, *Crabgrass*, 25–33. Pierrepont is quoted on p. 32.

5. Robert Fishman, *Bourgeois Utopias* (New York, 1987), 9. It is impossible to do justice to Fishman's elegant and sophisticated argument in a note, but his major point is that suburbs were a particular Anglo-American ideological choice arrived at by the upper middle-class. He illuminates his analysis with a comparison to the decision of the continental European bourgeoisie to remain urban. Henry Binford, *The First Suburbs* (Chicago, 1985), xiii. See also Clifford Clark, Jr., "Domestic Architecture as an Index to Social History: The Romantic Revival and the Cult of Domesticity in America, 1840–1870," *Journal of Interdisciplinary History* 7 (1) (Summer 1976): 35–56, and his more recent *American Family Home, 1800–1960* (Chapel Hill, N.C., 1986).

6. Binford, *First Suburbs*, 84, 139.

7. Ibid., 179. See also Fishman, *Bourgeois Utopias*, 122.

8. Christine Stansell, *City of Women: Sex and Class in New York, 1789–1860* (New York, 1986), 214.

9. Jan Cohn, *The Palace or the Poorhouse: The American Home as Cultural Symbol* (East Lansing Michigan, 1979) offers the best analysis of literary America's attitudes about the home.

10. Andrew Jackson Downing, *The Architecture of Country Houses* (1850; reprint, New York, 1969), xix, 270.

11. Fishman, in *Bourgeois Utopias*, notes on p. 123, that Downing "was especially indebted (to put it politely) to J. C. Loudon, . . . who was a dominant influence in England." See also Gwendolyn Wright, *Building the Dream* (New York, 1981), 80–84.

12. Ibid., 84–85; emphasis in original. Nathaniel Willis was the brother of novelist Fannie Fern.

13. Palliser, Palliser, & Co., *Palliser's Model Homes* (1878; reprint, Fenton, Calif. 1972), 38.

14. Joan Albee, *John Ruskin, The Passionate Moralist* (London, 1980), 330. See also Eileen Boris, *Art and Labor: Ruskin, Morris, and the Craftsman Ideal in America* (Philadelphia, 1986), esp. 3–7; John Ruskin, *The Seven Lamps of Architecture*, U.S. ed. (Philadelphia, 1849), 98–99 for his criticisms of domestic architecture.

15. Claudia Bushman, *A Good Poor Man's Wife* (Hanover, Conn., 1981), 117–119; John Stilgoe, *Metropolitan Corridor* (New Haven, Conn., 1983), 267–276.

16. Frank Scott, *The Art of Beautifying Suburban Home Grounds* (New York, 1870), 29. David Handlin, *The American Home: Architecture and Society, 1815–1915* (Boston, 1979), 171–177, has a very good summary of Scott's design philosophy.

17. Scott, *Suburban Home Grounds*, pp. 25–31.

18. The ideology of domesticity should not be confused with the broader doctrine of separate spheres, which ordained that men went out into the world while women stayed in the home. Perhaps in recent years the representation of gender-defined roles as "spheres" had been taken too literally to mean that men and women (here we speak of white men and women of the middle classes) inhabited different physical realms. Although to some extent that was true, we should not forget that men lived in the home and women shopped in town. The term "separate spheres" is a term of the nineteenth century that refers to the intellectual, emotional, and environmental territory that each sex dominated. Although the women who advocated the ideology of domesticity accepted the idea of gender separation, they insisted that it gave women important tasks in society, the most important of which was establishing and enforcing social morality. In the hands of domestic reformers, separate spheres could enjoin women to leave the home in order to "make the world more homelike," in the words of the great temperance leader Frances Willard. Kathryn Kish Sklar's *Catharine Beecher: A Study in Domesticity* (New Haven, 1973) remains the standard by which other studies of domesticity are judged. Also important is Nancy Cott, *The Bonds of Womanhood* (New Haven, 1977). Mary Kelley, *Private Woman, Public Stage* (New York, 1984), is an excel-

lent study of the use of domesticity by popular women authors of the nineteenth century.

19. Mary Beth Norton, *Liberty's Daughters: The Revolutionary Experience of American Women, 1750–1800* (Boston, 1980), 177–189. Linda Kerber, "The Republican Mother: Women and the Enlightenment—An American Perspective," *American Quarterly* 28 (1976): 187–205, and *Women of the Republic: Intellect and Ideology in Revolutionary America* (Chapel Hill, N.C., 1980).

20. Lydia Maria Child, *The American Frugal Housewife* (1829; reprint, New York, 1972), 92. Child's life changed dramatically when she began to advocate abolitionism with her *Appeal in Favor of that Class of Americans Called Africans* (Boston, 1833). For a while she was ostracized and suffered severe financial hardships, but she eventually recovered her reputation. As the editors of her letters have noted, she "was able to sustain her lifelong career as a professional author" (Milton Meltzer and Patricia G. Holland, eds. *Lydia Maria Child: Selected Letters, 1817–1880* [Amherst, Mass., 1982], xiii).

21. Child, *American Frugal Housewife,* 3, 4, 106 (emphasis in original).

22. Eliza Farrar, *The Young Lady's Friend* (1836; reprint, New York, 1975). Farrar wrote children's fiction and sketches, but this was her most popular work.

23. Cott, *Bonds of Womanhood,* 200.

24. Catharine Sedgwick, *Home* (1835; reprint, New York, 1890). On the popularity of *Home,* see Kelley, *Private Woman,* 13. Kelley is the originator of the term "literary domestic."

25. Sedgwick, *Home,* 50, 94–96; quote from Handlin, *American Family Home,* 14.

26. Ronald Hogeland, "The 'Female Appendage': Feminine Lifestyles in America, 1820–1860," *Civil War History* 17 (June 1971): 107.

27. Blaine McKinley, "Troublesome Comforts: The Housekeeper-Servant Relationship in Antebellum Didiactic Fiction," *Journal of American Culture* 5 (Summer 1982): 43.

28. Catharine Beecher, *Treatise on Domestic Economy* (1841; reprint, New York, 1970), 144.

29. Sklar, *Catharine Beecher,* 163.

30. Anna Cora Mowatt, *Fashion,* act V, scene 1.

31. L. H. G. Abell, *Woman in Her Various Relations* (New York, 1851), 99. Colleen McDannell, *The Christian Home in Victorian America* (Bloomington, Indiana, 1986), has an excellent discussion of the kinds of material goods (in both senses of the word) that graced Victorian middle-class houses.

32. Mary Ryan, *Cradle of the Middle-Class* (New York, 1981), 191.

33. Stansell, *City of Women,* 214. David Pivar, *Purity Crusade: Sexual Morality and Social Control, 1868–1900* (Westport, Conn., 1973), 109, 8–9.

34. Delores Hayden, *The Grand Domestic Revolution* (Cambridge, Mass., 1981), 79–82.

35. Ibid., 108.

36. Pivar, *Purity Crusade,* 275.

37. Victor Goheen, *Victorian Toronto* (Chicago, 1970), 73. My interpretation of the reasons for the time lag is different from his, but he clearly documents the existence of such a lag.

38. Handlin, *The American Home,* 216–231.

39. Charles T. Murray, "Living in the Suburbs," *Ladies Repository* 34 (1874): 437–438.

40. Catharine Beecher and Harriet Beecher Stowe, *The American Woman's Home* (1869; reprint, New York, 1971), 25.

41. Harriet Beecher Stowe was also ambivalent about urban life around the time she collaborated with her sister on *The American Woman's Home.* In her 1870 novel, *My Wife and I,* which I discuss in some detail later on, she moves her heroine and her husband to a neighborhood with all the physical earmarks of suburbia except one—it was located in Manhattan. Reluctant to give up the city, Stowe nevertheless created a suburban-like community within it.

42. Edward Bellamy, *Looking Backward* (Boston, 1887).

Chapter One: Moulding the Moral Nature

1. One of the best analyses of the utility of prescriptive literature is Clifford E. Clark, Jr., *The American Family Home, 1800–1960* (Chapel Hill, N.C., 1986), xiv–xv. Clark argues that while "[f]ew individuals . . . lived up to all the ideals espoused by the reformers, . . . [i]t is clear from the planbook houses actually built and the diaries and letters that survive that many if not most middle-class Americans accepted the reformers' central argument that the home was a personal and symbolic statement for the family that owned it."

2. For an excellent brief discussion of this process, see Mary Ryan, *Cradle of the Middle Class* (New York, 1981), 146, 188–189.

3. "The Open Hand," *Godey's Lady's Book* 27 (August, 1843), 69. See also Ryan, *Cradle,* 180–181.

4. Ellen DuBois, *Feminism and Suffrage* (Ithaca, N.Y., 1978), 15, argues powerfully that the early suffragists "expected the vote to lead to a total transformation of their lives." If early suffragism was radical, however, as it became a mass movement toward the end of the century that radicalism was blunted. Nancy Cott, *The Grounding of Modern Feminism* (New Haven, 1987), chap. 1, is the best recent treatment of the mass appeal of the woman's movement at the end of the nineteenth century.

5. Caroline Howard Gilman, *Recollections of a Southern Matron* (New York, 1852), 296–298. See Mary Kelley, *Private Woman, Public Stage* (New York, 1984), 14–16, 211, for a discussion of this novel.

6. Catharine Beecher and Harriet Beecher Stowe, *The American Woman's Home* (1869; reprint, New York, 1971). Kathryn Kish Sklar, *Catharine Beecher* (New Haven, 1973).

7. L. H. G. Abell, *Woman in Her Various Relations,* (New York, 1851), 209. See also, Ryan, *Cradle,* 180.

8. See Carl Degler, *At Odds* (New York, 1980), 34–42.

9. Carroll Smith-Rosenberg, *Disorderly Conduct: Visions of Gender in Victorian America* (New York, 1985),58.

10. Suzanne Lebsock, *The Free Women of Petersburg* (New York, 1984), 18; Ryan, *Cradle,* 196.

11. Abell, *Woman,* 14–15; Beecher and Stowe, *American Woman's Home,* 14; J. A. Banks, *Victorian Values* (London, 1981), 37.

12. Abell, *Woman,* 229; Beecher and Stowe, *American Woman's Home,* 220–221.

13. Beecher and Stowe, *American Woman's Home,* 216; also, Ryan, *Cradle,* 230–242.

14. The historian most responsible for our understanding of the subversive elements in the domestic ideal is Carroll Smith-Rosenberg. A representative selection of her essays has appeared as a book: *Disorderly Conduct,* cited earlier.

15. Ryan, *Cradle,* 232.

16. William Alcott, *The Young Husband* (Boston, 1839), 51; see also 136–149. Degler, *At Odds,* 269, discusses Alcott's popularity as a marital advice-giver.

17. Henry Ward Beecher, *Lectures to Young Men* (New York, 1849), 41, 152, 120–127; John Angell James, *The Young Man's Friend* (New York, 1860), esp. 50. Karen Halttunen, *Confidence Men and Painted Women* (New Haven, Conn., 1982), esp. 25–26, 47–48.

18. William Rathbone Grey, quoted in Banks, *Victorian Values,* 81. For an excellent example of the way women's advice differed, see Catharine Sedgwick, *Home* (1835; reprint, New York, 1890).

19. Timothy Arthur's series on "Model Husbands" appeared in *Godey's Lady's Book* 51 (January, 1855): 37–40; (February, 1855): 110–112; and (March, 1855): 206–208. Arthur argued that domestic happiness (or misery) was in the hands of the husband. The belief in the power of men to wreck the happiness of women is an important theme of the domestic novels of the mid-nineteenth century as well. Susan Warner's *Wide, Wide, World* (New York, 1852), the book that launched the concept of a best-seller, made this point explicitly; see esp. 12–13.

20. Catharine Beecher and Harriet Beecher Stowe, *American Woman's Home,* 203–204.

21. The book that has done the most to explain the connections between domestic religion and the spatial arrangements of the Victorian home is Colleen McDannell, *The Christian Home in Victorian America* (Bloomington, Indiana, 1986).

22. The sample is from pattern books, as listed in Table 2.1. The question might be raised: Did builders actually build the houses in the pattern books? The answer is that at least some did. See Catherine Bisher, "Jacob W. Holt: An American Builder," in Dell Upton and John Michael Vlatch, *Common Places: Readings in American Vernacular Architecture* (Athens, Georgia, 1986), 447–481. Clifford Clark (*American Family Home* [Chapel Hill, N.C., 1986], 77), notes that "thousands of Palliser buildings were constructed throughout the country."

23. Eugene C. Gardner, *The House that Jill Built (After Jack's Had Proved a Failure)* (Springfield, Mass., 1896), 15.

24. Robert Fishman, *Bourgeois Utopias* (New York, 1987), 56.

25. Many historians have commented on the way in which Beecher's model Christian home either resembled a seventeenth-century colonial house or prefigured the simplified floor plans of earlier twentieth-century houses.

But few have also noted that Beecher originally created this design for women teachers, who would perhaps need to teach in their parlor, and might have the opportunity, in areas where there was no church, to preach in it on Sunday. (See McDannell, *Christian Home,* 37). Others who discuss the design, but do not see it as specifically a house for women, include Delores Hayden, *The Grand Domestic Revolution* (Cambridge, Mass., 1981), 58, who discusses the use of "advanced" technology in design, and Clifford Clark, *American Home,* 33–34.

26. This idea about a "transitional" stage of architectural thinking is not original to me. Helen Lefkowitz Horowitz, in a talk in the mid-1980s before the Columbia University Seminar on the City, mentioned it; intrigued with the notion, I began to look for signs of it, and the idea appears to be a sound one.

27. Harriet Beecher Stowe, *My Wife and I* (New York, 1870), 98.

28. Abby M. Diaz, *A Domestic Problem* (1875; reprint, New York, 1974), 36–37. A good brief introduction to Diaz and her work in Jane Bernardete, "Abby Morton Diaz," in Langdon Lynne Faust, ed. *American Women Writers,* vol. 1, abridged (New York, 1983), 161–163.

29. Stowe, *My Wife and I,* 38, 229, 447 and 478; where Eva "propose[s] to introduce the country sitting room into our New York house." Stowe described the Hendersons' house, which was physically within the city limits, in unmistakably suburban terms; see 468–469.

30. Claudia Bushman, *A Good Poor Man's Wife* (Hanover, Conn., 1981), 86–87. The Robinson family is covered in detail in the next chapter.

31. Lydia Maria Child to her sister-in-law Lydia B. Child, 11 February 1875, in Milton Meltzer and Patricia Holland, eds., *Lydia Maria Child: Selected Letters* (Amherst, Mass., 1982), 530.

32. Bushman, *Good Wife,* 146, 200. My interpretation of Hattie Shattuck's growing resentment toward her husband's business failures differs from that of the family's biographer. On p. 200, Bushman argues that "Sid provided neither a living or a home. Hattie had no children and cleaved to her mother rather than her husband. Yet the family functioned well as a unit. All three pooled their resources and did not blame the others for their lacks." Hattie Shattuck's behavior, it seems to me, implied quite different feelings; she grew bitter and angry, and she refused to live with her husband during the long years of his reversals. I would guess that she was dissatisfied with her marriage.

33. Michael Katz, Michael Doucet, and Mark Stern, *The Social Organization of Early Industrial Capitalism* (Cambridge, Mass., 1982), 29. Also Smith-Rosenberg, *Disorderly Conduct,* 167–170.

34. Diaz, *A Domestic Problem,* 99, 115–116; Stowe, *My Wife and I,* 40. A very good new survey of changing family patterns is Steven Mintz and Susan Kellogg, *Domestic Revolutions* (New York, 1988). Although my research was conducted without benefit of their insights, in several instances we have come to similar conclusions. See esp. chaps. 2, 5.

35. Margaret Sangster, *The Art of Being Agreeable* (New York, 1897), 22. Sangster was a popular domestic writer whose works appeared in many popular journals and magazines.

36. The "sear and palsy" phrase is from Abell, *Woman in Her Various*

Relations, 214; the "just as important" phrase from Sangster, *Art of Being Agreeable*, 272–273; see also 49.

37. See Smith-Rosenberg, *Disorderly Conduct*, especially part 1, which includes her famous essay, "The Female World of Love and Ritual."

38. It may seem surprising that in what historians often see as an era in which women were increasingly home-bound, advice-givers urged women not to "build a wall around" the "sphere of domestic duties" because to do so would make them "narrow," and incapable of "having . . . prospects, interest, hopes or enjoyments beyond it." Those are L. H. G. Abell's words, in *Woman in Her Various Relations*, 22. Although a conservative advocate of domesticity, Abell believed that women needed "society" for their own emotional well-being; husbands did not come into it. By the end of the century things had changed. Readers might wish to contrast the ideas of "The Open Hand," discussed earlier in this chapter with a story in the *Ladies Home Journal* 38 (April 1908): 16, in which a young mother becomes so attached to her first baby that she neglects her husband. The young woman's mother advises her: "You should go out more and try to forget the baby for a time." Although shocked by her mother's advice, she follows it, and is rewarded by a better relationship with her husband and a happier child.

39. In addition to the material cited previously, see Bernard Mergen, *Play and Playthings* (Westport, Conn., 1983), 73–75, 105.

40. J. A. Banks, *Victorian Values* (London, 1981), 40–43; the other relevant studies are Edward Shorter, *The Making of the Modern Family* (New York, 1975); Laurence Stone, *The Family, Sex, and Marriage in New England* (London, 1977); Randolph Trumbach, *The Rise of the Egalitarian Family* (New York, 1976). For a challenge to those views, see Steven Ozment, *When Fathers Ruled: Family Life in Reformation Europe* (Cambridge, Mass., 1983).

41. Banks, *Victorian Values*, 132. Mark J. Stern, *Society and Family Strategy: Erie County, New York, 1850–1920* (Albany, 1987), 73–74.

42. Bernard Wishy, *The Child and the Republic* (Philadelphia, 1968). Henry Ward Beecher, *Lectures*, 54, 186–187.

43. John Angell James, *Young Man's Friend*, 276; see also 275–300, and 177. Abell, *Woman*, 44.

44. Beecher and Stowe, *American Woman's Home*, 278–280.

45. Abell, *Woman*, 53, 226–227; Beecher and Stowe, *American Woman's Home*, 207, 277.

46. Stowe, *My Wife and I*, 28–29.

47. Kate Wiggin, *Children's Rights* (Boston, 1890), 45.

48. Nora Smith, in Wiggin, *Children's Rights*, 119.

49. Sangster, *Art of Being Agreeable*, 60–61; Wiggin, *Children's Rights*, 15.

Chapter Two: The Minutiae of Domestic Life

1. Henry Binford, *The First Suburbs* (Chicago, 1985), xiii; Sam Bass Warner, *Streetcar Suburbs* (Cambridge, Mass., 1962), 14, also discussed the formation of the residential ideal, although he dated it considerably later. "The

rural ideal," argued Warner, "by its emphasis on the pleasures of private family life, on the security of a small community setting, and on the enjoyment of natural surroundings, encouraged the middle-class to build a wholly new residential environment: the modern suburb."

2. Harriet Hanson Robinson's papers are in the Schlesinger Library, Radcliffe College, and are available on microfilm. Relying principally on those papers, Claudia Bushman has written an absorbing chronicle of the Robinson family, *A Good Poor Man's Wife* (Hanover, Conn., 1981). Although my interpretation of Harriet Robinson's family relationships differs in some important points from Bushman's, I am indebted to her carefully researched and insightful volume. I have relied on her work for much of the factual material on the Robinson family that appears here.

3. See Bushman, esp. chaps. 5 and 6, and the Robinson Diary.

4. Binford, *The First Suburbs*, 91–92, on the rapidity of service between Lowell and Boston.

5. Bushman, *Good Wife*, 93. Harriet Robinson did not have an active social life in Concord either, although she did belong to the antislavery sewing society. See Robinson Diary, January 27, 1857. Her entry for June 23, 1858, after their move to Malden, showed that they found the people of Concord "snobbish" and "narrow," and that both of them wanted to be closer to, but not in, Boston.

6. *The Bicentennial Book of Malden* (Boston, 1850), 224.

7. For commuters' fares, see *Russell's Horse Railroad Guide for Boston and Vicinity* (Boston, 1862), and *The Strangers' Guide in the City of Boston* (Boston, 1849).

8. Michael Katz et al., *The Social Organization of Early Industrial Capitalism* (Cambridge, Mass., 1982), 29. Carroll Smith-Rosenberg makes the same point in *Disorderly Conduct: Visions of Gender in Victorian America* (New York, 1985), 167–170.

9. Bushman, *Good Wife*, 75, 117.

10. Robinson, influenced by Harriet Beecher Stowe's insistence in *House and Home Papers* (1864; reprint, New York, 1967), that a "lady" could "do her own work," vowed to do so. To late twentieth-century readers, the phrase "to do one's own work" no doubt conveys the idea that a woman did the cooking and cleaning herself. Not so: to do one's own work, for a middle-class wife, meant dispensing with live-in maids and instead hiring help by the day. As Claudia Bushman aptly phrased it (*Good Wife*, 109), "'Doing her own work' meant that a housewife supervised its completion, rather than doing it all personally."

11. *Manuscript Census Records*, Malden, Mass., 1880. Harriet Hanson Robinson was the census enumerator. Most of the household heads on Lincoln Street, which had only thirteen houses on it in 1880, were in clerical or sales work. One of the married women held a job outside the home, as did twelve of the eighteen single women living with their families. These women were clerks, saleswomen, and skilled workers such as dressmakers and milliners. In the larger neighborhood of which Lincoln Street was a part, 47 percent of the household heads (28 of 59) were professionals or proprietors. Another 18 percent (11 of 59) were in sales or clerical occupations. About a third of the households had live-in domestic help. As on Lincoln Street,

wives rarely held jobs outside the home; only one wife did so, as a teacher. The women who did hold jobs were either female household heads, adult daughters of the family, or other relatives. The jobs they held were as teachers, clerks, or skilled workers. Perhaps because Robinson was the enumerator, the attention paid to women's occupations was very careful, the most careful I have seen in census manuscripts of this period. Nevertheless, Robinson did not list herself as keeping a boarder, although she was doing so, nor did she list her daughter's part-time work as a writer. By 1900, when she still lived on Lincoln Street, Robinson listed herself in the manuscript census records as an "authoress."

12. Robinson's diary entries were loving towards her husband, and although she complained about different aspects of her life, she did not complain about him. See, for example, Robinson Diary, October 29, 1856, where she noted that her visiting relatives insisted that she has grown "handsome" since her marriage, unlike her cousin, who looked "all faded out, marriage has not improved her looks." Robinson credited "a happy marriage, like ours," for her improved appearance.

13. See Bushman, *Good Wife,* 157.

14. Harriet Robinson began her suffrage career as a supporter of Lucy Stone. After falling out with Stone because she believed she was not getting fair recognition, a falling out in which both husbands got involved, she switched her allegiance to the Stanton/Anthony faction. She never shared Stanton or Anthony's radicalism, however. The Boston Public Library has some *Calendars* from the Old and New Club. The members gave papers based on their own research, heard speakers, and held social events. It was a prominent club in Malden, and Harriet Robinson was a prominent member of it. See, for example, *Calendar: Old and New Club 1893–1894* (Boston, 1893). The Old and New joined the General Federation of Women's Clubs in 1890.

15. Harriet H. Robinson, *Loom and Spindle* (Boston, 1898), and *Early Factory Life in New England* (Boston, 1883). Robinson deserved a larger audience for these writings.

16. I pieced together the story of the lives of Mary Augusta and Charles Bradley Cumings from the following sources: First, and most heavily used, were the daybooks of M. Augusta Cumings, 1866–1880, in the Schlesinger Library; others included Boston City Directories, 1865–1907, Manuscript Census Records, *The Jamaica Plain News,* a local paper, and records of civic organizations and clubs.

17. Walter Muir Whitehall, *Boston: A Topographical History* (Cambridge, Mass., 1959), 136.

18. Albert B. Wolfe, *The Lodging House Problem in Boston* (Boston, 1906), 5–14.

19. *Boston and its Suburbs: A Guide Book* (Boston, 1886), 108–109. Charles Dole, *My Eighty Years* (New York, 1927), 189, 198–199.

20. Warner, *Streetcar Suburbs,* 41–43.

21. Dole, *My Eighty Years,* 199.

22. *Manuscript Census Records,* Boston, 1880. The household heads on Greenough Street were all men, their median age 45. (Charles was 42.) The Cumings family had two servants, and four of their neighbors had three. Most of the families had one or two children.

23. Cumings Daybook, February 18, 1867. There are a lot of gaps in the daybook. Often only a line or two is filled in. But there are extensive entries in the "notes" sections for many years. Although the information is sometimes sketchy, taken as a whole, the daybooks are very revealing, and the comparison between her entries and her husband's suggests their personalities as well as their interests.

24. Cumings Daybook, passim.

25. Ibid., October 16, 1871.

26. See, for example, Ibid., May 3, 1878.

27. *Jamaica Plain Tuesday Club* (Jamaica Plain, 1896). *Annual Reports, Jamaica Plain Friendly Visiting Society* (Boston, 1893–1903). The Society was founded in 1874. *Jamaica Plain News,* June 19, 1907: 4.

28. *Jamaica Plain News,* June 19, 1907: 4.

29. Cumings Daybook, 1876, dated notes in the memoranda section.

30. Dole, *My Eighty Years,* 276, 365; see also 287. When Dole wrote his memoirs, he did look back regretfully at some of his behavior, but he was very self-congratulatory about his actions as a husband and father.

31. Suzanne Lebsock, *The Free Women of Petersburg* (New York, 1984), 110, 170–178.

CHAPTER THREE: HOMEMAKERS MALE AND FEMALE

1. For a summary of suburban anti-urbanism, see Kenneth Jackson, *Crabgrass Frontier,* (New York, 1985), 68–72; also Clifford Clark, *American Family Home* (Chapel Hill, N.C., 1986), 179. Although Kathryn Kish Sklar's *Catharine Beecher* (New Haven, 1973), remains the best analysis of the ideology of domesticity, two other books clearly demonstrate the connection between the redefinition of urban life and the vision Beecher and others like her articulated: David Pivar, *Purity Crusade* (Westport, Conn., 1973), esp. 8–9, and Christine Stansell, *City of Women: Sex and Class in New York, 1789–1860* (New York, 1986), esp. 214.

2. By the early twentieth century the commuter railroad, perhaps more so than the streetcars, had made the city accessible to suburbanites, and suburban clubs brought the kind of social interaction valued by urban dwellers. Those clubs are discussed in detail in chap. 4. On accessibility, see Jon Teaford, *The Twentieth Century American City* (Baltimore, 1986), 21. It took eighteen minutes to go from suburban Queens to midtown Manhattan and twenty-three minutes to go from Riverside to downtown Chicago.

3. Christine Stansell, *City of Women,* 220. See also David Handlin, *The American Home* (Boston, 1979), 216–231; Sheila Rothman, *Woman's Proper Place* (New York, 1978): Mari Jo Buhle, *Women and American Socialism, 1870–1920* (Urbana, Ill., 1981), esp. 290–300.

4. Handlin, *American Home,* 220–230; Delores Hayden, *The Grand Domestic Revolution* (Cambridge, Mass., 1981), esp. 189 202.

5. Kate Upson Clark, *Bringing Up Boys* (New York, 1899), 193.

6. *American Homes and Gardens* (November 1905): 334; Joy Wheeler Dow, *American Renaissance: A Review of Domestic Architecture* (New York, 1904), 17.

When reviewing real estate brochures in the Huntington Library's Ephemera Collection, I noted that exclusionary covenants were the rule rather than the exception. The material surveyed dated from the early 1900s through the 1920s.

7. *Public Opinion* (May 14, 1988): 82. All radicals were suspect, but anarchists were more so. On the fear of anarchism in late nineteenth- and early twentieth-century America, see Margaret Marsh, *Anarchist Women, 1870–1920* (Philadelphia, 1981), 6–21.

8. For an analysis of the attitude that home ownership was an antidote to working-class and immigrant radicalism, see Carolyn Kirk and Gordon W. Kirk, Jr., "The Impact of the City on Home Ownership: A Comparison of Immigrants and Native Whites at the Turn of the Century," *Journal of Urban History* 7 (4) (August 1981): 474–475. Elainc Tyler May, *Great Expectations: Marriage and Divorce in Post Victorian America* (Chicago, 1980), 56.

9. *American Homes and Gardens* (September 1906): 148.

10. Richard Ely, Socialism in America," *North American Review* 355 (June 1886): 523.

11. In all of the anarchist violence in this country between 1886 and World War I twelve people were killed, among them three anarchists who died while making a bomb in a tenement on Lexington Avenue. This includes the Haymarket incident, for which eight innocent men were convicted and an anarchist who got away probably threw the bomb. The best book on Haymarket is Paul Avrich, *The Haymarket Tragedy* (Princeton, 1984). Avrich discusses the Lexington Avenue bombing in his *Modern School Movement* (Princeton, 1980); the popular philosophy writer Will Durant, who associated with anarchists in his younger days, wrote a fictionalized account of that bombing in a thinly disguised autobiographical novel, *Transitions* (New York, 1927), 206–213.

12. Marsh, *Anarchist Women,* 8–10.

13. It would probably be more correct to talk about the way in which "women's rights women" transformed the ideology of domesticity, and an important locus of that change was the women's club movement. The best discussion of the transformation wrought by club participation by women is Karen Blair, *The Clubwoman as Feminist: True Womanhood Redefined, 1868–1914* (New York, 1980).

14. Nancy Cott, *The Grounding of Modern Feminism* (New Haven, 1987), 4, 15.

15. Gilman, who had been influenced by the utopian visions of Edward Bellamy, designed an apartment house in which the domestic chores would be done by hired help. See Delores Hayden, *The Grand Domestic Revolution,* 188–192, on the substantial influence of Gilman's ideas, which Gilman perhaps laid out best in her book, *The Home, Its Work and Influence* (New York, 1903). Carl Degler, *At Odds: Women and the Family in America from the Revolution to the Present* (New York, 1980), also discusses Gilman, but he does not refer to her architectural ideas. Degler's fascinating and troubling book does, however, illuminate the great tensions between feminism and family life. Indeed, he asserted (p. 5) that "it is at once a primary argument and a basic assumption of the book that the equality of women and the institution of the family have long been at odds with each other."

16. See, for example, Mary Kelley, *Private Woman, Public Stage* (New York, 1984), especially chap. 6; on the Woman's Christian Temperance Union, see Ruth Bordin, *Woman and Temperance: The Quest for Power and Liberty* (Philadelphia, 1980); also Blair, *Clubwoman*.

17. *See Sheila Rothman, Woman's Proper Place*, 68–71, on the department stores. The best book dealing with the customers of the department stores, and the whole issue of the department store and middle-class culture, is about a Parisian store. See Michael Miller, *The Bon Marche: Bourgeois Culture and the Department Store* (Princeton, 1981). Susan Porter Benson, *Counter Cultures* (Urbana, 1986), places more emphasis on the employees.

18. See Rothman, *Woman's Proper Place*, esp. 14–18.

19. *American Homes and Gardens* 1 (July 1905): 46.

20. These apartment hotels appeared in all American cities, even in traditional and staid Philadelphia, but as David Handlin noted, *American Home*, 402, they "were especially popular in New York."

21. *Architectural Record* 13 (1) (January 1903): 85–91; quotes on p. 90.

22. One of the best kinds of primary sources to examine in order to understand this "duality" among such women is the women's club "scrapbook." Those of the famed Friday Morning Club of Los Angeles are well organized and accessible. This club was both reformist and pro-suffrage, yet many of its members identified themselves principally as wives and mothers. See for example, in vol. 1, 1910–1914, a clipping of an interview with a prominent clubwoman entitled "Womans Club, Man's Best Friend." The Friday Morning Club scrapbooks are in the Huntington Library, San Marino, California.

23. John Higham, "The Reorientation of American Culture in the 1890s," in John Higham, ed. *Writing American History*, (Bloomington, Indiana, 1970), 79.

24. See for example, Peter Gabriel Filene, *Him/Her/Self: Sex Roles in Modern America* (New York, 1974); T. J. Jackson Lears, *No Place of Grace: Antimodernism and the Transformation of American Culture, 1880–1920* (New York, 1981), esp. chap. 3; E. Anthony Rotundo, "Body and Soul: Changing Ideals of Middle-Class Manhood, 1770–1920," *Journal of Social History* 16 (Summer 1983): 32.

25. Jackson, *Crabgrass Frontier*, discusses suburban leisure on pp. 97–99, and on pp. 41–44 describes the inconveniences of commuting by horse-drawn omnibus in the mid-nineteenth century. By the early twentieth century, things had changed, and most suburbs were within thirty minutes, by rail, of their central cities. See *Thirty Miles Around Philadelphia on the Lines of the Pennsylvania Railroad* (Philadelphia, 1913). Since the deterioration of the railroad and other mass transit, and the advent of large scale traffic jams caused by the automobile and the changing commutation patterns, Americans have forgotten the convenience of early twentieth-century rail commuting. See also, John R. Stilgoe, *Metropolitan Corridor* (New Haven, Conn., 1983), 267–282.

26. Kathy Peiss, *Cheap Amusements: Working Women and Leisure in Turn-of-the-Century New York* (Philadelphia, 1986), 6. Her terms "homosocial" and "heterosocial" refer to a shift from men and women taking most of their leisure with their own sex to men and women spending leisure with each other. The term masculine domesticity is my invention. Contemporaries would have used words like "manly" and by 1910 or so "virile" rather than "mas-

culine." They would not have used the word domesticity in the context in which historians have come to use it. Early twentieth-century middle-class Americans would have spoken of the role of the "manly" man in the home.

27. As Nancy Cott has argued in *The Grounding of Modern Feminism*, 4–5, the question of what is, or is not, feminist is a very difficult one. If one would contend, for example, that all suffragists were feminists, or all those who advocated reform, then one could say that there were indeed some feminist aspects to masculine domesticity. Men's and women's defined roles did merge in perceptible ways. But if one defines feminism as an ideology that begins with a recognition that women are wrongfully denied full participation in the society, and demands equal rights and opportunities for women within that society, that is somewhat different, and is indeed the extension of the liberal argument of individualism to women. The latter definition seems more accurate for the early twentieth century; in that case, masculine domesticity was not feminist; it was an alternative to, or substitute for, feminism.

28. See, for example, Joan Seidl, "Consumers Choices: A Study of Household Furnishings, 1880–1920," *Minnesota History* 48 (Spring 1983); 183–197, for some examples of men and household chores. This article is particularly interesting in the way it documents a generational change. I am indebted to Daniel Horowitz for bringing it to my attention.

29. James Canfield, "The Philosophy of Staying in Harness," *Cosmopolitan* 39 (May 1905): 10–11; "A Father's View of the Home," *The Independent* 61 (1906): 912.

30. Richard Harding Davis, "Our Suburban Friends," *Harper's* 89 (January 1894): 55–57.

31. When historians take the word "companionate" into the early twentieth century, they run the risk of confusion. In the 1920s the term "companionate marriage" came to mean a specific type of trial marriage advocated by Judge Ben Lindsay of Colorado. In the context of this chapter, companionate has a more literal meaning, describing a marriage in which husband and wife were friends and companions.

32. Martha Bruère and Robert Bruère, *Increasing Home Efficiency* (New York, 1912), 292. To put the Bruères' work in context, it is important to have an understanding of the changing patterns of American consumption. The most important work in this area has been done by Daniel Horowitz. See his "Frugality or Comfort: Middle-Class Styles of Life in the Early Twentieth Century," *American Quarterly* 37 (Summer, 1985): 239–259; and his book *The Morality of Spending* (Baltimore, 1985). Horowitz discusses the blending of "comfort with cultivation" on p. 259 of the article.

33. The next chapter deals more specifically with the connection between "organization men" and the new suburban domestic ideal. See also Elaine Tyler May, *Great Expectations*, 49; and Peter Filene, *Him/Her/Self*, 80–83.

34. Bruère and Bruère, *Increasing Home Efficiency*, 291–292.

35. *American Homes and Gardens*, 1 (November 1905): editorial, and 1 (December 1905): editorial.

36. Quotes from Seidl, "Consumers' Choices," 186, 189.

37. Kate Wiggin, *Children's Rights* (Boston, 1890): 63–67.

38. See Filene, *Him/Her/Self*, 86–88. Allen Davis has an interesting analysis of manliness and war in *American Heroine* (New York, 1973), 240–241.

39. Ennis Richmond, *Boyhood: a Plea for Continuity in Education* (New York, 1898), 71–72. Carl Werner, *Bringing Up the Boy* (New York, 1913), esp. 69–83; Kate Upson Clark, *Bringing Up Boys*, 35; Margaret Sangster, *The Art of Being Agreeable* (New York, 1897), 55.

40. We need to know much more about such activities as scouting, particularly in terms of its impact on father-son relations. David Macleod, *Building Character in the American Boy* (Madison, Wis., 1983), presents some information on the number of fathers who were troop leaders, and says, on p. 268, that the organization made "ritual gestures" toward closer father-son relations, suggesting that there was some perceived rivalry between scout leaders and fathers. Foster Rhea Dulles, *America Learns to Play: A History of Popular Recreation, 1607–1940* (New York, 1940), chap. 11, esp. 194–201; quote on 198, T. J. Jackson Lears, *No Place of Grace*, chap. 3.

41. Albert J. Beveridge, *The Young Man and the World* (Buffalo, N.Y., 1907), 64–66.

42. Bernarr Macfadden's *Manhood and Marriage* (New York) was published in 1916; it was not until the 1920s that he became a publishing magnate.

43. Macfadden, *Manhood and Marriage*, 81; see also Clement Wood, *Bernarr Macfadden: A Study in Success* (New York, 1929), 14. Wood was an employee of Macfadden, so it is unlikely he would have said anything to displease him.

44. Beveridge, *Young Man and the World*, 164–166.

45. Beveridge is a good example. Although he supported women's greater participation in the life of the state, he made it absolutely clear that he did not expect (or desire) men and women to take on identical roles in the society. Beveridge, *Young Man and the World*, 175–177.

46. Papers and Proceedings, *Third Annual Meeting, American Sociological Society* (Chicago, 1909), esp. 167–168, 181–190. This organization was the predecessor of the American Sociological Association.

47. *Third Annual Meeting, American Sociological Society*, esp. 181–190.

48. House designs were published everywhere. *American Homes and Gardens*, *The Craftsman*, and *House Beautiful* focused on the home, but they and other shelter magazines were not the only places to show the new domestic architecture. To name just two examples, *The Ladies Home Journal* printed plans, and *Scientific American* for a time published a *Building Edition*.

49. Brendan Gill, *Many Masks: A Life of Frank Lloyd Wright*, (New York, 1987, 88–185, has a brilliant discussion of Wright's early career.

50. David Handlin, *The American Home*, analyzes Wright's early emphasis on family togetherness in his architecture as well as his later shift in emphasis to the individual, esp. 306–310; also Jan Cohn, *The Palace or the Poorhouse* (East Lansing, Mich., 1979), 106–107; and Gwendolyn Wright, *Moralism and the Model Home* (Chicago, 1980), 139. Gwendolyn Wright's pioneering scholarship is important for any understanding of the connection between architecture and patterns of culture. Her work emphasizes the importance of uniformity and simplicity abetted by technological sophistication and the influence of home economists. Of the home economists, she has argued, "[Their] bias toward the appearance of equality and self-restraint in domestic architecture derived in large part from the premise that such an image would help sustain an egalitarian society. This was clearly a naive assumption about

the power of an environment" (Wright, *Moralism*, 167). Wright also notes that expensive new technologies meant that many middle-class families could not afford larger houses. Although I do not disagree with Wright's analysis, my own view places less emphasis on the role of experts. I would suggest that it was principally a change in the ways in which suburban families spent their time together that shaped the new interior plans. The desire for a house that represented togetherness, in my view, spurred couples to demand such houses.

51. Such views are reflected even in the work of conservative architects like Joy Wheeler Dow. See "The Fascination of an English Cottage," *American Homes and Gardens* 8 (February 1911): 297.

52. Hayden, *The Grand Domestic Revolution*, 23.

53. *American Homes and Gardens* 2 (March 1906): 161–162. Durando Nichols wrote the article. The same passages appear, word for word, in Gustav Stickley, *Craftsman Homes* (1909; reprint, New York, 1979), 129, attributed to Stickley. On Stickley, see Eileen Boris, *Art and Labor: Ruskin, Morris, and the Craftsman Ideal in America* (Philadelphia, 1986), 53–81.

54. Frank Lloyd Wright, "The Cardboard House," originally published in 1930, in *The Future of Architecture* (New York, 1953), 152–153. Gwendolyn Wright, *Moralism*, 240–253.

55. Eugene Gardner, *The House that Jill Built (After Jack's Had Proved a Failure: A Book on Home Architecture)* (Springfield, Mass., 1896), 14–16.

56. Also, fewer middle-class families had live-in servants by the first decade of the twentieth century, so that the upper floors of the house might belong entirely to the family. See, for example, Olivier Zunz, *The Changing Face of Inequality: Urbanization, Industrial Development, and Immigrants in Detroit, 188–192* (Chicago, 1982), 169.

57. On the one hand, the enormous popularity of designs for children (as reflected in the home magazines and the child-rearing literature) suggests recognition of them as individuals. On the other hand, it shows how they are being set off from the private world of their parents. True, the Victorians had child-sized furniture, but early twentieth-century middle-class families went far beyond sizing furniture for children. In the Victorian household, children and women shared space, while the husband had a separate space. In the early twentieth century, husbands and wives shared intimate space with its own design, and children had their own defined space. This was evident on the second floor. The first floor was shared family space.

58. Zunz, *Changing Face of Inequality*, 152–153. Stephan Thernstrom, *Poverty and Progress: Social Mobility in a Nineteenth-Century City* (Cambridge, Mass., 1964). It is on the question of the relationship between middle-class status and home ownership that I am most at variance with other scholars who study houses and the people who live in them. Most of these scholars have viewed the purchase of a house as synonymous with middle-class status. See, for example, Clark, *American Family Home*, xiii. Gwendolyn, Wright, *Building the Dream* (New York, 1981), 175, suggests that a higher income meant greater home ownership in the early twentieth century. I think that the picture is much more complicated. Ownership, it seems, was central to middle-class status in Victorian America, and it would become so again a little while after World War I. But in the late nineteenth and early twentieth

century a different situation, the one that I describe here, made ownership much less important. Interestingly, Robert Fishman found a similar pattern several decades earlier in England. See *Bourgeois Utopias* (New York, 1987), 90–91.

59. Michael J. Doucet and John C. Weaver, "Material Culture and the North American House: The Era of the Common Man," *Journal of American History* 72 (December 1985): 561–564; and Roger Simon, *The City Building Process: Housing and Services in New Milwaukee Neighborhoods, 1880–1910* (Philadelphia, 1978).

60. See Daniel D. Luria, "Wealth, Capital, and Power: the Social Meaning of Home Ownership,"*Journal of Interdisciplinary History* 7 (Fall 1976), 261–282. Although I do not agree with all of Luria's analysis, this is a very provocative essay.

61. This issue will be discussed more fully in the next chapter. *Scientific American's Building Edition,* in 1898 and 1899, began to reflect a greater openness.

62. Foster Rhea Dulles, *America Learns to Play,* 194–201. For baseball on the suburban lawn, see Handlin, *American Family Home,* 181. Evidence from local sources will appear in the next chapter. Also, Cordelia Biddle, *My Philadelphia Father* (New York, 1955), 1, 40.

63. This ought not to be taken as an argument that in the years before World War I the suburbs had "won" the city/suburb conflict over which was the best place to live. It was not until the federal subsidies of the New Deal that the United States moved irrevocably toward becoming a nation of suburbs. What happened around the turn of the century was a victory of a different sort: Middle-class residential suburbs became identified with family togetherness, the new domesticity. But cities continued to compete. See, for example, Ruth Schwartz Cowan, *More Work for Mother: the Ironies of Household Technology from the Open Hearth to the Microwave* (New York, 1983), 108–109.

CHAPTER FOUR: BREATHING THE AIR OF DOMESTICITY

1. Robert Fishman, *Bourgeois Utopias: The Rise and Fall of Suburbia* (New York, 1987), chap. 5, quote on 139. The information about Henry Houston is from David Contosta, "George Woodward, Philadelphia Progressive," *Pennsylvania Magazine of History and Biography* 111 (July 1987): 341–370. Mary Corbin Sies, "American Country House Architecture in Context: The Suburban Ideal of Living in the East and Midwest" (Ph.D. diss., University of Michigan, 1987), has a chapter on Chestnut Hill.

2. John Stilgoe, *Metropolitan Corridor* (New Haven, Conn., 1983), 269.

3. Kenneth Jackson, *Crabgrass Frontier* (New York, 1985), 23–25. Margaret Marsh, "Suburbanization and the Search for Community," *Pennsylvania History* 44 (April 1977): 99–100.

4. *Property Atlas, Twenty-Fourth Ward,* (Philadelphia, 1st ed., 1879; 2d ed., 1884). Theodore Hershberg kindly lent me the volumes. These atlases show all the buildings and the land use of a particular area. In the 1880s, the Twenty-Fourth Ward encompassed West Philadelphia.

5. On Chestnut Hill see Sies, "American Country House Architecture"; Contosta, "George Woodward." On Rittenhouse Square, see Dennis Clark, "'Ramcat' and Rittenhouse Square: Related Communities," in Howard Gillette and William Cutler, III, eds., *The Divided Metropolis: Social and Spatial Dimensions of Philadelphia, 1800–1975* (Westport, Conn., 1980), 125–140.

6. *Walter Bassett Smith of Wendell and Smith at Ardmore* (Philadelphia, 1899), 6–8.

7. The land on which Overbrook Farms was built cost Drexel and Company $425,000 in 1893. For over a decade after construction started on Overbrook Farms, most of the land surrounding it remained undeveloped, and the new community retained an appearance of isolation, in spite of its proximity to the downtown. The community's memoirist was Tello J. d'Apery, *Overbrook Farms* (Philadelphia, 1936). See esp. 26. I am very much indebted to Jane Smith Taylor, the granddaughter of Walter Bassett Smith, who allowed me to use materials in her possession, including photographs, newspaper clippings, promotional material, maps, and miscellaneous information. As of the mid-1980s, these materials were still in her possession.

8. George E. Thomas, "Architectural Patronage and Social Stratification in Philadelphia between 1840 and 1920," in Howard Gillette and William Cutler, III, eds., *The Divided Metropolis: Social and Spatial Dimensions of Philadelphia, 1800–1975* (Westport, Conn., 1980), 109–111.

9. House prices were listed on the architect's drawing of Overbrook Farms houses in possession of Jane Smith Taylor.

10. The Woodward article was published in the *Architectural Record* in the early twentieth century; a copy of the article is in the files of the Historical Society of Pennsylvania.

11. Clipping File, Newspaper advertisements of Wendell and Smith, from Jane Smith Taylor. The builders kept a scrapbook of their advertisements in all of the Philadelphia papers.

12. For house prices in Philadelphia as a whole in the 1890s, see Frank H. Taylor and William B. McManus, *The City of Philadelphia as It Appears in the Year 1894* (Philadelphia, 1894), 186. Pennsylvania Railroad, *Thirty Miles Around Philadelphia on the Lines of the Pennsylvania Railroad* (Philadelphia, 1913), had housing costs for nearly all Philadelphia suburbs.

13. *Scientific American Building Edition* 26 (6) (1898): 92. The exact house shown was in Pelham, another Wendell and Smith development, but the same design was built in Overbrook Farms. Plans for several Overbrook Farms houses appeared in that edition.

14. Herman Wendell and Walter Bassett Smith, *A Little Talk with the Homeseeker* (Philadelphia, 1899), esp. 1–2, 12; Herman Wendell and Walter Bassett Smith, *Overbrook Farms: A Suburb Deluxe* (Philadelphia, 1905), 1, passim. The second advertising brochure is particularly fascinating in its highly sophisticated use of a suggestive visual technique. At the bottom outside corner of each page was a delicate line drawing, and the facing pages presented the contrast between the crowded, hectic, unhealthy city and the clean, pastoral, and restful suburb. Three examples are: a drawing of factories belching smoke opposite a golf-playing woman; a claw-like hand reaching for a glass of filthy dark liquid (impure water) opposite a graceful feminine hand stretching

forth for a glass of pure water in a country scene of hills, evergreens, and sunshine; and a hot, dirty man shoveling coal into a furnace opposite a well-dressed woman adjusting a thermostat.

15. The data comes from the *Manuscript Census Records, Twelfth Census of the United States,* 1900, Enumeration District 904, and from property maps lent me by Jane Smith Taylor. My sample included all the households.

16. *Manuscript Census Records,* 1900. Fifty-nine percent of the male household heads were between 30 and 50 in age, 14 percent were between 50 and 60, 12 percent were older than sixty, another 12 percent were younger than thirty, and 3 percent were unclassifiable. Of the female household heads, most were older than sixty. Of the thirty-eight daughters older than eighteen, thirty were simply "at home," in census parlance, five were in school or college, and three were teachers. The data on family size is interesting. Eighteen percent of the women who were currently or previously married had no children. The average number of children for women was 2.3, for those under forty-five, 1.9.

17. *Manuscript Census Records,* 1900. Exact percentages for servants break down as follows. Thirty-one percent of the households had one servant, 35 percent had two, 18 percent had three, and 5 percent had four or more.

18. *Manuscript Census Records for Ward 34 of Philadelphia, Thirteenth Census of the United States,* 1910. In 1910, 91 percent of Overbrook Farms families had live-in servants. Thirty-four percent had one, 32 percent had two, 17 percent had three, and 8 percent had four or more. The larger domestic staffs were on the north side; while just under 50 percent of the southsiders had one servant, nearly two-thirds of the northsiders had two or three.

19. In Wendell and Smith, *A Little Talk with the Homeseeker,* the developers claim that their planning would prevent any "wide diversity in the price of . . . houses erected—so wide, indeed, that the entire effect of a handsome mansion may be destroyed by a red-and-yellow structure next door." And in their newspaper advertisements they presented current residents as people "prominent in the intellectual, political, and mercantile walks of life" (Philadelphia *Press,* September 25, 1897, from W. B. Smith Clipping File, courtesy Jane Smith Taylor).

20. Colleen McDannell found advertisements for Overbrook Farms in Philadelphia Catholic newspapers of the period. The advertisements in the German language *Philadelphia Demokrat,* probably published between 1895 and 1900, are in the W. B. Smith Clipping File.

21. d'Apery's *Overbrook Farms,* is the most concise discussion of community life. See also *The Overbrook Farms Club, 1896–1946: Fiftieth Anniversary* (Philadelphia, 1946).

22. See d'Apery, *Overbrook Farms,* 70–80. Both d'Apery, *Overbrook Farms,* and the Pennsylvania Railroad, *Thirty Miles Around Philadelphia,* 19–20, agreed on the convenience of Overbrook Farms as a commuting suburb. Most men did commute downtown. Wendell and Smith printed a telephone directory in 1899, and I checked the business addresses of the men listed in the *Philadelphia Business Directory, 1899.* Seventy-six percent were indentifiable as downtown commuters.

23. d'Apery, *Overbrook Farms,* 76–79; also, Wendell and Smith, *Overbrook Farms, A Suburb Deluxe.*

24. d'Apery, *Overbrook Farms,* 78–79.

25. The men's club took the initiative in developing the community's athletic facilities and in organizing recreational and sporting events. The men's club also was involved in keeping the community's high status appearance intact. And it was in charge of some community "housekeeping" chores: the club arranged for snowplowing in winter, negotiated rates with the steam heat company (which heated all the houses), and successfully opposed the city's plan to run a trolley line through the community. See d'Apery, *Overbrook Farms,* 77–78, 97, and *Overbrook Farms Club,* 11–12.

26. *Civic Club Bulletin* 3 (7) (March 1910): 1; *Civic Club Bulletin* 12 (5) (January 1919): 10; *Fiftieth Anniversary, The Needlework Guild of America: Program* (Philadelphia, 1935), 6; d'Apery, *Overbrook Farms,* 90-93.

27. The Philadelphia Branch of the Needlework Guild, *Thirteenth Annual Report, Year Ending December 31, 1897,* 4; d'Apery, *Overbrook Farms,* 89–90.

28. A few of the men who lived in Overbrook Farms are listed in Ellis Paxson Oberholtzer, *History of Philadelphia,* vol. 3, *Biography* (Philadelphia, 1913), and these more prominent men do have city-wide interests as well as local ones. Also, d'Apery, *Overbrook Farms,* mentions that husbands and wives, sometimes in organized groups, patronized the downtown theatres.

29. There is a biography of Janet Sayward in *Who's Who in Philadelphia* (Philadelphia, 1920), 150. According to Jane Smith Taylor, the developer's granddaughter who grew up in Overbrook Farms, in the early twentieth century the girls went to Miss Sayward's School, while the boys went to private schools downtown or to the Friends School in Haverford. See also d'Apery, *Overbrook Farms,* 26.

30. d'Apery, *Overbrook Farms,* 71.

31. *Plan of the Haddonfield Ready Villa Association* (Philadelphia, 1854). Apparently there was already some small-scale commuting to Philadelphia from Haddonfield, as the planners of this community state that "businessmen who live in Haddonfield are generally in their counting houses [in Philadelphia] within thirty minutes of leaving the Haddonfield depot, refreshed by the morning ride and not fatigued by overwalking" (p. 11).

32. Ibid., 4.

33. Ibid., 3, 5–11. The Ready Villas were not the only land scheme in Haddonfield at the time, but it was the most thoroughgoing and ambitious. A more traditional speculative venture was the Haddonfield Land and Improvement Company, also founded in 1854. (The railroad came through in 1852.) This failed too, and the land was eventually sold at a sheriff's sale. See C. E. N. Hartel, "The Railroad Came" (typewritten MS, Haddonfield Historical Society, 1955.)

34. I am grateful to Collingswood historian George Palmer for sharing his research with me. Collingswood was incorporated in 1888. In the mid-1880s, sugar baron E. C. Knight, who was also a director of the Pennsylvania Railroad, hired his cousin, Richard Collings, as the actual developer of the community. Lots were platted and sold, and the community developed quickly into a middle-class suburb. By 1913, according to the Pennsylvania Railroad, *Thirty Miles Around Pennsylvania,* 140, Collingswood had become an "ideal suburb" for the "person of moderate means who seeks to combine the pleasures of suburban life with the conveniences of the city."

35. Analysis of *Manuscript Census Records, Twelfth Census of the United*

States, 1900, Haddonfield Borough, New Jersey, systematic sample of 20 percent of the households. By 1900, only 2 percent of the population were farmers.

36. In 1900, 25 percent of the men held sales or clerical jobs. Another 18.7 percent owned businesses, although their enterprises tended to be on a somewhat smaller scale than those of Overbrook Farms residents, and 8.4 percent were professionals. Corporate executives made up 2.8 percent of the population, and 5.6 percent referred to themselves as "capitalists" or as having an independent income. There were, in addition, a couple of farmers. Twenty-seven percent of the population in 1900 were working-class—16 percent skilled, 11 percent semi-skilled or unskilled—but their numbers were shortly to decline markedly. Analysis of *Manuscript Census Records, Twelfth Census of the United States*, 1900, and *Thirteenth Census of the United States*, 1910, Haddonfield Borough, New Jersey. For 1910, I used a systematic sample of 10 percent of the population.

37. Ruth Schwartz Cowan, *More Work for Mother: The Ironies of Household Technology from the Open Hearth to the Microwave* (New York, 1983), 157–158. According to Cowan (p. 99), nationally there was one servant for every fifteen households in 1900.

38. The black minister turned up in my census sample. The census data from 1900 and 1910 also showed a decline in Haddonfield residents who engaged in daily domestic work. As more middle-class families moved to it, living in Haddonfield became too prohibitive for the less prosperous, so they had to move across the creek or down the road, but outside the borough. It almost looks like early gentrification.

39. *Haddon Homesteads* (Haddonfield, n.d., but probably in the early 1920s), 4. Interview with George Palmer, August, 1986. Also, Pennsylvania Railroad, *Thirty Miles Around Philadelphia*, notes that commuting time between Haddonfield and Philadelphia was twenty-three minutes, including the ferry ride.

40. House prices, rentals, and commuter fares are from Pennsylvania Railroad, *Thirty Miles Around Philadelphia*.

41. *Manuscript Census Records*, 1900 and 1910, Haddonfield, New Jersey. Samples as described in notes 35 and 36.

42. Olivier Zunz, *The Changing Face of Inequality: Urbanization, Industrial Development, and Immigrants in Detroit, 1880–1920* (Chicago, 1982), 152–153; see also Roger Simon, *The City Building Process: Housing and Services in New Milwaukee Neighborhoods, 1880–1910* (Philadelphia, 1978), esp. 50–52.

43. Some of my information on the houses is from my own field work. Also, the Collingswood Public Library possesses some early twentieth-century plans of Haddonfield houses by local architect Clement Remington. See *Where To Live—Why?* (no place of publication or date, but internal evidence suggests early twentieth century.) The answer was a new development in Haddonfield called Haddonfield Manor. For the later teens and early twenties, see *Haddon Homesteads*.

44. Emma C. Gibson, *Pioneering Women of Historic Haddonfield* (West Collingswood, N.J., 1975?), 110, 120–130. Dr. Clement earned praise from the community when she suspended her practice to care for her child during a long illness; there were limits as to how important a woman's career could be.

St. Agnes was one of two Episcopal Boarding Schools that closed in the early twentieth century. See *Episcopal Schools: Forty-third School Year* (Haddonfield, N.J., 1902).

45. The Haddonfield Historical Society has the papers of the Natural Science Club. Some are undated, but are clearly from the early twentieth century, others are dated from 1908 to about 1914. There are membership lists, correspondence, and records of the minutes of meetings. Mixed in with these papers are those of the Debating Society.

46. Minutes of the Natural Science Club, 1914.

47. Papers of the Penn Literary Society, Haddonfield Historical Society. Like those of the Natural Science Club, these are miscellaneous materials from the early twentieth century, including minutes, some attendance figures, and the like.

48. *Haddonfield Gun Club: Second Annual Shoot at Targets* (Haddonfield, 1908). Papers of the Natural Science Club, 1911–1912. I am indebted to Kathy Tassini, the Librarian of the Haddonfield Historical Society, for the information about the early attempt to create a men's civic club.

49. Gibson, *Women of Historic Haddonfield,* profiles many of the early Fortnightly leaders. *Haddonfield Monthly* 1 (1) (March 1901): 8. *Haddonfield Monthly* 1 (2) (April 1901): 9.

50. Minutes of the Haddonfield Sewing Society, (handwritten), 1896–1903.

51. By-Laws of the Haddon Field Club [c. 1904–1910]. *Haddon Monthly* 1 (1) (March 1901): 10.

52. An excellent illustration is the Moore Family Scrapbooks, esp. 1902–1908. Haddonfield Historical Society.

53. Edith Shelhorn's scrapbook, 1914, in the Haddonfield Historical Society, has a wealth of information about the social life of adolescents. Shelhorn was a student at Haddonfield High School. See also the program for the high school's 1907 graduation.

Chapter Five: A Version of America

1. On the housing industry in the twenties, see Gwendolyn Wright, *Building the Dream: A Social History of Housing in America* (Cambridge, Mass., 1981), 193–214. The most exciting recent treatment of the way in which women, under the guise of "free choice," were lured back into domesticity is Nancy Cott, *The Grounding of Modern Feminism* (New Haven, Conn., 1987), 145–174. Historians do not generally think that the First World War had a tremendous impact on housing; for example, Clifford E. Clark's *American Family Home* (Chapel Hill, N.C., 1987), does not have an index entry for World War I, although World War II receives considerable coverage.

2. Sam Bass Warner, *The Urban Wilderness* (New York, 1972), 224. United States Bureau of the Census, *Historical Statistics of the United States, Colonial Times to the Present* (Washington, D.C., 1960), 393. Although the actual housing picture is somewhat more complex than Warner suggests, his argument has merit. According to the above-referenced census figures, from 1906 through 1908 there was a steady if slight decrease in housing starts, followed by a rise in 1909. After that, until the United States entered the war in 1917,

housing starts increased very slowly, by an average of only 6 percent a year. In 1917 the decline became very serious. Housing starts that year were 45 percent below what they had been in 1916, and those in 1918 were 50 percent below those of 1917. If we consider the decade as a whole, it is clear that there was a real problem. Between 1910 and 1920 the population of the United States increased by about 15 percent, while the housing starts during the same period witnessed an overall decline of 1.7 percent.

3. According to the Philadelphia Housing Association, one of its investigators canvassed an extensive area of West Philadelphia into which some black families had been accepted before the war. Now, only one agent would rent to blacks, and he had only one house. Philadelphia Housing Association, "Negro Migration Study," (typewritten MS, Philadelphia, ca. 1920).

4. Racial and ethnic covenants were not entirely new in the 1920s, but they proliferated enormously. My survey of real-estate ephemera in the Huntington Library for this period suggests that they were the rule rather than the exception in California. Carol O'Connor, in *A Sort of Utopia* (Albany, 1983), found Scarsdale, New York, also to be exclusionary.

5. Warner, *Urban Wilderness*, 222. I am indebted to Gail Radford, who is writing a dissertation for Columbia University on twentieth-century reform housing, for sharing her knowledge with me.

6. Franklin K. Lane, quoted in William Smythe, *City Homes on Country Lanes* (New York, 1921), 66–67.

7. Ibid., 213.

8. Ibid., 183.

9. Ibid., 190–191.

10. Mark Foster, *From Streetcar to Superhighway* (Philadelphia, 1981), 47.

11. Ibid., 46–48.

12. United States Bureau of the Census, *Historical Statistics*, 393. United States Department of Commerce, *Statistical Abstract of the United States, 52d Number, 1930* (Washington, 1930), 92. Gwendolyn Wright, *Building the Dream*, 193, notes the national government's interest in home ownership, but errs in stating that during the twenties, "the percentage of homeowners had been steadily declining."

13. United States Bureau of the Census, *Historical Statistics*, 396.

14. Information on house prices from *American Home*, 1928–1932.

15. Self-amortizing mortgages did not become used until the 1930s, when the federal lending agencies paved the way. In the 1920s, it was common for people to have two mortgages. A few financial advisors suggested that with a fairly substantial down payment, families might be able to buy a house that cost three times their annual income.

16. The professions surveyed were physician, lawyer, engineer, dentist, and college professor. *Historical Statistics*, 97.

17. See, for example, Warner, *Urban Wilderness*, 224.

18. Margaret Slattery, *The American Girl and Her Community* (Boston, 1918), 150.

19. Slattery, *American Girl*, 108, 164.

20. Beatrice Forbes Robinson Hale, *What's Wrong with Our Girls?* (New York, 1923), 41.

21. For a summary of "post-feminism," 1920s style, see Cott, *Grounding of Modern Feminism*, 273–283.

22. Penina Migdal Glazer and Miriam Slater, *Unequal Colleagues: the Entrance of Women into the Professions* (New Brunswick, 1987).

23. Mary Hinman Abel, *Successful Family Life on the Moderate Income* 2d ed. (Philadelphia, 1927), 71–73, 197–198, 237.

24. Cott, *Grounding of Modern Feminism*, 174.

25. Cosgrove, *Mothers and Daughters*, 29–30.

26. Hale, *What's Wrong?*, 13, 14, 83–87. See especially these *Good Housekeeping* stories: Faith Baldwin, "Garden Oats" (January through April, 1929), and Margaret Widden, "Rhinestones" (August through December, 1928).

27. Abel, *Successful Family Life*, 238. Also, "We Will Buy These for you in New York," *Good Housekeeping* (July 1932). The work week for middle-class adults had shrunk to forty five hours a week by the end of the twenties. See George Lundberg, *Leisure* (New York, 1934): 96–98.

28. Mary Thayer Bixler, "The Affiliated Nursery School—the Parents' View," in *The Nursery School as a Social Experiment* (Northampton, Mass., 1928), 27–29.

29. Elaine Tyler May, *Great Expectations: Marriage and Divorce in Post Victorian America* (Chicago, 1980).

30. One of the best illustrations is "Forgotten Magic," *Good Housekeeping* (April 1928): 52–55 ff.

31. Philip Howard, *Father and Son: an Intimate Study* (New York, 1922), 10–19.

32. Howard might have been surprised to find that by the end of the decade at least one young son of immigrant parents considered that the model he proposed was the "American way" of family life. There is no indication that the pseudonymous "Ralph," one of the sons of immigrant parents studied by youth worker Ryland Boorman, had ever heard of Howard, but his perception of an emotional distance between himself and his parents led him to adopt what Boorman called "significant changes in the customs of his home [that] came primarily from American practice" (*Personality in its Teens* [New York, 1931], 38). Ralph wrote Boorman: "Up to a short time ago, our family was not as happy and intimate as other families I have seen." Ralph decided to initiate a closer relationship with his parents by showing affection for and confiding in them. What is so interesting about this is that Ralph believed that in so doing he was making his family more "American."

33. *Good Housekeeping* (August 1928): 40–41 ff. The illustration that accompanied this article shows a woman working at a desk, while the husband sits on the floor playing with a child.

34. *Outlook Magazine* 148 (May 2, 1928): 8, 501.

35. Ibid.

36. Christine Frederick's fascinating book, which in my view is the most shockingly cynical marketing tract to come out of the 1920s, is *Selling Mrs. Consumer* (New York, 1929). Hermann Keyserling, the self-styled "Count Keyserling" who apparently wrote a widely read book on marriage, arrived in the United States in 1928 for a much publicized lecture tour. In an interview for *Good Housekeeping* (April 1928), 30–31 ff, he lamented how much power women had over men in this country. The United States, he proclaimed, had become a "matriarchate," where "women are the real rulers. . . . American husbands today make just as abject an impression as oppressed woman ever

did." If the stereotype of the henpecked husband did not fully come into its own until the 1950s, Hermann Keyserling gave his American audience an early version, blaming women for "throw[ing] the sexes out of adjustment" (*Good Housekeeping* [April 1928], 247).

37. *American Home* 3 (November 1929): 146, is an excellent example.

38. It is probably not a coincidence that Colonial Williamsburg was a creation of the 1920s, and that Winterthur (an historic mansion) was also opened then.

39. *American Home* 4 (August 1930): 493. In Marcia Mead, *Homes of Character* (New York, 1926), 122, is a quote from John Ruskin that nearly every American writer on domestic architecture had been quoting since the 1880s: "I would have our ordinary dwelling houses built to last and built to be lovely; as rich and full of pleasantness as may be, within and without." By the 1920s, Ruskin had become a little shopworn, but still serviceable.

40. Eugene Gardner, *The House that Jill Built (After Jack's Had Proved a Failure)* (Springfield, Mass., 1896), 93; emphasis in original. Emily Post, *The Personality of a House* (New York, 1930), 297.

41. *American Home* 4 (April 1930): 44.

42. Mead, *Homes of Character*, 196–197.

43. *American Home* 1 (March 1929): 518; Also, *American Home* 3 (September 1929), 73–74; 7 (March 1932), 342–343 ff. C. Madeline Dixon, *Children Are Like That* (New York, 1930), 5.

44. Caroline Bartlett Crane, *Everyman's House* (New York, 1925), 1. The house cost $7,300 to build in the midwest. Herbert Hoover wrote the forward to the book. Pauline Duff, "Consider the Children," *American Home* 5 (November 1930): 127–128 f.

45. Dixon, *Children*, 17–18.

46. Andrew Jackson Downing, *The Architecture of Country Houses* (1852; reprint, New York, 1969), xix, 270; Nathaniel Willis is quoted in Wright, *Building the Dream*, 84–85.

47. *American Home* 3 (July 1929): 463, editorial.

48. *American Home* 1 (October 1928); 8, quotes and discusses the acceptance speech of candidate Hoover.

49. Wright, *Building the Dream*, 196, 204.

50. This survey was taken by a building and loan association, and was reported in *American Home* 1 (February 1929), 390 ff. Quote from 390.

51. *American Home* 1 (December 1928): 209. Walter Pritchard, the month before, had condemned urban dwellers to a "poor, pale, ghost of the old" Thanksgiving celebrations as well. *American Home* 1 (November 1928): 111. Similar kinds of sentiments appear in the same magazine as follows: 2 (June 1929), 319; 3 (November 1929), 129; 1 (January 1929), 287; and 2 (December 1929), 243.

52. The best analysis of Hoover's policies, in my view, remains Albert U. Romasco, *The Poverty of Abundance* (New York, 1967).

53. Frederick, *Selling Mrs. Consumer*, 395–396. Frederick's views are fascinating not because they are either coherent or intellectually compelling—they are neither—but because her mission in life was to get families to spend money, which was more important to her than holding on to any particular set of values. Her cynicism is breathtaking. For instance, on p. 397 she argued

that it was urban women who worked after marriage, and they did so for the sake of having more purchasing power for the family. After stating what she called this "fact" at considerable length, she went on to contradict herself and suggest that young married women held jobs because they were unwilling to "be in the position of complete economic subjugation to man." The long quotation from Frederick is on p. 393.

54. Frederick, *Selling Mrs. Consumer*, 393–394.

55. Christine Frederick, "Is Suburban Living a Delusion?" *Outlook Magazine* 148 (February 22, 1928): 290–291, 313.

56. Lundberg, *Leisure*, 45, 50.

57. Ethel Longworth Smith, "In Defense of Suburbia," *Outlook Magazine* (April 4, 1928), 543, 558.

58. Lundberg, *Leisure*, 47–48.

59. See, for example, Daniel Schaffer, *Garden Cities of America: The Radburn Experience* (Philadelphia, 1982), 69–75.

60. Lewis Mumford, "The Wilderness of Suburbia," *New Republic* 21 (September 7, 1921): 45. Catherine Bauer, *Modern Housing*, (New York, 1934), is her most comprehensive critique of conventional housing.

61. Mark Foster, *From Streetcar to Superhighway*, 65–68, 70.

62. Schaffer, *Garden Cities*, 46–47.

63. Schaffer, *Garden Cities*, 161; Bauer, *Modern Housing*, 239.

64. Radburn residents George Sporn and William Elbow, quoted in Schaffer, *Garden Cities*, 167, 169.

65. Ibid., 174–176.

66. *Historical Statistics*, 393.

67. *American Home* 4 (September 1930): 558. For some of the less expensive houses, see *American Home* 6 (June 1931) and 7 (March 1932): passim. On remodeling, see, for example, *American Home* 4 (June 1930), 303; and for advice on interiors 6 (September 1931), 370–374, 208 ff, and 7 (February 1932), 261 ff.

68. *American Home* 6 (September 1931): 349, for the optimistic assessment of one editor. See also *American Home* 7 (December 1931): 145.

69. President Hoover's speech quoted in *American Home* 7 (February 1932): 253, and discussed on 273–274.

70. Bauer, *Modern Housing*, 272.

71. The "curious mixture" quotation is from Jan Cohn, *The Palace or the Poorhouse* (East Lansing, Mich., 1979), 110. Tom Wolfe, whose very barbed *From Bauhaus to Our House* (New York, 1981) is a scathing critique of modern architecture and design, lauds Wright's ability to understand suburban Americans.

72. Kenneth Jackson, *The Crabgrass Frontier* (New York, 1985), 196.

73. Jackson, *Crabgrass Frontier*, 203.

74. Kenneth Jackson's work on the FHA is particularly illuminating. See *Crabgrass Frontier*, 204–218.

75. Foster, *Streetcar to Superhighway*, 166. Foster's chapters on the New Deal's urban and transportation policies are excellent. On the Greenbelt towns, Joseph Arnold, *The New Deal in the Suburbs* (Columbus, Ohio, 1971), remains the most comprehensive work. See Arnold R. Alanin and Joseph Eden, *Main Street Ready Made* (Madison, Wisc., 1987), on Greedale.

CHAPTER SIX: THE SUBURBAN CITY BEAUTIFUL

1. Robert Fogelson, *The Fragmented Metropolis: Los Angeles, 1850–1930* (Cambridge, Mass., 1967), 144, 157. Quote on 157. In 1880 the Los Angeles population was 11,183; to make an intra-state comparison, over 200,000 people lived in San Francisco. By 1920, both Los Angeles and San Francisco topped the half million mark. But ten years later, while San Francisco had grown only to 634,000, and its metropolitan area to 1,290,000 the city of Los Angeles had 1.2 million residents, and its metropolitan area 2.3 million. Fogelson, *Fragmented Metropolis,* 21, 79. Throughout this period, Los Angeles was a city in which native white Protestant midwesterners dominated the original settlers, in which European immigrants were a relatively small proportion of the population, and where Mexican, Asian, and black Americans were excluded from the mainstream. In 1930, while New York's immigrants totalled a third of the population, and Chicago's a quarter, in Los Angeles immigrants formed only 15 percent of the population. Fogelson, *Fragmented Metropolis,* 80–82.

2. *Grand Auction Sale: The Malabar Tract* (Los Angeles, 1886). *Alhambra* (broadside, n.d.). In Ephemera Collection, Huntington Library, San Marino, California. The Huntington has dozens of similar broadsides, real estate brochures, and the like, for different subdivisions and suburban tracts, all of which have a similar message. See Robert Fishman, *Bourgeois Utopias* (New York, 1987), 155–160, for a good brief discussion of early Los Angeles.

3. Broadsides from the Moran Tract (1887) and Orangedale (1896), Ephemera Collection, Huntington Library.

4. The collapse of the land boom discouraged investors only briefly. Prosperity returned and by 1894 the business community was even able to poke fun at itself. In that year's La Fiesta Parade (La Fiesta was a promotional event designed to draw tourists, investments, and new residents to Los Angeles) there was a float that satirized the feverish boom that had collapsed just seven years earlier. The float carried an auctioneer and a little crowd. Its signs proclaimed, "Corner Lots only $1000 per Inch," and "Free Water, only $10 per Gallon," and "Tenderfeet Wanted." See *La Fiesta Program* (Los Angeles, 1894). That businessmen, who sponsored the parade, could make fun of a recent collapse suggests that they now felt on pretty secure ground. See also Fogelson, *Fragmented Metropolis,* 78, and Fishman, *Bourgeois Utopias,* 159–162.

5. Dana Bartlett, *The Better City: A Sociological Study of a Modern American City* (Los Angeles, 1907), 7. Southern Pacific Railroad, *California: South of Tehachopi* (San Francisco, 1908), 11–19. Quotes on 11, 18.

6. Smythe, quoted in Fogelson, *Fragmented Metropolis,* 137. This is the same Smythe who wrote *City Homes on Country Lanes* (New York, 1921). Elaine Tyler May, *Great Expectations* (Chicago, 1980), 54.

7. Fogelson, *Fragmented Metropolis,* 2, 157. Fishman, *Bourgeois Utopias,* 169.

8. Augusta Fink, *Time and the Terraced Land* (Berkeley, Calif., 1966), 107–109. *Palos Verdes* (Los Angeles, 1922). E. G. Lewis noted that he had pre-

viously developed the Los Angeles suburb of Atascadero, and University City in St. Louis, Missouri.

9. Robert Sherwood, "Palos Verdes," in Robert M. Stern, ed., *The Anglo-American Suburb* (London, 1981), 80. *Palos Verdes,* 22.

10. *Palos Verdes Bulletin* 2 (11) (November 1926): 3. The Huntington Library has nearly a complete set of these bulletins into the 1930s.

11. *Palos Verdes of Today* (Los Angeles, 1926), introduction.

12. "Palos Verdes Carries Its Town Plan into Execution," *American City Magazine* 33 (December 1925), 667. The magazine commended the suburb's "protective restrictions," regarding lot size, setback regulations, and minimum construction costs, but they did not mention the more sinister racial and ethnic exclusion. But these existed, not only in Palos Verdes, but also nationwide. Many California suburbs excluded "negroes [sic], Asiatics, and people of other than the white or caucasian race, except in the capacity of domestic servants." That last category included most Mexican-Americans, the one exception being those descendants of early settlers who could claim pure Spanish heritage. See *Protective Restrictions, Palos Verdes Estates* (Los Angeles, 1923), 4. In the east, restrictive covenants were also extended to Jews, but Los Angeles did not have any significant Jewish population in this period. Although restrictive covenants were not entirely new in the twenties, their use had become very much more widespread. More informal methods of exclusion, practiced by the previous generation of suburbanites, had apparently ceased to be as effective.

13. *Protective Restrictions, Palos Verdes Estates, Tract 6885* (Los Angeles, 1923), 3–4.

14. *Protective Restrictions,* 1. Although in many ways Palos Verdes was like other Los Angeles suburbs, the developers made it clear that they would not allow the idea of a "garden suburb" to be carried to the extent that some Los Angelenos liked—that is, in some suburbs, the concept of garden suburb meant that residents could create tiny farms. Many subdivision advertisements in the Ephemera Collection at the Huntington Library explicitly encouraged the growing of produce for sale, or the keeping of rabbits, chickens, or other small livestock. One prominent Los Angeles clubwoman even gave a newspaper interview from her home in Glendale in which she boasted of her 200 chickens, which provided her a small business. Friday Morning Club Scrapbook vol. 1 (1910–1914), 164, available at the Huntington Library, San Marino, California. She would not have been allowed to do that in Palos Verdes. Residents were forbidden to have rabbits, chickens, or other livestock, except in unbuilt areas, for their private use, and with express permission of the Homes Association. *Protective Restrictions,* 4.

15. Frederick Law Olmsted, Jr., "Palos Verdes Estates," *Landscape Architecture* 17 (July 1927): 256. *Protective Restrictions,* for tracts 6885, 6890, and 7537.

16. "Palos Verdes Carries its Town Plan into Execution," 667. *Palos Verdes Bulletin* 7 (5) (May 1931): 37–38. Throughout the period the *Palos Verdes Bulletin* profiled various residents.

17. *Meetings of Underwriting Subscribers of Palos Verdes Project: Report of Proceedings and Addresses* (Los Angeles, 1922), 6, 18. *Palos Verdes Bulletin* 7 (2) (February 1931): 8.

18. See, for example, *Palos Verdes of Today*, 3. Also, the monthly *Bulletin* published numerous photographs.

19. *Palos Verdes Bulletin* 3 (10) (October 1926): 6, and 6 (11) (November 1930): 5. Fishman, *Bourgeois Utopias*, 170.

20. The Margate section is described in *Palos Verdes Bulletin* 7 (1) (January 1931): 1.

21. *Protective Restrictions*, 5.

22. *Palos Verdes of Today*.

23. *Palos Verdes Bulletin* 2, 11 (November 1926): 3. George Lundberg et al., *Leisure* (New York, 1934), 184. The suburbanites of Westchester County, New York, which Lundberg and his team studied, were remarkably like the residents of Palos Verdes—family-centered (most of the men spent every evening with their wives and children), outdoors-loving, and choosing the suburbs because they believed that suburbia would allow them to develop closer ties to their children and to nature.

24. See, for example, the following *Palos Verdes Bulletins:* 3 (9) (October 1927): 4; 6 (11) (November 1930): 1; and 5 (10) (October 1929): 8.

25. *Palos Verdes Bulletin* 2 (2) (February 1926): 1, and 2 (3) (March 1926): 3.

26. Carol O'Connor, *A Sort of Utopia: Scarsdale New York* (Albany, New York, 1983). *Palos Verdes Bulletin* 3 (4) (April 1927): 7; 5 (5) (May 1929): 6; and 6 (11) (November 1930): 4.

27. See, for example, *Palos Verdes Bulletin* 2 (6) (June 1926): 1.

28.*Palos Verdes Bulletin* 2 (1) (January 1926): 1.

29. *Palos Verdes Bulletin* 3 (1) (January 1927): 5; 4 (1) (January 1928): 3; 5 (1) (January 1929): 4.

30. *Palos Verdes Bulletin* 7 (1) (January 1931): 5.

31. For example, *Palos Verdes Bulletin* 6 (4) (April 1930): 1. The Ball was held in February.

32. *Palos Verdes Bulletin* 6 (4) (April 1930): 4.

33. Friday Morning Club, Scrapbook 1 January 1909–February 1910, and 2, 1912. The clippings was unidentified further.

34. Clipping from *Los Angeles Examiner* April 25, 1915, in Friday Morning Club, Scrapbook 3, January 1914 through January 1916, 84; see also 91. In 1915, for example, there was a hotly contested election for club president, in which one candidate was criticized because her opponents feared she would insist on "too many political programs in the club or too great an infusion of outside interests." The candidate so criticized was "Mrs. Seward" Simons. She won, but the election generated enough heat to be covered by the major Los Angeles daily newspaper. Clipping from *Los Angeles Times*, June 23, 1923, in Friday Morning Club, Scrapbook 8, January 1923 through August 1927. Clipping from *Los Angeles Herald*, June 6, 1924, also in vol. 8.

35. These are impressions from my reading of the Friday Morning Club Scrapbook 8 (1923–1927), 10 (January 1926–July 1928), 12 (1930 and 1931), and 16 (1934 and 1935.)

36. *Palos Verdes Bulletin* 5 (4) (April 1929): 3, and 6 (11) (November 1930): 5.

37. *Palos Verdes Bulletin* 6 (11) (November 1930): 2–4, and 5 (10) (October 1929): 1.

38. *Palos Verdes Bulletin* 3 (1) (January 1927): 2. Palos Verdes was not

much different in its lack of interest in church-going from Los Angeles as a whole, where only about 20 percent of adults were religiously affiliated. See Fogelson, *Fragmented Metropolis,* 194. Nationally, about 44 percent of Americans belonged to a congregation in the twenties. See George H. Singleton, *Religion in the City of Angels* (Ann Arbor, Michigan, 1979), 213. Lundberg's statistics are extremely interesting. Only 43 percent of the families in Westchester county as a whole had at least one family member who attended religious services on a regular basis, and that did not necessarily mean an adult member. No one ever mentions synogogues. Jews were not welcome in these suburbs, although there were some Jewish families in parts of Westchester county. Catholics seem invisible as well.

39. See the following *Palos Verdes Bulletins:* 2 (5) (May 1926): 4; 2 (6) (June 1926): 3; 2 (9) (September 1926): 6; 2 (10) (October 1926): 2; and 2 (12) (December 1926): 2. There was no church in Palos Verdes until well after World War II, when a nondenominational "community church" was established.

40. *Palos Verdes Bulletin* 2 (9) (September 1926): 3; 6 (11) (November 1930): 4; and 5 (10) (October 1929): 8.

41. *Palos Verdes Bulletin* 1 (8) (August 1925): 3. Again, the families of Palos Verdes seem to resemble those of suburban Westchester county. Lundberg's quantitative data matches the more impressionistic information on Palos Verdes. In both communities, the families spent their leisure time together. In Lundberg's study, 56 percent of the commuting husbands spent every evening with their wives, and another 34 percent spent at least five evenings a week in that manner. Of the children, Lundberg said: "So far as the children of commuting families are concerned, they, too tend to spend the evening at home. On one particular evening of a school day, 71 percent of the boys and girls were at home with their families." Lundberg, *Leisure,* 184–185. Eighty-five percent of Lundberg's families ate dinner together *every* evening, and 47 percent of those families had both breakfast and dinner together. Lundberg and his colleagues, despite these impressive figures, seemed worried about family togetherness, partly because women's interest in their own clubs seemed to take them away from the interests they might otherwise be sharing with their husbands, and also because adolescents spent their afternoon hours after school in activities with their peers. His data would not seem to support such a conclusion, but I also believe that in the 1920s the marital togetherness that had been so important for the previous generation had become less intense and more routinized, and the intensity that had gone into that relationship was now focused on the family as a whole. My perception is based more on qualitative evidence than on statistics, and perhaps Lundberg and his associates sensed something that they could not quantify. See especially 112, 129, and 145.

42. Nancy Cott is superb on this point. *The Grounding of Modern Feminism* (New Haven, Conn., 1987), 156–167.

Epilogue: The Mystique of Fulfillment

1. Kenneth Jackson, *The Crabgrass Frontier,* 232–234. The following are good examples of the various points of view about the suburbs of the fifties

and sixties. Most observers were critical of suburbia, and this too is a change from the viewpoint of social commentators in the days when suburban life was open principally to the upper middle class. John Keats, *The Crack in the Picture Window* (Boston, 1956), has its amusing moments, but its intent is deadly serious. Keats believed that "the dwelling shapes the dweller," which is architectural determinism at its most severe. William H. Whyte, *The Organization Man* (New York, 1956), made a similar point, arguing that the corporation and the men (then the corporate world was a male world) who served it had destroyed American individualism. Even John Seely et al., *Crestwood Heights* (New York, 1956), generally a more sympathetic portrayal of suburban life, regarded suburbanites as conformist and status-seeking. William Dobriner, *The Suburban Community* (New York, 1958). Bennett Berger, *Working Class Suburb* (Berkeley, 1960) was the first study of a working class residential suburb. It and Herbert Gans, *The Levittowners* (New York, 1967) are, in my view, the best suburban studies of the decade, in large part because they attempt to understand suburban communities from the point of view of the suburbanites. Another sympathetic account is Scott Donaldson, *The Suburban Myth* (New York, 1969.)

2. See, for example, the Interview with Count Keyserling in *Good Housekeeping* (April 1928), 30–31 ff; also Nancy Cott, *The Grounding of Modern Feminism* (New Haven, Conn., 1987), 272–273.

3. Cott, *Grounding*, 183. D'Ann Campbell, *Women at War with America* (Cambridge, Mass., 1984), 247.

4. See Ferdinand Lundberg and Marynia Farnham, *Modern Woman: the Lost Sex* (New York, 1947); Betty Friedan, *The Feminine Mystique* (1963; reprint, New York, 1973), 111. Mary Ryan gives an excellent overview of this issue in *Womanhood in America* (New York, 1983).

5. For an understanding of the domestic architecture of the 1950s two good sources are Gwendolyn Wright, *Building the Dream* (New York, 1981), chap. 13; and Clifford Clark, *The American Family Home* (Chapel Hill, N.C., 1986), chap. 8.

6. According to Friedan, *McCall's Magazine* claimed to have coined the term in 1954. See *Feminine Mystique*, 40–41, 232. Elaine Tyler May's fascinating new work, *Homeward Bound: America Families in the Cold War Era* (New York, 1988), suggests that the 1950s were in many ways a break with the past rather than a continuation of it, and she pays particular attention to the impact of the Cold War. See esp. 7–9. That emphasis on the Cold War is extremely persuasive, and might account for the peculiar character of 1950s "togetherness." Still, the continuities seem to me to be substantial.

7. *Glamour* (April, 1953), quoted in U.S. Department of Labor, "The Status of Women in the United States, 1953", *Women's Bureau Bulletin* 249 (Washington, D.C., 1953): 13.

8. U.S. Department of Labor, "'Older' Women as Office Workers," *Women's Bureau Bulletin* 248 (Washington, D.C., 1953): 35–36. Zane Miller, *Suburb* (Knoxville, Tenn., 1981), 127–129. Sara E. Rix, ed., *The American Woman, 1987–1988* (New York, 1987), 87, 107.

9. Robert Fishman, "American Suburbs/English Suburbs: A Transatlantic Comparison, *Journal of Urban History* 13 (May, 1987), 238–239. See also Fishman, *Bourgeois Utopias* (New York, 1987), chap. 7. Peter O. Muller, *Con-*

temporary Suburban America, (Englewood Cliffs, N.J., 1981), x, has made a similar assessment. During the 1970s, he argues, "the traditional metropolis—composed of a dominant central city and a subservient ring of suburbs—was both turned inside out and split asunder. See also Mark Gottdiener, *Planned Sprawl: Private and Public Interests in Suburbia* (Beverly Hills, 1977).

10. Social scientists are beginning to give the demographics of the new suburbia serious attention; a good recent example of such work is Hugh Wilson, "The Family in Suburbia: From Familism to Pluralism," paper delivered at the Hofstra Conference commemorating the fortieth anniversary of Levittown. For some solutions to the design problems of the changing suburbs see Delores Hayden, *Redesigning the American Dream* (New York, 1984), especially part 3.

11. At the Hofstra Conference, suggestive papers included Jenni Buhr, "Levittown as Utopian Community" and Michael Fifield, "Transitional Spaces: Design Considerations for a New Generation of Housing." Barbara Kelly of the Long Island Studies Institute directed the conference; inquiries should be directed to the Institute. The museum administrator's comment came at a session of a workshop on the Interpretation of Home and Family was conducted by the American Association of State and Local History at the Strong Museum on April 26 through 30, 1987.

I N D E X